PRAISE FOR

# THIS THIN VEIL BETWEEN US

"Award-winning author Eunice Boeve has a firm, unquestioning belief in God. In *This Thin Veil Between Us,* she discusses the numerous ways He has shown His love by permitting those who have passed to communicate with their loved ones. Beginning when she was just five, Boeve has received signs from passed family members and friends and recounts here not only her own experience of these episodes but that of others as well. Part memoir, part treatise on these encounters, *This Thin Veil Between Us* will encourage the doubtful to believe and reassure the disciples of an afterlife."

—Andi Downing, Author of *Always on My Mind*

"*This Thin Veil Between Us* is the memoir of a mystic blessed with a psychic gift. The story crosses generations and realms with a powerful message of hope and unity. The stories wonderfully conveyed by the author helped me to see that we all end up in the same place, so let's take care of each other in the here and now, and occasionally, when we need it most, we may get some help from those in the great beyond, reaching through this thin veil between us. It's worth the read."

—Tracy Morgan, Commissioned Minister, First Christian Church, Loveland, CO CC(Doc)

"'[Eunice] Boeve is a natural storyteller,' a reviewer wrote, commenting on *Along Winding Trails*, a novel that Boeve published in 2015. *This Thin Veil Between Us* is not a novel but rather the story of Boeve's life; but once again, her gift for storytelling is apparent. This is especially true when she describes her childhood, growing up on Libby Creek in Montana, and I found the word pictures she painted of this time in her life particularly evocative. . . . My own experience was different from Boeve's (no creek, no horse, etc.), but when I read these words, I was suddenly filled with nostalgia for the freedom of childhood, my childhood—though I wished that I could share her childhood memories of Libby Creek and its freedom, as well."

—Winona Howe, Author of *Sita and the Prince of Tigers*

"Eunice 'Eunie' Boeve's fiction is well known for her unforgettable characters, her impeccable historical detail, and her lyrical descriptions of setting. Her newest book, *The Thin Veil Between Us*, a nonfiction memoir, has many of these qualities; but here, she uses a mix of stream of consciousness and reportorial narrative. Thus, she's able to weave her autobiography, biographical information about her parents' lives and family genealogical detail, wondrous events of her own out-of-body experiences and interactions with her late husband's spirit, touching stories of children's interaction with the spirit world and angels, and comments on life after death and worldwide religion into one astounding work. If any of these things interest you, this is a book worth reading and rereading. Read it through from start to finish or any chapter. You will be not only touched but also enlightened.

—Marilyn Hope Lake, Author of *Our Mothers' Ghosts and Other Stories*

"It takes courage to write about a subject many don't even share with family or friends. Eunice Boeve shares her personal story and those of others who have connected with the departed, to reassure all of us that loved ones can support us, even after they have physically left us. She also reminds us how young children can tune in to aspects of spirits that most of us cannot perceive. As a young child, she overcame hardship and fear of those gathering for her father to pass. But after her husband passed, he helped heal her fears and embrace his presence and support. This 'thin veil' that separates us from lost family and friends needs a closer look, as does this charming memoir from someone brave enough to share her peek into this alluring topic."

—Richard LaMotte, Author of *Follow His Lead*, *Pure Sea Glass*, and *The Lure of Sea Glass*

"A great book for everyone to read. So insightful! Those who are caring for a loved one at the end of life or those who have had a loved one die ought to read this book to better understand the *Thin Veil Between Us*. I am anxious to share this with hospice staff and families."

—Sandy Kuhlman, Hospice CEO

"*This Veil Between Us* is a significant and exciting text that takes you on a journey of discovery. I would confidently say the book is a gift to humanity, one of a kind. Anyone who is struggling with the question of 'after life' should read this text whereby Eunice Boeve shares her firsthand experience with death. In my view, *This Thin Veil Between Us* is a handbook that can be beneficial to those dealing with a phobia of confronting the subject of death. The text is an additional resource for scholars and general readers who wish to have an additional tool for discussion and practical life."

—Rev. David Manyara, Pastor, United Methodist Church

"Boeve takes us through the mists of time and grief until we find surprising comfort and encouragement."

—Vicki Constable, Retired Journalism Teacher

"*This Thin Veil Between Us* is a glowing and passionate affirmation of the ability of deceased loved ones to connect with the living. Born a 'sensitive,' Boeve's disturbing account of childhood attempts to cope with a flood of paranormal images following the loss of her father is a poignant testimony to the isolation of gifted children. This haunting narrative whisks away all barriers between heaven and earth."

—Charlotte Hinger, Author, Winner of 2021 Colorado Author's Hall of Fame, Will Rogers Gold Medallion, and "The Book Mama" Kansas Notable Book Award

*This Thin Veil Between Us*
by Eunice Boeve

© Copyright 2023 Eunice Boeve

ISBN 979-8-88824-117-2

All rights reserved. No part of this publication may be reproduced, stored in a retrieval system, or transmitted in any form or by any means—electronic, mechanical, photocopy, recording, or any other—except for brief quotations in printed reviews, without the prior written permission of the author.

Published by

3705 Shore Drive
Virginia Beach, VA 23455
800-435-4811
www.koehlerbooks.com

# THIS THIN VEIL BETWEEN US

EUNICE BOEVE

VIRGINIA BEACH
CAPE CHARLES

# TABLE OF CONTENTS

Introduction .................................................................................. 1

Chapter 1: Daddy's Mustache ....................................................... 3

Chapter 2: The People .................................................................. 10

Chapter 3: Tears ............................................................................ 17

Chapter 4: Our Mother's Breakdown ............................................ 22

Chapter 5: Hard Days Ahead ........................................................ 28

Chapter 6: The Welfare Stigma .................................................... 35

Chapter 7: Dad's Book .................................................................. 42

Chapter 8: The People Disappear ................................................. 49

Chapter 9: Those Panic Attacks and Fainting Spells .................... 56

Chapter 10: Bonners Ferry ........................................................... 62

Chapter 11: Scrawny Ronnie and Puny Eunie .............................. 70

Chapter 12: Mom's Illness ............................................................ 77

Chapter 13: We Move to Kansas .................................................. 84

Chapter 14: Ron's Growing-Up Years .......................................... 94

Chapter 15: I Begin Writing ......................................................... 103

Chapter 16: I Am Set Free! .......................................................... 111

Chapter 17: The Funeral Home .................................................... 119

Chapter 18: A Near-Death Experience ........................................ 127

Chapter 19: Ron's Myasthenia Gravis and Danny ....................... 135

Chapter 20: Ron's Battle with Myasthenia Gravis ............................. 145

Chapter 21: Ron's Last Earthbound Days ........................................ 152

Chapter 22: Wonderful Evidence ...................................................... 161

Chapter 23: A Kiss Goodbye, My Birthday,
 and the Big Dream ........................................................... 170

Chapter 24: The Heart Chakra and More ....................................... 179

Chapter 25: Jax's Birth ...................................................................... 185

Chapter 26: The Cardinals and The Winfield Contest .................. 193

Chapter 27: The Psychic and Doubling ........................................... 201

Chapter 28: More Signs and My House Sells ................................. 210

Chapter 29: Angels ............................................................................. 219

Chapter 30: Quarantine, Jax, Papa, and Cooper ............................ 227

Chapter 31: Our Song and the Angel Boy ...................................... 235

Epilogue: It Happens Every Day ...................................................... 242

# INTRODUCTION

**I BELIEVE DEATH** simply means we are no longer earth dwellers. We are still alive, we've just changed our place of residence, and as Shakespeare's Hamlet put it, we have "shuffled off this mortal coil"—this human body—which in our new home would just be a drag. I also believe that our loved ones who have passed never really leave us, that they are still with us, still cognizant of our continued journey through life and will be there to greet us when we, too, have shuffled off this mortal coil.

I also believe that those who have passed, as well as God, Jesus, and angels, can and do reach out to us from time to time. I have been so blessed over the years to have experienced this, but I would never ever have imagined how prolific a loved one could be until my husband of sixty-two years, my love, my Ron passed from this life on January 25, 2018, and began to make contact in an astounding number and variety of ways—all of which eventually led me to writing this book.

This book is a memoir that begins when I was five and had my first remembered premonition—a sudden frightening knowledge that my daddy was soon to leave us. That premonition was the catalyst that led to me having panic attacks and fainting spells for forty-three more years. Then an out-of-body experience set me free, and what had been a curse became a gift—a blessing that in later years let me see my mother for a few seconds, standing before me in solid form, smiling with love and pride in her eyes. Because of this blessing, my brother Danny could send me a vision of his passing in the company of our parents, and of course Ron's almost continued contact with me that has left no doubt but that there is an afterlife. Well, when he's not here working on me to write this book. This was his idea, and he was the driving force behind it. I call him my "ghostwriter."

Years ago I began collecting stories from others whose experiences testify to the existence of life after what we call death, as well as evidence that God, Jesus, and angels also pierce this thin veil between us. Some of those stories are in the memoir, the others are in the epilogue. In all the stories, except those in Ron's and my immediate family, if I use a name, it is only a first name and fictional at that. There are some who contributed their stories that requested I use their true first names. A few who shared their stories with me did not want their story or stories told at all, even if fictionalized, and of course, I honored their request.

My hope is that this memoir and the added stories in the epilogue will bring comfort to those who have lost loved ones and give additional confirmation to those who believe or know without question that life continues after death. I also hope that for those who do not believe in life after death or are skeptics, this book will at least cause them to consider the possibility. I'm very guilty of not having shared experiences in the past. I, like many others, was afraid I'd be considered, at best, a little odd. Now, with Ron's continued encouragement, I have no such doubts. Perhaps my sharing through this book will free others to share with friends and family, and even strangers, thus spreading the word that although such stories cannot yet be proven scientifically, they do give an abundance of anecdotal evidence that there is only a thin veil between us earthbound and those who now reside in the world of the afterlife.

# CHAPTER 1

# DADDY'S MUSTACHE

**MEMORIES OF MY** father are few, most remembered now in small flashback scenes of the five and a half years I knew him. The most detailed and longest memory is of an afternoon in late summer or early fall in 1942, when he decided to shave off his big gray mustache. That afternoon we were all gathered around to watch the event, smiling, happy, for we all knew our daddy would entertain us in the process.

In those days we lived in northwest Montana's forested country of mountains and hills, lakes and rivers and streams. Logging country, but also a country of farms and ranches. Our father was neither rancher, farmer, nor logger. He had "cowboyed" across the west in his earlier years, but now settled in one place with a family to support, he operated his own string of pack horses for the US Forest Service. He rode those mountain trails, leading his pack string loaded with supplies for lookouts, trail crews, and fire camps and was often gone for days at a time. He also worked for the local fish hatchery and in winter followed a trap line. His name was Harry Goyen.

Dad and Mom purchased our home on Libby Creek, south of the town of Libby, in May of 1937 for seventy-five dollars from a couple named Staley when I was a month old. Those forty acres, complete with a small, four-roomed wood-sided house, a barn, woodshed and other outbuildings, had once been a stage stop on the old original road. Now Highway 2, that old road came south out of Libby for seven miles, then it turned east and, a mile farther on crossed Libby

Creek on a wide wood planked bridge. The road then passed by that old stage stop we'd one day call home and on up a long winding hill, called Trainer Hill. From there it continued on toward Kalispell and other towns along the way. A man named C.M. Doty lived at the top of Trainer Hill and in those winter months of deep snow, when motors began to replace horses, he and his team were often called on to pull those stalled vehicles up that last steep grade. That old road was rerouted in 1934 to continue on south and east, bypassing Libby Creek and Trainer Hill and two years later, flood waters washed away that wide, wood-planked bridge.

I remember the old Doty cabin. It had been abandoned for years and by the time we came along, what had once been the door and a couple of windows, were just openings in those log walls. We often played in that old cabin, although one day we encountered a black bear inside, so we played elsewhere that day.

The logging industry began in the area in the late 1800s, cutting down the trees that had grown there for centuries. In the 1920s, that flat between Libby Creek and Trainer Hill, where we'd one day live, was a railroad camp for the logging company. The families lived in house-like train cars that were moved from camp to camp on flat cars. In those early days, the logs were sent sliding down the mountains on long wooden chutes, and in those first years, hauled to the mill by teams of four to six horses. Eventually, the lumber company replaced the horses with a train to haul the logs. The train tracks were gone by the time we moved there, but the old trestle over a deep ravine just northeast of our house was still there and great fun for us kids to play on.

That small brown four-room house, that old stage stop, was a happy home in those years before our dad passed on that winter night in 1943. The three older kids have the most memories and recall our dad as a hands-on father who might entertain them with a story, coax our mother out into the dusk of evening to play hide and seek with them and, in other ways create happy memories. Margaret, who was a tiny child and not much bigger when grown-up, remembers Dad swimming in the creek with her on his back, her little arms clasped around his neck. Some of Earl's fond memories were going with Dad on some of his packing trips with supplies for lookouts and trail crews. Mabel told me that she and Earl and Margaret were assigned a part of the garden to weed, comparable to their size and age, the job to be done by Sunday. One Sunday, we'd been invited to dinner at our aunt and uncle's and Mabel's part of the garden still sprouted weeds. Her punishment was to stay home and pull those weeds, but Dad stayed home and helped her. I wonder if having our dad all to herself that day, was even more of a treat than that Sunday dinner would have been.

Those three older ones have many more memories of our father, while the three younger ones, Larry, Danny, and June have none. I, who was five when he passed, have a few, including the day he shaved off his mustache and I had my first remembered premonition—a terrifying glimpse into the future that froze me to my chair. Then Daddy squatted beside me and whispered a plan to play a trick on my mother and my fear soon changed to joy.

Why our daddy decided to shave off his mustache that afternoon has passed with him. Now, with TV and other forms of entertainment, one might consider the shaving of a mustache hardly worthy of an audience, but this wasn't just getting rid of some whiskers, for this man was a born showman who would entertain us in the process. Besides, we were just kids. We had no other kids to play with and we loved our daddy.

That day in late summer or early fall of 1942, we had all gathered in a corner of the kitchen, for without plumbing of any kind, it was where we washed our hands and faces in an enamel wash basin that set on a wooden washstand, and where Daddy shaved his cheeks and chin, but not his big gray mustache—until that day. I remember how the slanting rays of the afternoon sun shone through the screened-in porch that afternoon, splashing its golden rays of light across the threshold of the open kitchen door. I remember the warmth of being a part of a whole: the smiles, the grins, the anticipation of the "show" that was about to begin. My older siblings must have pulled over the kitchen chairs, for I remember sitting on one. Although we were all gathered around to watch our daddy, my memory has not retained a clear vision of my siblings. I'm sure my focus was on Daddy, the star of the show. I also remember my mother standing behind us, holding baby June in her arms. At thirty-nine, her blond hair may have been threaded with a few strands of gray, from a gene passed down on her mother's side that causes one to gray early. I didn't know that then, of course, or that I also carried the gene. Her name was Hazel, née Cline.

We were a family of nine. My three brothers were: Earl, fourteen, Larry, three, and Danny, nearly two. My three sisters were: Mabel, twelve, Margaret ten, and baby June, just a few months old. I was, at five, the exact middle child.

I sat on that kitchen chair, bare feet dangling, a sun-browned towhead in a cotton dress, likely a faded hand-me-down from my two older sisters, and I, like my mother and my siblings, watched this man we all adored, our faces lit with smiles.

I don't remember the details of how our daddy used that simple act of shaving off his mustache to create his one-man show. I just know we weren't disappointed, for I remember the smiles, the laughter that permeated our sunlit kitchen that afternoon.

Perhaps, our daddy first peered into the mirror that hung on the wall above the wash basin at his full gray mustache, the only evidence of his fifty-five years, his hair still dark, his body slender. I doubt if I ever saw my reflection in that mirror as a young child, but a few times I may have seen my small face in my mother's hand-held mirror. It had been a set, with a matching hairbrush and comb. I have the mirror now, but the brush and comb are long gone.

Few pictures were taken of us in our growing-up years. I had my first and only—until my teenage years—taken in 1939 or '40, so I was two or three. Uncle Charley, Dad's brother, was visiting from Wyoming. I remember being told that he had come to persuade Dad to move back and work on this ranch where he was the foreman and co-owner. Dad declined for whatever reason. I think of how, if he'd said yes and we had moved to Wyoming, I'd never have met my Ron and I would not now be writing this book. In fact, we would all have lived different lives. That day, Mom took two group pictures of Dad and his brother with my three older siblings and me. Our little brother Larry was a baby and napping, so he missed being in the pictures, something he regrets, as I would have too. In those photos, our father has that large gray mustache he shaved off that sunny afternoon.

I have no memory of how he entertained us. Maybe, after he used Mother's scissors to clip the extra hair from his mustache, he offered to give my two older sisters haircuts that would have no need for comb or brush, and only a quick dip to be clean. If so, they would have shrunk back, laughing, shaking their heads as he advanced, scissors in hand, their hands flying up to protect their hair.

I imagine he teased some more before turning back to the process of shaving. Mixing a little water with the soap in his shaving mug, he worked his shaving brush around and around until the bristles were soft and foamy. Perhaps then, he reached out with the brush and dabbed a spot of foam on his youngest son's nose. His other small son, dark eyes sparkling, knowing he was next, shrinking back, laughing when Daddy turned to him, and the dab of white soap landed elsewhere, maybe on his chin.

Now Daddy may have told a joke or a small, funny story, for he was a storyteller. Then, turning back to the mirror, he brushed the white foam on those remaining hairs and using the long blade of his straight razor shaved off the last of his once full, gray mustache.

I don't remember how he showed off his new look. Perhaps he turned with a sweeping bow to accept accolades from his audience, but all I remember as he turned toward us, my laughter ready to bubble out, was a sudden jolt of cold fear.

Although I will never know this side of Heaven what I "saw"

or "heard" that day that so frightened me. All I know was in some way, maybe a voice, maybe a vision, I knew this man we so loved and who gave so freely of his love for us, was soon to be gone from our lives—maybe not how or when, but somehow I knew, and I was terrified. Over the years, I'd have other premonitions, not many, but some, although thankfully, none so terrifying.

The rest of the kids scattered after the show, but I sat stiff and still on that kitchen chair, my whole being filled with fear. Then Daddy squatted beside me and whispered a joke to play on my mother.

Of course, he would have had no idea as to what had frightened me. I imagine he thought it was seeing him without the mustache. Soon I would not remember either, for in that time of pure delight, I would lose, for forty-three years, all conscious memory of that horribly frightening premonition.

I don't know when that fear left me that afternoon. Perhaps it vanished at the sight of his smiling face, the twinkle in his dark brown eyes and his whispered words about playing a joke on my mother. Or maybe when he lifted me from the chair and we hurried off to the girls' bedroom, where at night I slept between my two big sisters and where Mother kept a wardrobe of clothes for her and Daddy. Perhaps it was when he sat me down on the bed and turned and pulled a dress of Mother's from that wardrobe and slipped it on, his pants legs and boots showing below the hemline. I remember the giggles spilling out of me and of falling over backward on the bed and rolling over to sit back up, still laughing. I think then, if any memory of whatever had so terrified me remained, it was swallowed up in those giggles of pure delight.

Now, with one of Mother's scarves covering his dark hair and another over my blond curls, he lifted me up and put me through the open bedroom window and set me feet first down on the ground below and climbed out after me. We sneaked around the house, two conspirators, hand in hand, hunched low, seeking our prey.

At the door of the screened-in porch off the kitchen, I imagine

Daddy grinned at me as he raised his hand and knocked on the wooden edge of the screen door.

Mother stepped out onto the porch and came to greet us, looking at us as if we were indeed strangers. Now my siblings had gathered around, some standing outside a few feet away, the rest following our mother out on the porch. I imagine they all grinned at seeing our daddy dressed as he was, but I was entranced, filled completely with pure joy.

The gist of Daddy's story was that he was a widowed lady with this sweet, precious child to raise and could our mother give him a job. I wiggled and giggled as he spoke those words of woe and in that small span of time I'd become not the middle child, one of seven, but the only child, the most beloved.

Years later, I will note the irony of that happy time, for on a January night a few months later, it would be our mother who would be left to raise alone not just one child, but seven.

# CHAPTER 2

# THE PEOPLE

**WE HAD GATHERED** in the living room the evening of January 6, 1943, as we always did on winter evenings after supper, the fire dying out in the kitchen stove. Our mother, Earl, and Mabel back from doing the chores, were now in the living room, their caps and coats hanging along the west wall in the kitchen. Margaret had stayed inside to tend to us small ones, especially baby June. Larry and Danny and I probably played on the floor with a few toys. Our daddy, who had not felt well for some time, lay in his and Mother's bed. With the two bedrooms occupied, one by the boys, the other by us girls, our parents' bed was in the southeast corner of the living room.

Darkness comes early to Montana in winter, and the kerosene lamp on the table in the living room gave us light as we settled in for the evening. The heating stove, filled with chunks of wood, gave off its welcoming warmth, and outside the temperature dropped and the snow covering the fields and hills cast a deep silence over the land.

Before our daddy took sick, winter evenings had been warm and cozy. Daddy might tell us a story or join my three older siblings in a game of cards or checkers. Maybe he held one or both little boys on his lap. I probably played with a doll. Mother might be tending to the baby or reading one of the many books she checked out of the library, or re-reading one from her own small collection—among them, perhaps, a book of poems, for she loved poetry and could recite many by heart. Sometimes our mother and daddy talked and smiled and laughed together. I liked how they looked at each other then, for it filled me with a comforting happiness.

Those evenings of the last days of our father's life had to have been more subdued—without laughter, our faces solemn—our mother tending to Daddy, soothing him with cool washcloths on his forehead and medicine to quiet his coughs. Our older brother Earl may have quietly entertained Larry, the oldest little boy, while Margaret took care of Danny. Mabel may have tended to little June, now six months old. I do not know if there was some degree of anxiety in those older siblings that night. I wonder now if they were worried about Daddy, or believed he'd get better and soon be up and around again, the fever, the chills, the aches, gone. But, if so, it was not to be. He would pass in the early morning hours while we were sleeping.

I was surely growing sleepy by the time Daddy began to speak in soft mumbled words, his eyes open and looking as if he were seeing someone I could not see. Then I sensed the presence of others, and I looked around the room, but no one was there—just us. I looked to the windows, and I thought they must be there, outside in the snow, looking in at us, and I was afraid.

My eyes kept wanting to look up at the windows, but fear kept my head down, my eyes on my doll. Sometimes, I looked up at my mother for reassurance—of what, I'm not sure. Maybe that it was okay for those people to be there outside in the snow—at the windows. But her eyes were always on Daddy.

Our daddy was an outdoors man and did not like curtains at the windows. He said they hid his view of the outdoors. We had but few neighbors, the closest, a mile or so away, so curtains weren't really needed, although after Daddy was gone, our mother hung them at all the windows.

That night I clutched my doll tighter, wanting to tell my mother about the people—wanting her to hang blankets over those blank, dark panes of glass—wanting to tell her that I was afraid of the people, but the words would not come.

Of course, I didn't know then, nor would I know for years about the dying sometimes seeming to see loved ones who had already passed, some believing it was true, others that the dying one was just hallucinating.

I don't remember being worried or afraid of the people when we went to bed that night. Maybe, knowing I had sensed them, they had backed off, so I'd not be afraid and waited to come for him while we were sleeping. I slept between my two big sisters. Our mother warmed our beds on winter nights with the heavy flat irons she used to smooth the wrinkles from our clothes. Heated on the stove, wrapped in old rags, and tucked down by our feet, they helped chase away the chill.

Years later I asked my sister, Mabel, who had been twelve at the time, if she remembered Daddy talking as if others were in the room or maybe outside looking in the window. I didn't tell her that I'd sensed the people that night. I told her I had imagined there were people outside in the snow looking in at us and I had wanted Mom to hang blankets at the window, but I'd been too scared to ask. Mabel did not remember our dad talking as if to some invisible beings. He had mumbled some, she knew, but he most likely had a fever.

I don't know when our daddy took sick, but I remember being worried about him on Christmas Day. I don't remember what I got for Christmas that year, but Larry and Danny got toy pistols. What I remember is our daddy getting really cross with them for pointing their guns at each other. He told them you never pointed a gun at another person unless you intended to shoot them. That he seemed so upset with both little boys had disturbed me.

My Daddy had looked so tired that Christmas Day. I remember he wore something like a robe, probably a light blanket or shawl, for I can't imagine he ever owned a bathrobe. But that covering draped about him was out of the ordinary and that also bothered me.

I think it was shortly after Christmas that our daddy began to be in bed all day. On one of those days, he got up and dressed and came into the kitchen. Mother had made my two little brothers and me a bowl of uncooked sage dressing and had set the bowl on the seat of a kitchen chair. We three were standing by the chair, spooning the tasty, flavored bread into our little mouths when Daddy came into the room. He told Mother he was tired of being cooped up inside and was going outside for some fresh air. She pleaded with him not to go, but he brushed aside her concerns and, taking his coat and gray felt cowboy hat from the hook by the door, went out in the cold of that winter day.

Sometime after Daddy passed, we got a telephone. It hung on the wall in the living room. To dial a number, one turned the crank on the side. The numbers were a variety of long and short cranks. I don't remember ours, but a number might be one long—a vigorous continuous turning of the crank several times—and two shorts—two quick turns of the crank. The phones rang in every home on that party line, as it was called, and others on that line might listen in at times. One day my mother was on the telephone with her sister, our Aunt Teddie, and I heard her say she believed that our daddy going out that cold winter day had led to his death.

Aunt Teddie, her husband, and their two sons were our only relatives in Montana. We called her Aunt Teddie, although her name was Zella. Her husband we simply called by his first name Blaze, without prefacing it with Uncle. Their two sons, John and Bill, were twenty-three and sixteen that winter of 1943 when our father passed from this world.

Dad's parents had died years before I was born, and I knew little about them. I was somewhere in my forties when I joined our town's local genealogical society to find out about my dad's ancestors. I knew he had been born in Pratt County, Kansas, and the first time I came to a meeting I told them with a grin that I'd joined because of this one strange connection I had with my dad. He was born in Kansas and died in Montana, whereas I was born in Montana, and it looked like I'd probably die here in Kansas. As a member of our local group of family-tree builders, I started searching for members of dad's family. Luckily one cousin was also researching the family history.

Along with the genealogical data, that cousin also sent a copy of a letter written in 1879 by my dad's grandmother. The letter was to Dad's mother, telling her that her father had passed. He had been injured while working with a horse in the barn and had passed a few days later. This is a quote from the letter: *A little while before he passed, he said, "Someone is coming, and I must go."* Then with his last breath, he said, *"Glory!"* I'm sure my dad's grandfather was seeing deceased loved ones from the spirit world, those "people" my daddy had talked to and who I thought stood outside in the snow. Although at that time, I no longer had conscious memory of the people. That memory had slipped into my subconscious when a woman was run over at our school when I was in the second grade. I would not regain conscious memory of them until I'd have an out-of-body experience when I was forty-eight years old.

I believe that the "someone" Great-Granddad had seen were passed loved ones who had come for him. And the word, "Glory!" was a glimpse of Heaven as he left this earth. I thought it was interesting that Great-Grandmother wrote of that as a fact, and didn't preface it with such words as, *he must have been hallucinating.* Many do believe we go to Heaven, but to be able to return to earth, even just briefly to escort a dying loved one into the next life, might for some be a bit of a stretch.

There are many stories that lend credence to what many believe, me included, that we do not die alone but pass in the company of those who have gone before. Sometimes the dying, especially children, will speak of Jesus being at their bedside a little while before they pass. I'm sure there are many such stories, but few speak of them outside of the family, if even then. The following are some of those stories I've collected from family, acquaintances, and friends.

My husband Ron's Aunt Hattie, his dad's sister, was dying in the hospital when she suddenly announced the presence of her mother. Her daughter, who was sitting with her mother, reminded her that her mother could not be there as she had died many years before.

"Yes, she is," Aunt Hattie told her, "She's right over there," and she gestured toward that part of her hospital room where evidently she could see her mother. I wonder if the family accepted that as an actual event, that the mother was truly there for her daughter, or if it was thought to be a hallucination. I don't remember where or when I heard about it, but it came to me as I was writing this chapter. I passed it on to a granddaughter who had never heard the story.

Allen passed through this thin veil between us, of cancer, at age thirteen. He spent his last days at home with his loving parents and sister. One day, he said to his parents, "Jesus is here. He is standing by my bed." His parents told him to go with Him, that it was okay for him to go, but Allen said, "No. He said, 'Not yet, but soon.'" Allen passed the next day.

Years ago, a hospice nurse told me this story about a little girl in their care. The day she passed, the child was propped up in her hospital bed, her parents hovering nearby, when suddenly she started smiling and looking all around the room, now and then nodding as if seeing something or someone neither the parents nor the nurse could see. Her mother asked if there were others besides them in the room." "Oh, yes!" she said, "lots of people. There are so many, there's not even enough chairs for them all." Then she added, "The kids are all playing. They told me I can't go over the hill yet." Later that day, she was sitting on her grandfather's lap when she looked up at him and said, "It's time to go over the hill." Then she slumped in his arms and was gone.

Mae and Betty and Grace had been friends for forty or more years, when after a short illness Betty passed. A year later, Mae became ill, and the doctor told the family she had, at best, only a few weeks to live. Then Mae's other old friend, Grace, succumbed to an illness. Because Mae was so ill, her family did not tell her that this friend, too, had passed. The last few days of her earthly life, Mae was in and out of consciousness and the family gathered around knowing the end was near. Then a few hours before she passed, Mae suddenly opened her eyes and said, "Hello, Betty." And then she added, "There's Grace! I didn't know she was gone." Sometime later, she lapsed into an unconscious state and soon passed. At the funeral service, the minister spoke of Mae acknowledging her friends those last few hours of her earthly life, especially seeing Grace, whom she had not known was also gone.

Tim also had a friend come for him. Bob had passed from cancer some years before and now Tim was terminally ill. A few hours before Tim passed, his family at his bedside, he suddenly said, "Well, there's Bob." The family told him that Bob had passed some years ago, didn't he remember? He nodded his head and said, "Well, yes, but just now he's standing at the foot of my bed."

Many of these stories we never hear, but when I am ready to shuffle off this mortal coil, I know Ron will be there, and probably Mom and Dad and maybe some others. I hope if my family members are privileged to hear such an exchange between me and someone who has passed, they will record it in my obituary and be sure the newspapers don't leave that part out when they print it, and the minister will speak of it at my funeral, like Mae's did at hers.

# CHAPTER 3

# TEARS

**IN THE TWENTY** years I knew my mother, I never saw her cry. Once, I saw tears spring to her eyes, but I never saw her break down and cry. Those tears, I remember, came one day in the spring after the people had come for our daddy. Mom's milk cow was due to calve and when she went out to look for her, she found that the cow had delivered, but the newborn was dead. I didn't know it then, of course, but as an adult I know what that dead calf had cost her, for later it could have brought in some much-needed cash, even food on the table. That loss must have been evident on her face, even without tears, for I remember how her face, her voice, seemed different somehow. She started to come into the house but stumbled on the thick slab of wood that led out from the screened-in porch, serving as a sidewalk, and fell. It was then that I saw the tears spring to her eyes and a terrible fear gripped me, for if my mother gave way to tears, I knew that somehow we were lost. But she did not cry. She blinked back those tears, got to her feet, and came on into the house.

I do not remember anyone in our family ever crying. I cried a few times, but never where anyone could see me. Once, I ran to the creek where a thick stand of willows grew and amid those willows gave way to tears. I imagine my mother and my older siblings also cried in secret.

My mother, I'm sure shed many tears for a long time after losing our father. The little boys must have shed tears in frustration and anger when very young, but if so, I do not remember. We were a stoic lot. A part of not giving way to tears, I'm sure, was also the times we lived in when a stiff upper lip was admired and tears a sign of weakness.

I have no memory of tears that morning our daddy was taken from us. I woke with the soft glow of lamplight spilling in through the doorway of our bedroom, just off from the kitchen, my mother standing in the doorway. I always slept between my two big sisters and either they told me, or our mother told all three of us that our daddy had died while we were sleeping. That memory is fragmented and hazy, as if enclosed in whisper-thin shadows. I didn't think of those people then, those people who I believed had stood outside in the snow. In my next memory I am dressed and sitting on a chair in front of the kitchen stove, the fire crackling, spreading its warmth. My siblings are also there in the kitchen, as is our mother, but my memory sees them only as shadowy movements, not distinct beings. I'm sure there were tears, but silent ones, deep inside, our eyes dry. Our mother had to be barely holding it together for our sakes. Later though, her grief and fear would take her down.

I remember the silence and the shadows. If words were spoken, they were probably soft, quiet ones, but I remember the shadows cast by the kerosene lamp upon the ceiling and walls as my mother and sisters moved about dressing the little boys and my baby sister. I have a shadowy memory of Blaze, our uncle, sitting back by the water bucket and wash basin, waiting to take us to his home. We would stay with them until after the funeral. I have no memory of going to their house.

Years later I would learn that with the snow so deep and only the highway plowed, the funeral director had left the hearse at the highway and walked the mile to our place. Blaze had returned from taking us kids to Aunt Teddie's and a neighbor had snow-shoed over to help. They hitched the team to the wagon and took Dad's body across the creek and up to the highway.

When our daddy passed in that early morning hour, our mother sent our brother Earl to tell Aunt Teddie and Blaze. They had a telephone, but we did not. Just fourteen, he waded that mile through deep snow on that cold, dark morning and one can imagine the tears he had to constantly wipe away. Still, some must have frozen on his cheeks. Years later, our cousin Bill, who was sixteen that winter, told me he woke up when my brother knocked on the front door. It had surprised him. "No one ever came to our front door, and it was still night! Still dark!" Earl had probably gone to that door rather than the back door, for he'd have known they'd be asleep and their bed, like that of our parents, was in the living room. Their sons had shared the one bedroom, but John was then either in college or the military, as our country was at war. This cousin, hearing him, said he got out of bed to see what was going on. "I saw Mom wrapping a blanket around Earl and Dad building up the fire in the heating stove. Earl was shivering and looked so miserable, so forlorn. Then Dad said, "How's your dad?"

"Oh," Earl said. "He's dead."

"Those words," Bill told me, "so flat, so emotionless, his entire being numb, his heart breaking, tears threatening, but held back, for he dared not let his grief, his emotions spill out. He had come with the news that your mother needed them, but he could not say the words until he was asked." Bill paused and looked away, as if seeing that scene from those long-ago years. Then he turned back to me and added, "I felt so sorry for him."

Blaze brought Earl home and then waited to take us to his house, to Aunt Teddie, before coming back to help our mother. I had slipped into my coat and scarf and had pulled on my rubber boots, reaching into my coat pockets for my mittens. Then I remembered that I had played awhile in the snow yesterday afternoon. We usually dried our mittens behind the kitchen stove, draped over the wood box, but yesterday, I'd left mine by the stove in the living room. Just last night, my daddy had been in bed in that room and now my mother had told us he'd died. But somehow I'd not made the connection or couldn't yet bear to do so, for without thought, I ran to open the living room door to retrieve my mittens. As I reached to push open the door, my mother was beside me, questioning me. I explained about my mittens and was puzzled when she said to go back and wait, that she would get them for me. Her words surprised me. I was big enough to get my own mittens and had done so lots of times. We were taught early on to be as self-sufficient as we were able. Now my mother was getting my mittens for me. I was five; I could do it myself.

She opened the door just enough to slip inside and I saw the room was in darkness and suddenly I knew! *My daddy was in there!* I'd given no thought to where he was now, now that he was dead, but now I knew, he was still there, still in bed, but he was dead. It was then that I remembered the people, and I knew they had come in while we were sleeping and had made him die. I also knew that whatever they had done to him had made him look so awful, so scary—not warm, not loving, not like my daddy anymore, and that's why my mother did not want me to see him. I went back and waited with the others and my mother brought me my mittens.

We stayed at Aunt Teddie and Blaze's home for several days. The day of the funeral, a woman came to stay with us. I don't remember if she was young or old or in between. I have only one fuzzy image of her changing my baby sister's diaper. Many years later, my aunt told me on one of those days we stayed with them, that I told her I could still hear my daddy's voice, but I guess it was just in my head. "You looked so sad," she said, "but you did not cry."

I have no trouble now with tears, for I learned from Ron and his family the value of hugs, verbally expressed love, and the healing power of tears. Also, society now accepts tears of sadness and sorrow, as well as shows of affection more readily than in my childhood days. (Our dad may have been the exception, but Mom was more reserved.)

Seventy-one years after my father died, I attended the funeral service for a young mother who had died in an auto accident, leaving a five-year-old son behind. When I arrived at the church for the service for this young mother, the sanctuary was full, so I was seated with others in the balcony. I had an aisle seat, a young man—a stranger to me—on my right. From my seat, I had full view of the family below, the little boy clutching a teddy bear almost as big as he was, going back and forth from his father's lap to his stepmother's, plainly restless and in distress.

Sometime during that service, I was no longer in the church sitting in the balcony but standing in my aunt and uncle's kitchen in Montana, and I was a little girl again, looking up at the window over the sink. In this out-of-body experience, I was all alone and was scared and desperately in need of my mother. I knew it was the day of my father's funeral, and I knew that was where my mother had gone. I looked up at that kitchen window, for although I was too small to see out of it, I knew the road went that way, past the garage, the barn, up the road to the highway, and on into town. And that was where my mother had gone, and it was how she would come back to me. I knew nothing of funerals or cemeteries. I'm sure I heard that "Daddy's funeral" was in town. (Or maybe my adult brain was still partly functioning and had that information.)

Perhaps I made a sound, maybe a sob, for the man beside me touched my arm and with his touch, I was back in the church in Kansas and back in present time. He held out a folded tissue, and I made good use of it, for it was hard now to stem my tears. I kept my eyes down, so as not to see the family, especially that little boy, and I created an image of my father riding his horse through the mountains, across a stream and through a forest of aspen and birch trees, the sun shining, a breeze ruffling the leaves on the trees.

When the service was over, I stood outside with others until the procession left for the cemetery. Back in my car, I cried until I was empty of tears. Some sorrow lingered, sorrow for the little boy who had lost his mother, and for the rest of the family, but I had no lingering sorrow for the little girl who, long ago, had so desperately needed her mother.

# CHAPTER 4

# OUR MOTHER'S BREAKDOWN

**I DON'T KNOW** how long we stayed with Aunt Teddie and Blaze before we went back home. My memory begins with stepping in through the front door that opened into the living room and the smell that slammed into me—a smell so foreign, so unexpected that it terrified me. I'd learn years later that our mother and aunt had come over and cleaned the house the day before, so the cleaning solution was probably the source of the odor. But being a child, I did not know that, and the smell only added to my anxiety at coming home—home to a house without Daddy. I remember, too, that empty bed in the living room. I imagine all our eyes were drawn to that bed the second we stepped through the door. The blankets straight now, the pillows as smooth as if he had never been there at all.

I don't remember if I thought the people had come back while we were at our aunt and uncle's home and had left that scary smell, but I do know that it was that smell, along with the empty bed, that was suddenly so overwhelming that despite our family's stiff upper lip, I burst into tears. Those tears gushed out of me—tears I could not hold back. Then my mother sat down on the foot of that bed and pulled me up on her lap and silently, gently, held me close in her arms until my tears subsided.

I know my mother held me as a baby, maybe even as a toddler, but I have no memory of her ever holding me before that day. I do have two very clear memories of Daddy holding me, once sitting at the kitchen table with me on his lap, looking out the window at the horses he'd brought down from the hills as they milled around in the long fenced-in area we called the lane. The other time was when I woke in the night with an earache. He held me, rocked me, and blew cigarette smoke in my ear, an old-time remedy that evidently worked. Although probably, Mother also added some drops of warm sweet oil. Those two times that I remember Dad holding me, were, I'm sure, not the only times. Also, my sisters have told me that Dad often entertained us with stories while Mother cooked our supper. Those times, he held the small ones on his lap as he sat in the kitchen, the older kids gathered close to soak up the warmth of belonging, of parental love in action. So, at one time, I had to have been one of the small ones.

As I mentioned, back in my growing-up years, people didn't hug each other like they do now, and probably even less so in my mother's generation. It also depended on the families. Not giving those shows of affection did not mean that families loved each other any less. Although, our mother never showed us physical affection, that I remember. She did not hug or kiss us, yet she was, in so many ways, an excellent, loving mother. But even the best of mothers, the strongest, the most loving, can break, and our mother broke, sometime after we came home from our father's funeral.

On our first night home from Aunt Teddie and Blaze's, Mabel, who was twelve at the time, told me years later that our mother asked her to sleep with her, and all night long she tossed and turned and moaned and cried out in her sleep. "I was so scared," Mabel said, "so afraid she was dying." Sometime, maybe the next day, maybe later, our mother took baby June and moved into our girls' room and we girls moved to our parent's former bed in the living room. Now, our mother began to stay in bed most of the day, getting up only to tend to the baby, but even then, she was withdrawn and silent.

I retained no conscious memory of those days and nights our mother spent broken in grief and the fear of what lay ahead. I did not know, of course, that my mother was grieving or even what grieving was, nor would I have understood how helpless, how scared she had to have felt not knowing how she could provide financially for her children. I thought she was sick, like my daddy had been, and I began to fear that the people would come for her one night while we were sleeping and kill her too. Sometime in those days before she recovered, that terrible fear became too much for me and like the premonition I had that our daddy would leave us, it too went into my subconscious, and I lost all conscious memory of our mother's breakdown.

Mabel and Margaret, twelve and ten, dropped out of school and took over the care of us little ones and managed the household as best they could while our mother was lost in her grief and fear. To ease the burden, Earl, then fourteen, also dropped out of school and went to live with an old man back up in the hills and worked for his room and board, and possibly a few dollars.

My heart aches for those children, so broken-hearted, so worried, so overwhelmed. Life's events can alter a child's perception of how they see themselves and life around them and shapes the adults they will become. Those years that followed our father's passing were tough ones for us all, especially for those three older ones, and of course, our mother. My sister Mabel said of that time, "We lost our childhood then."

Even though I lost all conscious memory of our mother and even my baby sister, during that terrifying time when I feared the people who had killed my daddy would come one night and kill her too, I do remember how my sisters took care of our little brothers just like they were their mothers, feeding and dressing them, bathing them, and tucking them into bed. Mabel always took care of Larry and Margaret always tended to Danny. I also knew that those two young girls brought in the wood each night for the stoves and carried our water up from the spring in buckets too heavy for me, at five, to even lift. I knew they fed the chickens and tossed down hay to the cow, and the horses. They milked the cow and cooked for us and shoveled the new snow from the paths to and from the outbuildings, the spring, and the outhouse. I know they did all that, but only as an adult did I understand the herculean task those two young girls met and mastered each day, and if they were ever cross with us, I don't remember.

Of course, at five I had no clue as to how hard it had been for them or that my little brothers needed more care than me, and I grew jealous of those little boys who each had a sister to care for them, just as if they were their mothers, while I had no one. Of course, I wanted to be special too, but I came to believe I was special to no one anymore. I knew I'd been special to Daddy. But, of course, we'd all been special to Daddy.

I think of our mother now, how devastating to not only lose the man she dearly loved, but to have to rebuild her life and her children's lives without his help and without his income. She had to have felt so helpless, so hopeless. However, the day came when she left her bed and became our mother again. And here, I want share some of my growing-up memories of our mother.

I don't remember her ever being cross with us. I don't know if we ever needed much in the way of correction, or maybe I've forgotten.

Once when Larry and I were confined to the living room with the measles, or maybe it was the mumps, or the chicken pox—we had them all—Larry, restless, bored, and cranky, took our crayons and scribbled on the wall. I'm sure Mother was distressed, but if she reprimanded Larry, it was with understanding. Any harshness, I'm pretty sure I would have remembered.

Through the years she read to us in the evenings after the chores were done and we were settled in for the night. We'd gather around her as she read from the light of the kerosene lamp. When Larry and I had pink eye, we did not go to the doctor, probably not that unusual in those days, especially when money was so scarce. Overnight, a scabby crust would form, so by morning our eyes would be stuck shut. Each morning, Mom washed the crust from our eyes with a solution of boric acid and warm water. One of those mornings, as she washed our eyes, she sang the church hymn, "Open My Eyes That I May See."

To protect our eyes those days of the pink eye, we had to stay in the living room, the windows covered during the day to keep out as much light as possible. During those days confined to that room, our mother would often sit on the kitchen side of the closed door and read to us.

As I remember, Larry's eyes healed sooner than mine, so I think he was back in school when Mom sent me back. The teacher sent me to the school nurse, who sent me to the doctor. The hospital was at the opposite end of town. I walked, of course, and it was a cold November day, snow on the ground. I was sure my eyes were healed, but the doctor wasn't, so I walked back to the school. I don't remember if I stayed in the nurses' office the rest of the day, or if Blaze came and took me home. However, I got home, I know it was by way of Libby Creek, for I was crossing the footbridge carrying my math book (the teacher had sent home with me to work on), when somehow it slipped from my arms and fell into the water. I stood there in dismay as the book rolled and tumbled on down those flowing cold waters and out of sight. My mother did not reprimand me nor speak of my carelessness. It was an accident, and we all have accidents. I don't know if she had to pay for the book or not, but if so, she never told me.

Even when we tried to be naughty, it didn't shake her up a bit. Once we conspired to shock her with a string of cuss words. She just laughed and told us we sounded like a couple of old muleskinners. That pretty much took the fun out of that.

Once she bought a flat of tomatoes and let us eat them until they were gone, no hoarding, no drawing it out, no saving some for tomorrow. It was a special treat, and we could eat all we wanted.

One night, she roused us from bed to come out to see an extra brilliant display of the Northern Lights.

I remember she bought me a Kewpie doll for no reason other than that she knew I had coveted that doll, eyeing it with longing whenever we went to town, which was seldom. I was smitten with that doll, and during lunch hours at school, I'd run uptown to see it, hoping it would still be there.

We didn't get birthday gifts, but now and then we'd get something special, like that doll. That she loved us dearly, I came to know after I grew up and had children of my own. She was gone by then to be with our dad and other loved ones, passing in April before our first baby was born in September.

On the Fourth of July, we always went on a picnic with Blaze and Aunt Teddie. Mom always ordered three big kegs of ice cream—vanilla, chocolate, and strawberry from the creamery in Libby. The kegs were wrapped in what looked like burlap to keep the contents cold, usually through the picnic, but as the afternoon passed, what little was left would melt. I loved to spoon up that creamy melted sweetness from the bottom of those kegs. Mom always ordered our ice cream early, but one year they already had all the orders they could handle. That day she ordered next year's ice cream and every year after, when she picked up her ice cream, she placed her order for the next year.

Our mother valued education, and although only having an eighth-grade education herself, she was a voracious reader. Probably every one of us first saw the inside of a library while still cradled in her arms. I remembered the pleasure it gave her to be able to buy us a set of encyclopedias and a very large dictionary when I was about fourteen. Our mother also loved music and loved to sing. She had left her pump organ in Wyoming with a sister when she married our father and moved to Montana. Many years later, an older cousin gave it to my brother, Larry, and his wife, Pat. It was offered to me, but I declined, as I had inherited none of Mom's musical talent—not even a smidgen.

## CHAPTER 5

# HARD DAYS AHEAD

**I HAD NO** conscious memory of our mother's breakdown until I had that out-of-body experience at age forty-eight. I will write of that experience in full detail in a later chapter. It was the fear of the people—who I believed had killed my daddy and who I feared would now come for my mother—that had been too much to bear for the child I was then, and it had slipped from my conscious mind into my subconscious.

When I regained conscious memory of our mother's breakdown those many years later, I recalled how I'd always stayed close to my mother and when she would get up to tend to the baby and rock her awhile before going back to bed, I'd stay where she could see me, waiting for some indication that she still cared for me.

I am sure that in her eyes and small weak smiles, I saw her grief, her hopelessness, but I did not understand that she was mourning our father, and dreadfully afraid of the days ahead, for how could she feed and clothe her seven children? How could she find a job? And how to get to that job unless she went by buggy, horseback, or walked—and it was seven miles into town. And if a job was to be had to bring in the money she would need to care for us, then what about the little ones? She couldn't leave them alone, and the older kids needed to get back to school.

Of course, I knew none of that. I thought she was sick like my daddy had been, and I was afraid—afraid the people would come for her as they had for him. I know, too, that my big sisters' mothering of my two little brothers fed in me a sense of isolation and abandonment. They each had their own little brother to care for, and my mother had June. Everyone had someone, except me. *And then, there were the people.* Those terrible people who had killed my daddy and I was so afraid would now come for my mother.

Probably, also, was the memory of the morning our father had passed, and my mother had not let me get my mittens. *What had those people done to him? What would they now do to my mother?*

Years later, I'd think how if I'd been taken to the funeral and seen my dad in his casket, I would have realized he'd not been mutilated by those people. I might even have heard from those gathered there how he had died from an illness, not killed by those people at the window. It could have made so much difference.

I had wanted my mother to hang blankets at the windows the night the people came for our daddy. I may have wanted my sisters to hang a blanket now at this bedroom window, but if so, I didn't ask. I might have believed they would come in anyway, or that with the blanket at the window, covering that blank, dark pane of glass, they could be there, and I wouldn't be able to feel their presence. I don't, of course, know my exact thoughts of those evenings before bedtime, as I waited for the people to come for my mother. Neither do I remember when the fear of those people became so unbearable that it slipped into my subconscious memory.

When I did regain the memory of my mother's breakdown forty-three years later, I knew that as darkness gathered each evening, I stayed beside her in that bedroom and waited—waited for her to start talking to someone I could not see, and when I sensed their presence I would know they waited outside in the snow and when we were in bed asleep, they would come in and kill my mother. But, if it was bedtime and she had not mumbled words to someone I could not see, and I had not sensed their presence, then I would know she would be safe for that night.

I have no memory of when our mother returned to us and of course, no knowledge of when she came to know that her only choice was to apply for assistance. I do, however, clearly remember the day the welfare man came. By then Mabel and Margaret were back in school. Earl, who had left home to ease the burden on Mom, was also in school, although he still lived with the old man. I'm sure those years Earl lived with him, he had to have felt so isolated and in some way even abandoned. He had been so close to our dad. Besides those packing trips for the Forest Service when he was out of school for the summer, during huckleberry season they'd camp a few days in the mountains, going by horseback and leading a packhorse, two long narrow wooden boxes lashed to the sides of the pack saddle to bring the berries home. Now, his father gone and that old man's house just a roof over his head, I'm sure he shed many tears out in the hills, among the sheltering trees, or in the barn against the coat of one of the several dogs the old man kept.

I know Earl was home at haying time and to get in the winter supply of wood and other times as well. One day, I think it was the spring after dad passed, I was sitting on the top rail of the corral watching my big brother working with some horses. Then the mare, Flossie, kicked him in the chest, and he fell and lay motionless on the corral floor. I climbed down off that top rail and ran to the house and crawled under a bed, for I knew he was dead. Sometime later, my mother found me there huddled in fear.

When our mother returned emotionally to us, my two sisters were for me, just big sisters again, but for the little boys, the line had blurred and for every want or need, both boys turned to the sister who had cared for him those days of our mother's breakdown, and I believed both sisters favored them as well. That attachment continued in my eyes for several years. I also believed our mother favored our little sister June. Those factors continued to feed a sense of isolation in me, of being an extra child and special to no one.

For some months after our mother was up and about, I needed her physical presence to feel any measure of security. I still consciously remembered the people, knew they had killed my daddy, but I had no conscious memory of my mother's breakdown or the people coming for her. I still feared for her because in my subconscious she was still in that bed, the people still coming to kill her.

That spring we would visit Daddy's grave and I'd think the people were there, down in his grave, and now they were after me. I was in the second grade when a woman was run over and killed just outside our school. It was then that I came to believe that the people were everywhere and that we were all in danger and the fear grew to be too much for the child I was, and the people, like my mother's breakdown, slipped from my conscious memory into my subconscious and there those memories stayed and sometime later, I have no idea when, I began having panic attacks and fainting spells. My triggers were death, dying, the blood running through the veins, the heart beating, vaccinations, etc. However, except for vaccinations, I rarely encountered those triggers until I grew older. I remember lining up at school to get our vaccinations, but I would soon begin to panic and the nurse or the teacher would pull me out of the line before I fainted.

Now, because of that subconscious fear of the killers, I stayed close to my mother, and I was in the kitchen with her the day the welfare man came. My sisters were probably in school, baby June napping, perhaps the little boys, too, or maybe playing in the living room.

She was baking her weekly batch of bread that day, mixing the dough in the big bowl she always used. She seated him at the kitchen table, and I assume she explained her situation with the bread and went back across the room to her work counter and turning the dough out onto the wooden breadboard, she began to work the dough. I always liked to watch my mother knead bread, her flour-dusted hands turning the dough over and around and over and around on the flat wooden bread board. For me, it was a satisfying soothing rhythm of motion, but not that day. Now there was no rhythm, just hard jerky movements, like she was mad at that lump of white dough in her hands.

Sometimes, when she answered the man at the table across the room, she paused, lifted her hands from the bread dough and turned to face him, but sometimes she flung her words back over her shoulder as if they were bullets and I believed the man's words, words I did not understand, were mean words, words to make her angry. He did not sound angry or mean, but my mother was very upset. Although I didn't know it then, I suspect she was angry at the situation she was caught in and fighting tears.

I have no memory of the man's physical appearance, or when he climbed back in his car and drove away, probably relieved to have that interview over. But to this day, I remember his name.

I don't know when I learned about welfare and that the man had been a case worker and now our mother would begin to receive money to help her feed and clothe her family. I may have been six by then, my birthday in April, too young to understand what that exchange between my mother and that man was all about. Maybe later, I overheard words between her and our Aunt Teddie, and especially if my mother was still upset, maybe ashamed of needing assistance, maybe angry, her grief still so raw.

Mom had an old box camera and when I was about twelve or thirteen, I started using it. One picture I took was of my mom and it's my favorite of her. She had come up from the spring, carrying two buckets of water and was just outside the house when I called to her to stop so I could take her picture. *She stands there in that photo holding those buckets, and she laughs in the face of the camera.* In the background one can see that the barn roof is beginning to sag, the side walls shored up with old scrap lumber and behind her a pile of debris, remnants of the blacksmith shop that had recently burned to the ground. As an adult looking back, my mother gone to be with her love, I came to admire that woman who, instead of growing bitter, had learned to laugh in the face of adversity.

One day, years later, I showed the photo to a woman who had come into the family after Mom had passed, so she never knew my mother.

Sometimes, we say words in a moment of thoughtlessness and I'm sure she did that day. I don't now recall my words, but in essence I said, "I love this picture of my mother. I love that she is laughing. My mother always laughed." I was stunned, and of course angry when she replied, "The poor dear. She didn't know any better."

Of course, she knew better. In no way was she ignorant of the limitations of her life, but she knew that what you cannot change, you need to accept and carry on the best you can, for if you are to succeed in life, that is your only choice. And if you laugh and look for the joy in life, acceptance is easier. Mom used to tell us kids when one or more of us expressed a desire beyond our reach, "If wishes were ponies, then beggars would ride." Another saying was, "It's not what you like that makes you fat, it's what you get."

Ron's mother had a saying I love, not just for the truth of it, but also for the silly picture it raises in one's mind, "Want in one hand and pee in the other and see which one gets filled first." Neither one of them had an easy life and both died of cancer in their fifties. But they were strong women, loving women—mothers to be proud of.

My mother passed from this earth in 1957 after a long illness at age fifty-three. Fifty-one years later, on July 21, 2008, she appeared to me in full form in the kitchen of our summer vacation home in Montana that we had purchased in 1995. She was smiling at me with love and pride in her eyes. Then in seconds, she vanished. I felt so loved, so blessed.

I wish I'd been closer to my mother growing up, but it was the initial fear of the people—not understanding they were passed loved ones who had come for my daddy—that had created a subconscious emotional barrier between me and my mother. The subconscious is a powerful thing, for even as I saw her, saw her look at me, heard her voice, her laugh and on a conscious level knew she was no longer in that bed with the baby, and I was no longer five years old and waiting in fear for the people, my subconscious still held on to that belief.

It's amazing how the brain works, how it processes the information taken in, and especially if you are a child and have limited knowledge of the world around you, and you are faced with a fear so overwhelming you can no longer endure it, how the subconscious takes over. At least, it did for me. The brain takes the object of the fear and hides it from one's conscious memory, where it will continue to influence our thoughts, which influences our behavior, until something changes those thoughts and fears. As noted at the beginning of this chapter, I will write later about how an out-of-body experience took me back forty-three years to being a five-year-old child again, standing by my mother's bedside in our old home in Montana. I knew then that this was why I'd had those panic attacks and fainting spells for most of my life. Once it was brought to my conscious mind, I knew she was not still in that bed. In fact, by that time she had been in Heaven for twenty-eight of those years.

# CHAPTER 6

# THE WELFARE STIGMA

**THE WELFARE MAN** did not magically change our lives that April day, allowing us lots of money so no one had to work. Earl stayed with the old man a few more years before getting other jobs that allowed him to live on his own. He did a couple of grades in high school and then dropped out to work. When my sisters reached high school, they began working for others. Margaret worked in homes while Mabel chose to do ranch or farm work. Both lived with their employers, and both graduated from high school. For all three, those years had to have been so very difficult.

I'm sure my mother knew what being on welfare signified, how many looked upon welfare recipients as deadbeats, too lazy to work, preferring to live off the money others paid in taxes. I would learn. In fact, just a few months ago I was reminded again when I met a couple I knew casually while out shopping. We chatted a bit and then something triggered the wife's disgust of welfare recipients, and she spouted that same old song and dance about those folks being too lazy to work. I listened to her a short while and then with a pleasant smile, I lied and said I needed to get home.

Of course, we all know there are those who will take advantage of any system they can, even among those who are extremely rich. There is a billionaire (I guess that's what he is) currently in the news who appears to have been cheating for financial gain for years, and it seems to be finally catching up to him. One wonders if a subconscious belief is lying to him, maybe from a shattered childhood, telling him he needs more and more and more or he will die. I'd not be surprised, for the subconscious, hidden from our conscious mind, can have us believing the impossible, the outrageous. It can make us believe anything at all.

Two incidents with men who had stores uptown when I was in grade school left me feeling that I was somehow inferior or unlikable, but I didn't know why. It might have been the welfare stigma, for there are few secrets in a small town. Or maybe they were just bullies. The first experience was in the variety store, then called a *Dime Store* or a *Five and Ten*. Our school was at the end of the main business section of town, and after lunch we were free to do as we pleased, so long as we were in our classrooms when the afternoon sessions began. Mostly we stayed on the playground, but one day I'd brought a small bit of money to school to spend uptown on my lunch hour.

To have any money at all was a rarity and I have no idea now how I'd acquired it. So, after eating my lunch, I hurried up to the variety store to make my purchase. I looked every item within my price range over carefully and then made my selection and took it up to the man who stood behind the counter. Not realizing I'd made a mistake and was a few cents short, I laid the item (I don't now remember what it was) and my few coins down in front of him. The man looked at the money and then at me and in a harsh voice told me it was not enough.

I looked up at his face, cold, unsmiling, and stammered an apology. "I... I didn't know. I ... I thought..." His face stayed hard and cold, and he said, as I remember, "Sure you did." His words and tone of voice conveyed to me that he thought I knew and was trying to cheat him. I scooped up those few coins and head hanging, I scurried from the store.

The man who owned the drug store had evidently been cut from the same cloth as the man in the Dime Store. I remember always feeling uneasy around him, but I can't say if I did before the following incident.

I was probably about twelve that day in the drugstore with my mother when, bored with waiting for her to finish making her purchases, I wandered over to the other end of the store where there was a display of magazines and I picked up one to look through. Suddenly the man stood there, looking down at me, and in a hard-edged voice asked if I intended to buy it. Totally intimidated, I shook my head. "Then put it back," he said in that same nasty voice. I did and went back to stand by my mother. She never said anything to me, so I don't know if she heard that exchange or not. I shouldn't have been looking at the magazine knowing I wasn't going to buy it, but the man could have been a whole lot nicer about it.

This was a few days before Christmas, and when Mom went to pay for the items she needed, the man set a box up on the counter and told her that someone had left it there for her. I saw her face stiffen and her chin tilt a little higher. Then Blaze came to drive us back home, and we left the store.

I knew my mother was not happy with the box, but on the way home, I mentally dug inside, imagining cakes, cookies, and other sweet delights. Now, the box sat on the kitchen table, and I waited in anticipation. Finally, she stepped up, pulled back the flaps, and began to laugh. Her laughter surprised and stunned me. What could possibly be in that box to make my mother laugh? Then, smiling, a sparkle in her blue eyes, she reached in and pulled out a bottle of wine.

I don't remember what else was in that box, but I'm sure it was something we kids found especially delicious, for I'm sure whoever packed that box wasn't the stingy, mean-spirited kind. I was totally amazed when she got us four kids cups from the cupboard and poured a tiny bit of wine into each—even in June's, who would probably have been about seven. We only got a drop or two in our cups and she poured only a small bit in her own. Then she had us touch our cups together, hold them up high and she offered a toast to this unknown friend who had given us this gift box for Christmas. I remember how we sputtered and spit, while our mother laughed. When the neighbor

Margaret worked for brought her home for Christmas, Mom gave the rest of the bottle to him.

One summer day, a couple of women brought us a box of used clothing. Mom invited them inside and we four kids stood around while they visited for a while. I have no memory of whether the clothes were suitable, or if there was anything at all we could wear. What I remember was the look of pity on the women's faces, and I did not understand. I was probably eight or ten and I thought it must be because of where we lived and that made no sense at all to me, for I thought we lived in a wonderful place with hills to roam, trees to climb, and a creek where we swam on hot summer days and where the trout lingered in the shadows, rising to take the bait from our hooks. In summer we had plenty of wild berries, sweet and tasty, to feast on, a long hill to coast down in winter, and even a horse to ride. I thought we lived in paradise, and when we moved from there to Bonners Ferry, Idaho to a house in town when I was fourteen, I was dreadfully homesick for a time, as were Larry and Danny. I don't know about the boys, but I didn't miss our old house, for this house was bigger, had electricity, running water, an indoor toilet, and even a bathtub. But, for a long time, I did miss all those hills and trees and especially the creek.

Our forty acres on Libby Creek had included a small bit of land across the creek and Dad had made it into a park, free to all, and kept it mowed with a hand scythe. Afterward, I expect Earl maintained it. I don't remember ever having a picnic there, but over the years, a lot of people from town used it, their kids splashing in the creek.

One day in late summer, I was across the creek from the park when the young woman who would become my fifth-grade teacher that fall was there with her family for a picnic. She came down to the creek and when she saw me, she waded across at a shallow spot to introduce herself. Her name was Daisy Hunter and I felt quite special when we gathered in the classroom that morning of the first day of school, for I'd already met that beautiful, smiling young woman.

The firemen had a picnic there every summer where, from the sounds of it, they had a heck of a good time. This annual picnic, we heard, was also when the new recruits were brought into the fold with a "baptism" of sorts in which strong arms grabbed on to them, lifted them up, and tossed them into the water. Of course, we saw none of this. We could sit outside and listen to the sounds of merriment, and when hearing a splash, imagine the baptism, but Mom wouldn't let us go where we could see any action. After the picnic as a thank you for using our park, the fire chief would bring over a box of what they called leftovers. However, I imagine that box had been filled separately at the store when they purchased their picnic supplies. I have a memory of the fire chief walking across the narrow foot bridge carrying that cardboard box one of those years. I was always excited about those boxes of food the firemen gave us, for our mother smiled and laughed as she exchanged words with the man. That wonderful, delicious food in those yearly boxes was free and clear, no shame attached.

I carried that stigma of being on welfare for years. I was probably in my late thirties or early forties when I admitted to a couple of my friends that I had been raised on welfare and the roof didn't cave in. In fact, it was no big deal to them. I think their acceptance helped me lay some of that shame to rest, but one last sting still lay in wait.

Ron and I were both retired when we went to the movies with another couple to see *The Help*, which is about some Black women in the sixties—long after slavery, but still subservient, still not equal to Whites in society. They worked as domestics in White homes and were treated as inferior beings. Afterward, we stopped at a restaurant. Somehow the conversation turned to those days of my childhood. And the husband asked how my mother had managed to raise seven children alone. With his words, something snapped in me and in anger, I said, "There is such a thing as welfare, you know!"

Our friends were embarrassed, and Ron was embarrassed—terribly so, I'm sure—but bless his heart, he never, ever said anything to me. Then one of them changed the subject and I sat silent, holding fast to my tears. I could have sunk away into the depths of the sea, had there been one to sink into. Looking back, I am sure it was the movie's subject matter that had triggered that long-hidden shame. Thankfully, I never ever had another episode. Now, I would say, "Well, we had to go on welfare. Mom hated it, but she had no choice." I don't exactly know why I carried that stigma for so long, but I did.

I did start out in this world on shaky ground, so maybe that's also a part of it all. I don't really know. I was born at home, the fifth child of my parents. Their fourth child had been a big, healthy-looking little boy, who despite his appearance, died when he was six days old. I have no idea how old I was when I heard the story of my birth and the birth of the child before me.

"You were so ugly. You looked like a monkey. We thought about throwing you into that swampy place down by the river." Those words were from my siblings, speaking as kids will do, especially siblings—teasing words, but words with a ring of truth.

My mother had hepatitis when I was born and that may have been why my skin was tinged with jaundice. I was, of course, born at home, my breathing shallow and weak. To aid in my breathing, I was placed before an open window so the April breezes could blow across my tiny face.

My siblings were then nine, seven, and five. Margaret's memory of that baby boy was probably hazy at best. Mabel had probably retained some memory of him, and certainly Earl did. Emotional stress highlights our memories and sometimes distorts them.

Kelly, our third child, was no older than six weeks when she had her first bout with tonsillitis, and every two weeks it returned. The doctor did not want to remove her tonsils until she was two and he urged us to take every precaution to keep her from getting sick. We did, but she continued to get sick, and her last bout, when she was just a few months shy of two years, made him feel he couldn't hold off any longer. The operation cured her, although for a while her throat was so sore that she was totally mad at me.

Through those nearly two years, Kathy, our oldest child, age five when Kelly was born, seeing her little sister so ill all the time, maybe even because of the unpleasant smell of her little head (caused by the infection and medications), began to believe her little sister was going to die. She told us many years later that the fear of her little sister dying had kept her from wanting to have anything at all to do with her.

I believe this fear was the same fear that made my siblings shut themselves off from me. Like Kathy, I am certain they believed I would die, like the baby before me who had looked so healthy but had lived only six days and was buried the day before Christmas. This one, weak and sickly, most likely wasn't going to be around very long either. Hearing those stories, I remember feeling some survivor guilt. He was a big, beautiful, healthy child, did he not deserve to live more than me?

I was about thirteen when one day I came into the living room and saw my mother standing at the window, looking out at the snow. It had just begun, that first of the season, a light fluttering of large white flakes cascading down on the fields, the trees, the hills, and I heard her murmur, "And still fluttered down the snow." She noticed me then and smiled and I asked what she'd said. She told me it was from a poem entitled *The First Snowfall* by James Russell Lowell and she brought out one of her poetry books and read it to me. The poem is about that first snow of the season and that one line she had murmured as she stood looking out the window, "and still fluttered down the snow," was what I always remember, rather than the title. About midway through the poem, it tells of a little headstone, the snowflakes folding gently around it. The last lines are of how she'd kissed her daughter, but the kiss had not been for her, but for the child's baby sister, lying under the deepening snow. I wondered then if she was thinking about that baby boy, who by all rights, should have survived instead of me. Years later, I bought a book of poetry just for that single poem, and I still have it.

# CHAPTER 7

# DAD'S BOOK

**I DIDN'T KNOW** about cemeteries, or where my daddy was buried, and for a time I tried to pretend he had not died, that he was away on a packing trip that had taken him far into the mountains, but someday he'd come home. Of course, I knew he was dead, that the people had come for him, but in my need to deny that he was gone from us forever, I'd tell my two little brothers the packing trip story. Then sometime after our mother recovered, maybe March, for in my memory, it is still cold, but the ground is bare of snow, I saw our mother carrying a shovel. She wore her heavy, wool plaid winter work coat, a knit cap on her head. It was the shovel that made me think that our daddy was buried somewhere up in the hills. Although I knew the funeral had been in town, I didn't know what a funeral was, but I evidently knew about burials. Maybe I'd heard that the big, healthy baby boy who was born before me was buried in the Libby cemetery. I had known about burying, but a cemetery would be just a word, until Blaze would take us there in May and I would see my daddy's grave for the first time.

Dad came into the world on July 10, 1887, near Cairo in Pratt County, Kansas, but six years later, his family moved by covered wagon to Oklahoma, where they took a homestead near Richmond in Woodward County. Dad's Goyen grandparents were from England, his father born in Canada. Later, they moved to Ohio, where his parents met and were married. Sometime later, they moved from

Ohio to Iowa and eventually left Iowa, traveling by train to Kansas.

According to cousins, Dad's mother was quite stern, a church-going woman who served the community as a midwife. They also said she had favorites among her children, and my dad was the least of them. I was told that when their father passed, their mother made out her will, leaving everything to Ben, the youngest. Then WWI broke out and Ben got called to serve, as did our dad. Ben died in the army camp in New Jersey of the 1918 flu pandemic. At the time, Dad was stationed at Camp Freemont in California. He escaped going to war, as it ended just as his unit was being called up to go overseas. With Ben gone, their mother chose their sister Emma to inherit everything. I guess she was the next favorite. However, when their mother passed, Emma shared equally with all her siblings, even my dad.

Although the country school provided eight years of education, it was not required and a lot of farm boys either dropped out early, or only attended sporadically during times when the farm work eased. I've been told that our dad only went through the fifth grade. He left home at about eighteen, returning at least once for his father's funeral. I never heard if he came back for his mother's.

According to my cousins, the grandparents were relativity affluent and had a nice house and what was described to me as lovely Havilland China in the cupboards and a parlor with a settee and other nice furniture. It might not have been a happy home—at least in later years. From what I gathered from those cousins, all of them much older than me, our grandmother may have had a mental disorder. Her preference for one child at a time is an indication as well as being harsh even with the grandchildren. One cousin said that when we came with our parents to visit, she did not greet us—even us little ones—with a smile or endearing words, but some command, like "Wipe your feet." She also said that the family was seated in the parlor, even the kids, and that the settee, stuffed with horsehair, itched.

I think of the advances in medicine and mental health in the years since and wonder if she were living now if she could have been helped.

Our dad roamed the west working as a cowboy for the next eighteen to twenty years. Army records show he was working out of Lusk, Wyoming, when he was drafted into the Army during WWI, but otherwise there is no information on those early years, until 1925–26 when we know he was in Wyoming in the Wheatland and Chugwater area because that's where our parents met. Dad's brother, Charley, was the foreman and co-owner of a ranch there, and we know Mom had worked for Charley's first wife, who passed away early in life.

Our mother was born near Mystic, Appanoose County, Iowa on June 28, 1903, and came to Wyoming on the train with her parents and other family in 1914 to settle on the homestead her father had taken the year before. The land was south of Chugwater, near Diamond, a small town that no longer exists. She attended country schools through the eighth grade and was an avid reader all her life. Besides having worked for Charley's wife, Mom had at one time worked in the store at Diamond. I don't know how or when our parents met, but both places would have presented the opportunity. Dad was sixteen years older than Mom, but it was without doubt a love match.

They were married in Greeley, Colorado on December 5, 1927, and moved into their first home, a cabin near Rock River, Wyoming. Soon afterward they moved to Montana, where a few years before, Aunt Teddie and Blaze had bought a home and acreage south of Libby. They rented several places before buying the place on Libby Creek in 1937.

I don't know when Dad started writing his book about his cowboy days, but when he had it finished, he showed it to Libby's librarian. I have kept notebooks for years in which I write family stories, jokes, and other miscellaneous items of interest to me. One entry in August of 1976, I wrote of being in Libby and visiting with the librarian about Dad's book. Inez Ratekin Herrig had been the librarian for years and was one of Libby's outstanding citizens, who loved the town, its history, and its people. She recalled for me the day Dad came to her with his handwritten book for her to read. She remembered the year was 1936. She said he was shy, almost apologetic, as if he hoped he wasn't wasting her time. She thought the story was very good and insisted on typing it for him. She also urged him to send it out, which he did—one time, but it was rejected.

"Now you know," she said, her brown eyes enormous, dark, and shining behind thick glasses, "many good books have been sent out as often as twenty times before they've sold. I wish I had encouraged him more." She told me that when he wrote about the horses he'd known and the world of the cowboy, that his words made pictures that brought the story to life and drew the reader into the story.

She called Dad the last of the old-time cowboys. "His walk was that sort of rolling gait peculiar to the cowboy from wearing boots and spending so much time in the saddle." She also told me that he was one who had the ability to see animals as individuals and his writing was such that the reader could see it, too. "He also had a really good sense of humor," she said. "I so enjoyed visiting with him."

I told her I had read Dad's book when I was thirteen and I am glad I didn't wait any longer, for the next year it was lost during our move to Bonners Ferry, Idaho.

Disappointed to hear that, she said, "I wish I'd kept the original when I typed it, but of course, I couldn't have done that."

I wish she had, too, and still had it to give to me.

There were color illustrations in Dad's story that depicted the life of the cowboy—the horses, riders, and range stock. I have no clear memory of those pictures, but I have the impression that I, as a young girl, thought they were very good. I always thought that Dad had drawn and painted those scenes, but one day I asked Mabel, and she told me she thought Mom had done them. So she probably did, Mabel being older and more likely to have remembered. I imagine Mom helped with spelling and punctuation, for she was well-read, and valuing education as she did, she'd have to have kept up on all that.

I don't remember the book's title, but the main character was a cowboy who went by the name of Prairie. He got that nickname because he always changed the lyrics of that old cowboy lament, "Oh Bury Me Not on the Lone Prairie" from "where the coyotes howl, and the wind blows free" to "For some dry farmer will plant corn over me."

Both Dad and Prairie were known to have said, "If God had wanted the sod to be turned upside down, He would have made it that way."

Although Dad went by that fictitious name, the stories were his own. Prairie had a one-man horse that only he could ride and one Saturday night, the cowboys in from the ranch had gathered in the local saloon. Sometime that night, Prairie, having imbibed a bit too much and needing a place to sleep it off, went out and crawled under his horse. In the book, he wrote how his friends tried to pull him out from under his horse, but the horse stood them off, with ears laid back and teeth bared. A real story or made up? Well, Dad had a way with horses, but he was also a storyteller.

I remember hearing that Dad had played the clown in the local rodeo, distracting the bull away from the rider and entertaining the audience in the process. I also heard that he rode a horse in the local parade advertising a car dealership, even though he had no use for cars. One of his acts, Earl told me, was riding a horse without saddle or bridle and backward, using the horse's tail for reins and pretending to have nipped too heavily on the sauce, he would periodically fall off his horse and then run after it in high-stepping strides, grab the horse by the tail to stop him, climb up on its bare back, again backward, and farther up the street, repeat the process.

Dad did love his horses. I had to have been five or under when I heard him tell Mother about this horse named Red who had fallen off the side of a mountain (or so I recall), breaking his leg, and my daddy had to shoot him. Being so small and seeing my daddy's obvious distress, I thought Red was a person and my daddy's best friend. I felt so sad for my daddy having to shoot his best friend. I don't know when I learned that Red was a horse.

I imagine the term "horse whisperer" was coined for just such a man as our daddy. With a good horse under him—and they were all good under him—he must have loved his job packing for the Forest Service. In the old days, he'd happily herd a bunch of cows, but, like the true cowboy of his day, he'd not be caught milking them. Neither he nor Prairie would have ever been happy farming.

Because Dad loved horses and the open range of the old west, he would have loved the book, *The Longhorn Cowboy* by James Cook and Howard Driggs, published in 1942. One of the stories is about when the subject of the book, James Cook, rode out from camp one day and came across a small herd of ten buffalo. Without hesitation and contrary to his normal reactions, in which he would have just ridden on by, he pulled out his rifle and killed six of them.

"I never killed game I couldn't use. We had plenty of meat and no use for the hides," he wrote. Disgusted with himself, he rode back to camp and told the other men what he had done. They agreed it was a damn fool thing to do.

They broke camp and rode on and soon met a wagon train whose people were suffering from hunger and thirst, having found no water or game for days. The cowboys led them to a good-sized creek and then to the six dead buffalo. They helped the people skin and butcher the animals and preserve the meat to take with them. The author had acted totally out of character. Was it divine intervention—an answer to pleading prayers from those in the wagon train?

Although it didn't dawn on me until many years later when I ran across the entry in an old diary, I think Ron and I were once an answer to prayer. Sometime after we retired and were traveling more, we met a man who asked for money, but we did not feel safe in that situation to open purse or wallet, so we shook our heads and went on. After that we started taking out fifty dollars in fives and tens, each carrying some in our pockets, so if asked, there'd be little if any risk. When that ran out, we'd take out fifty more. We called it the Lord's money.

That year, we still had the last fifty dollars when we headed home from Montana in our motor home, our car on a trailer behind. At Billings, we stopped for gas, Ron exiting at a Flying J. He pulled up to the pumps, turned off the motor, and we heard a *clunk*. The trailer hitch had broken. Not on the interstate, but right there, the very moment we stopped. We knew we had escaped an accident, maybe injury, even death, and we gave grateful thanks to the Lord. Ron called a repair shop and when they came for the trailer, we moved the motor home and the car over next to the building, out of the way, and settled in to wait.

When we pulled off the interstate, we'd seen a couple with two children about ten and twelve on the eastbound ramp trying to hitch a ride. From where we had parked to wait for the trailer, we had a clear view of them standing there. They were still there an hour later. Then the woman and the girl came over, we assume to use the restroom, and it was then that we remembered the fifty dollars. So, when they came out a short time later, I gave it to them. She was so appreciative and thanked me over and over. About five or ten minutes after she and the girl returned to the man and boy, all four came over and went into the restaurant. We wondered if they would have eaten at all that day had it not been for the Lord's money. Within fifteen minutes of them returning to the off-ramp to find a ride, Ron looked out the motor home's windshield and saw that they were gone.

# CHAPTER 8

# THE PEOPLE DISAPPEAR

**THAT SPRING OF** 1943 after our dad passed in January, I assume it was on Memorial Day, Blaze drove us to the cemetery in Libby. There for the first time, I saw my daddy's grave and realized he wasn't buried up in the hills, but in this place called a cemetery.

We'd brought wild pink roses from the hills and maybe some purple irises (we called them flags), from the bed that grew south of the house, but I only remember the roses. I had turned six in April and would go to the first grade in September. I suppose I was anxious to see what a cemetery was and how Daddy's grave would look. However, my excitement died at the sight of that grave. It was a WWI veteran's grave—like all the others there in rows in that part of the cemetery. The men's names and information were etched in the upright identical white slabs of stone, but it was the sight of Daddy's grave that chilled me. For in that moment, I suddenly thought of the people who I believed had come that night and killed him. A jolt of fear slammed into me, for I knew they were there in the grave waiting. Waiting for me. My conscious memory no longer remembered my mother's breakdown and my fear that the people would come for her, but I'd not forgotten how they had come and killed my daddy. Dad had passed in January, so the grass had not yet covered that long narrow patch of earth, and maybe that was why I thought the people were hiding down there in the grave and if I stepped too close they'd thrust their hands up through the dirt, grab me, and pull me under. I stepped back far enough away to feel safe and waited. I was so relieved when we were all back in the car and Blaze was driving us away.

One might wonder why, if I thought those people were down in Daddy's grave, I thought they would grab me. Why not my mother? She was there at the cemetery with me. Well, consciously I knew my mother was no longer in that bed with my little sister and there were no evil people coming to kill her, but my subconscious still believed otherwise and what my subconscious believed ruled me without my knowing. So, *subconsciously* I believed that the people would come for her there, in that bed at home, not here at the cemetery.

I don't recall ever visiting the cemetery again until we buried our mother there fourteen years later in 1957. Six years before that, our mother had moved us four younger kids to Bonners Ferry, Idaho, and she had died there of cancer. Because our dad was buried in the WWI veteran's section, she could not be buried beside him, but at least she was in the same cemetery.

I did not fear Dad's grave when we buried our mother, for the people were no longer a conscious memory. However my subconscious still had my mother in that bed back in that old house on Libby Creek and I don't recall feeling any emotion when we buried my mother there that day.

I was six or seven when I has my tonsils out and that experience reinforced the fear that had started at my dad's grave, that the people were now after me. I'd never been in a hospital before. I don't know if I'd ever even seen a doctor; if so, I don't remember. I know I was quite apprehensive as I waited in a small room with my mother. My memory sees her sitting in a chair and me standing close to her and I'm wearing a long white gown. When they came for me and led me away, I looked back at her one last time. They laid me on a table and shone bright lights in my eyes. They wore white caps on their heads and white masks on their faces, so all I could see of them were their eyes.

"Breathe deep," a voice said, a kind, gentle voice, and clapped an ether pack over my face. Terror flooded my being! They had tricked me! I fought for my life in those seconds before I went under.

I woke up in a bed and my mother was there smiling at me, her voice soft, gentle, and I knew I was safe. My throat hurt but I had escaped from the people. There was a bed beside mine, and a little girl no bigger than me lay in it crying. "Don't cry," her mother, who was sitting in a chair beside my mother, said, "See, that little girl isn't crying." My throat was hurting really bad, but I did not cry. I wanted to cry, but I couldn't. We didn't cry in our family. Besides, I knew I had to be brave for that little girl and, maybe also, so my mother would be proud of me.

We didn't have kindergarten, so I started school in the first grade. I was terrified of being left alone in that classroom, so my mother stayed with me that first day. At least that is what I always thought, until now, writing this, all these years later. I think what really terrified me was leaving my mother at home where my subconscious still had her in bed with baby June, the people still coming for her. *What if they came while I was gone?* I don't remember how I got to school that first day, but since I was too scared to leave my mother, I'm sure Blaze drove us into town and then came back for us when school was out. Aunt Teddie probably kept the three little ones. The next day, Mom told me I had to ride the bus, that she needed to stay home with the boys and baby June. Mabel or Margaret or both probably took me into the building and to my classroom before going to theirs. I don't remember that day, but I'm sure I was relieved when we got home to find my mother still there and still alive. Eventually, I must have lost my fear of being away from my mother. As far as I remember, I liked school, and I got along well with the kids, except for this one girl with short, curly red hair. She harassed me out on the playground, chasing me, pushing me, yanking my long, curly blond hair, and calling me an "old witch."

Because I didn't like her pulling my hair, I asked Mom to cut mine short and she did. That did it and "Red" and I became close friends all through grade school and junior high. I went to high school in Idaho.

I was in the second grade when the truck that delivered coal for the school's furnaces hit a woman and killed her. It was just as school was being let out. We had been given instructions on how to leave the school—the town kids to go to their homes one way, the bus kids another.

I don't know if I got the directions wrong, but I know that on my way to the bus, I saw that blanket-covered body lying on the ground at the entrance of the blacktop between those two grade school buildings—and I see it still. I'm certain it wasn't just my imagination, for how would I know a dead body would be covered?

That woman's death at the school terrified me, for I now believed the people were everywhere. They had even come to our school to kill her. Maybe they had pushed her in front of the coal truck, or maybe they were driving it. I knew then that there was no place where we would be safe from them.

That belief had ratcheted up my fear and anxiety to such a high level that I lost all conscious memory of the people—even that they had killed my daddy, were coming for my mother, and twice had tried to get me. Although I no longer remembered the people consciously, my subconscious did and kept my mother in that bed for many more years. Within a few years (I don't remember exactly when they started), I began to have panic attacks and fainting spells.

As I remember, the first time I had one of those panic attacks and fainting spells was when we were lined up for one of our childhood vaccinations. As I stood in that line, the panic rose and soon I grew lightheaded and wobbly. A teacher or someone, seeing my distress, pulled me out of the line, and it happened every time. I was in the fifth or sixth grade as I remember when we got the smallpox vaccinations. I think it was explained as a kind of a scratch, for I never felt a bit of panic and I was so proud of myself.

For some reason, I didn't have any of those attacks while in high school in Bonners Ferry. But four months out of high school, when Ron and I went to get our blood tests, a requirement for getting a marriage license. I got panicky, then wobbly as my blood was drawn, and Ron had to practically carry me out of the doctor's office. Outside, I immediately recovered.

Two months after we were married and we were living in Canada where Ron, who was in the Air Force, had been reassigned, I wanted to go to the hospital to visit a fellow Air Force spouse to see their new baby. Ron drove me, as I had not yet learned to drive and wouldn't until two years later. I was happy that day. I was with my love and going to visit my friend and see her new baby. I had no inkling at all of what was to happen when I stepped through the door of the hospital and that smell hit me. The smell of ether.

It was like when we came back to our house after my father's funeral and that foreign smell, maybe along with the bed all made up as if my daddy had never been there at all had triggered the fear of the people who I believed had killed him. But this smell was the smell of ether, although I didn't realize it then, and it took me back subconsciously to that hospital operating room when I was a child, and I thought those masked people who took my tonsils out had tried to kill me. That they were those people who had killed my daddy and would have pulled me down into his grave if I hadn't stepped back out of their reach, and those people who drove the coal truck and killed that woman at my school. As well as those people who I still subconsciously believed were coming for my mother. I know now, but I didn't know it then, that it was the smell of ether that triggered that memory of the people, those evil ones who although gone from my conscious mind, remained a terror in my subconscious.

I had just stepped through the entrance of that hospital when immediately I grew panicky, dizzy, and faint and I knew if I didn't get back outside, I would pass out. I turned and stumbled back toward the door, my vision fading. Ron grabbed me and helped me outside, where away from that smell, I soon recovered. But even after the dizziness was gone, and my vision had cleared, I could not go back in there. Not even to see my friend and her baby, so Ron drove me back to our apartment while I sat huddled beside him in silence, holding back the tears of shame. He never asked me about it, and I could not have explained if he had, for I didn't even know myself. Although I'd begun to have those panic attacks and fainting spells sometime in grade school, for years, I had no clue as to why.

Eventually I would learn that my triggers were death, dying, the thought of the heart beating and of blood running through the veins, images brought to my mind in my science books beginning in grade school, vaccinations, and now the smell of ether. However, I would never encounter that smell again, as other sedatives were fast taking ether's place. Ron never asked me about either of those spells, nor would he about any future episodes. I am sure he knew each time that I was ashamed. Perhaps, he also suspected that even if he had asked why, I had no explanation to give him.

After Mom passed in 1957, we moved here to Ron's hometown of Phillipsburg, Kansas. Within a month or so, the hospital held an open house to show some new additions to the facility and Ron thought we should go. I was reluctant, but I couldn't tell him I was afraid this hospital would smell like the one in Canada, or that something else would trigger an attack. And if I did get panicky and start to pass out, he'd have to drag me from the building in front of those he'd grown up with, most who had known him and his family for years—some all his life. I did not share with him or anyone then this weakness, this weirdness of mine I didn't even understand myself. I went, praying desperately that this one would not have that smell. The only other hospital I'd been in since that one in Canada was the one in Bonners Ferry, Idaho, where my mother had surgery for a broken hip, and where fourteen months later she would leave us, but thankfully it had not smelled of ether.

Our tour of the Phillipsburg hospital went well, no ether smell, no panic attacks, no fainting spells. It was a good thing, too, because two months later I'd be there giving birth to our first child. Our second little girl also arrived at that hospital, as did our third. Our son was born at the hospital in Norton, as our hospital was, at that time, short of doctors. I had no trouble there either.

Ron's sister, Shirley had delivered her two sons using hypnosis and she sang its praises, and so I decided to give it a try with our third baby. Each time the doctor started the process, within minutes I'd panic and feel like I was going to throw up, and finally he gave up. I never forgot what he said then, almost as if he were angry, as if somehow, I had failed him. "You're going to have to learn to relax and I don't know how the hell you're going do it, but you've got to." He did give me some relaxation exercises to practice and those served me well in labor, until I got a huge cramp in my leg and had to be sedated.

Later, when our daughter Kathy was about six or seven, she had warts all over her hands. This doctor suggested hypnosis and I felt a rush of panic and I knew I couldn't help her. So, her daddy put her through the daily routine of relaxing and soothing the warts away. I don't remember how long, maybe a month or six weeks, but in a relatively short time, the warts were gone.

I don't know if I ever thought why I reacted as I did to being hypnotized. That is until now as I write these words. The doctor had me lay on the examining table, look up at a spot on the ceiling, and count backward. I could not get very far before I'd have to sit up, feeling sick, the gorge rising in my throat. I know now it was that subconscious fear that kept my level of anxiety so high, I could not relax, as the doctor said I needed to do.

CHAPTER 9

# THOSE PANIC ATTACKS AND FAINTING SPELLS

**THE PEOPLE HAVING** slipped into my subconscious memory meant that I no longer remembered that I thought they had killed my daddy or were waiting for my mother or had been in Dad's grave when we visited the cemetery or were the ether-bearing masked ones in the hospital or had killed the woman at my school. They now lived in my subconscious where I had no control, no memory on a conscious level, and there my subconscious continued to plague me.

Although my conscious memory no longer remembered, my subconscious retained that awful fear of the people, and if I'd encounter one of my triggers, I'd begin to panic and then, if I couldn't escape, I'd faint.

However, these triggers only applied to humans. I'd seen plenty of death in animals—a young steer butchered, a deer cut up to feed us, the heads of chickens cut off. I even helped pull off the feathers. Once our cousins John and Bill Echo killed a bear and brought it to us, skinned and creepy looking. For a time, Mabel raised rabbits and I watched them being killed and skinned for our dinner. Once my brother and I killed a couple of frogs, cut off their legs and asked Mom to fry them for us. We'd heard of people eating frog legs, so we thought we'd give it a try. Yuck! We took one small bite and promptly spit it out. We never did that again! We trapped gophers and sometimes shot them with the .22, not for sport, but because they dug holes in our alfalfa fields. The deaths of those animals were a part of normal life. It was human death that terrified me, that those terrible, evil, bad ones who had killed our daddy and were waiting to kill my mother and had tried to kill me would come again. That's what scared me. Even though, since the second grade when the woman got run over at my school they had left my conscious mind. My subconscious still believed, and that belief directed my thoughts and actions.

Eventually, the school must have notified my mother that I had missed my vaccinations because she had Mabel take me to town one day to begin getting those dreaded shots. We didn't have a car, so she took me by horseback. We were about halfway to Libby when the latigo, the leather strap that held the cinch in place, broke or came loose and the saddle slipped, and we both fell off on to the edge of the highway. Somehow Mabel fixed it so the saddle wouldn't slip again, and we rode on, but by then I'd begun to feel apprehensive, and by the time we'd reached Libby, I was getting panicky.

In those days, there was a place behind the stores that lined the west side of the main street where one could leave their horses. By the time my sister had our horse tied, she could see I was in distress. Hoping to soothe me and calm my fears, she left me with the horse and ran across the street to a grocery store and came back with an orange. I loved oranges, actually all fruit, and I sat down on the ground and devoured it. Then Mabel took my hands and pulled me to my feet. Now we had to go over to the hospital a block away and get my shots. I took a couple of steps in that direction and threw up the orange. Mabel untied the horse, put me back behind the saddle, and we went home. I don't know whether my lack of vaccination status fell through the cracks, the school looked the other way, or there were no requirements in those days. When that out-of-body experience cured me of my "spells" I went to the clinic and got the vaccinations I would have ordinarily had.

My first full-blown fainting spell was in the fifth grade. That day, the teacher had us open our science books to a certain page to begin our lesson. I opened my book and saw the full-page picture of a human heart with all its veins and ventricles. I don't even remember the rise of panic before I fainted and fell out of my desk to the floor. I woke with the teacher and all the kids gathered about, peering down at me. The teacher sent me to the nurse's office, assuming I'm sure, that I was ill, and by the time the nurse decided I wasn't and sent me back, science class had ended.

I remember several times when we studied the workings of the inner body in the sixth, seventh, and eigth grades when I'd feel the panic rise, my sight growing dim. Those times I escaped through urgent bathroom visits, which I came to rely on as my escape mechanism. All I'd need was to get outside the room and immediately my panic would subside, the dizziness fade, and I'd fully recover. I assume I lingered awhile in those bathrooms until science class was over.

In the eighth grade during science class one day, the teacher was leading us in a discussion of the material we had been assigned to read the day before, but because of the subject matter (the inner workings of the human body), I'd not read a word of it. During the classroom discussion I tried to talk inside my head to shut out the words, but at some point, that failed me, and I felt the panic rise. My vision blurring I raised my hand to be excused to go to the bathroom.

The teacher did not see my hand, or else he ignored it. Finally, desperate to get out of the room, I bolted from my desk and then, barely able to see as the dizziness fogged my sight, I staggered between desks to the door. The teacher caught me just before I fell and took me on out into the hall where I immediately recovered. He took me to the nurse's office, which was next to the principal's office, and except for being extremely embarrassed, I was fine. I heard him tell the principal about the classroom's subject matter and that he'd heard of people who fainted at the sight of blood, or when getting a shot, or visiting the doctor, and he thought that might be my problem. In a way, I felt a kind of relief, hearing his words, for if there were others like me, then maybe I wasn't such a freak after all.

I didn't have any panic or fainting episodes in Bonners Ferry when I was in high school. I remember we dissected a frog one time, but that was not a human creature. If we had any studies of the human body, I don't recall them, so we must not have had any or I was absent, or the bathroom was handy.

One of the problems with this affliction was that when we moved to Kansas after my mother passed, Ron bought into a funeral home then owned and operated by the Olliffs, Arel and Minnie, and their son, Darel, who had married Ron's sister, Shirley. Ron and Darel had first bought out the old McKinley Furniture Store and a year later, the store doing well and the senior Olliffs retiring, Ron then purchased shares in the funeral home and the name was changed to Olliff-Boeve Memorial Chapel.

Generally, I had little trouble being at the funeral home, a three-story structure, for it was also home to Darel and Shirley and their two little boys, as well as Arel and Minnie. Shirley would have me over for coffee in her kitchen and our kids would play together. Sometimes Darel and Ron would join us. I remember once when the bathroom, just off from the kitchen, came in handy. That day the guys joined us for coffee after they had been on an ambulance trip—a car wreck where a man had been decapitated.

In those years before I was cured, one odd episode happened while Ron and I were visiting friends in Colorado Springs. Sometime during that visit, the couple began to tell us about some people who were on a family vacation— people they knew, I assumed. The family had taken the grandmother along, but she died on the way in the back seat of the car, so they tied her on top of the car, and left her sitting on a chair in another family member's patio as the family wasn't home at the time. How much of that I heard I don't remember for I tried not to listen, but soon I had to excuse myself and head for the bathroom. Thankfully, the subject had changed by the time I got back.

Some years later, I saw the Chevy Chase movie *Vacation* on TV, and I realized they had been talking about that movie. If I had known it was just a movie it wouldn't have bothered me, for it was not real. The problem was that I was always so hypervigilant about my affliction that I'd stop listening if the talk turned to something I feared would trigger an attack, and I'd try to drown out their words with self-talk inside my head.

I had never told Ron about my "spells." I was too ashamed of my weakness, as that was what I believed those spells were—just a flaw in me. Even after I realized, sometime later, maybe months later, that those friends had been talking about a movie, I couldn't say anything to him, for I was still hiding my shame. Also, to learn it was just a movie, made me doubly embarrassed. I assume Ron never knew why I had escaped to the bathroom that evening and those other times—at least I don't think he did, but sometimes he must have wondered about me.

In writing this chapter, I looked up that movie's release date. It was 1983. I was forty-six years old. In two more years, my sister, Mabel, and her husband, John, would come from Montana to visit us and she would speak the words that would bring about that out-of-body experience that would take me back to my childhood home, a five-year-old again, and where I'd learn the reason for my panic attacks and fainting spells. That knowledge would set me free.

When one's father passed some forty years ago, it's rare that anyone asks details of his passing, and even if they do, it doesn't usually pose a problem. But a few weeks before Mabel and John visited us that summer of my forty-eighth year, Darel, Ron's sister's husband, and Ron's partner in the furniture store and funeral home, asked about my dad's death. As his words became more probing, I was gripped with an overwhelming sadness, and I broke down and cried. It embarrassed us both.

If Darel had waited a few more weeks until I'd had that out-of-body experience to ask about my daddy, I would have been fine. That experience showed me the source of my subconscious belief and a deep and long-lasting unresolved grief. All of which had been the cause of my panic attacks and fainting spells.

I never had another panic attack or fainting spell ever again, and that old, deep sadness from childhood had dissipated too. A little less than a year later, I was able to work at the funeral home and I'm positive I could have even had hypnosis then, but I didn't have warts and I was too old for babies.

In writing this and remembering those years I'd feared the people, I've come to understand a bit more about how those events affected me. It began not so much with my father's death, but that next morning when Blaze was waiting to take us back to stay with Aunt Teddie and I was needing my mittens. It was then that I came to believe that the people who had killed my daddy had made him look so awful that my mother had not wanted me to see him. And I never did, thus sealing in my mind what could have been so easily prevented. I'd thought the woman who was run over at the school had been covered with the blanket because the people had made her look so awful when they killed her, just like they had my daddy.

If I had left my mittens by the kitchen stove to dry instead of in the living room, the people probably would have just faded from my memory. And with no memory of the people and what I thought they had done to my daddy, I might have worried about my mother when she had her breakdown, but no more than any child and certainly not to that degree. Also, when the woman was run over at my school, it would have been just an accident. Without those people, I would have been able to get all my vaccinations. Without those people I wouldn't have suffered those years of fainting spells and panic attacks.

*Just one little pair of mittens.*

CHAPTER 10

# BONNERS FERRY

**ONE SPRING DAY** we got off the bus at the top of the hill just above the fish hatchery to walk those two miles home on that old road, once traveled by stagecoaches. That old road that led us down Trainer Hill and home was now named Swede Mountain Road. At the top of Trainer Hill it now turned east, toward the mountain it was named for and where the lookout, at its top, is still manned during fire season, as it has been for years.

That day in 1951, as we kids, Larry, Danny, June, and I walked down Trainer Hill toward our home, I had no inkling that our lives were about to change. When we stepped into the house, our mother was waiting for us, waiting to tell us she'd sold our home and we would soon be moving to Bonners Ferry, Idaho, a small town fifty miles west of Libby. We knew we were eventually moving. We knew Mom had listed our place and we had gone with her to look for a new home there, a home in town, but I don't recall having any thoughts about it until, at the bottom of Trainer Hill, we left the road to crawl through the barbed-wire fence and cut across what we called "the new alfalfa field" to the house. It was then, as I crawled through the fence, that I had a premonition. I suddenly knew my world was changing, but not how or why, just that something was happening. And, for a second or two or more, it was as if I were standing there watching myself climb through the fence and start walking across the field toward the house. Mom was sitting in her rocking chair in the living room waiting for us, and as soon as we stepped through the door, she said, "I sold the place today."

That spring day in 1951 would be the start of a huge life-changing event for me. In three more years, I would meet Ron, but, that moment of knowing might have been only that we were moving, that the place had sold.

It seems to me that on most of those school days, we walked that old road those two miles from our place at the bottom of Trainer Hill to ride the school bus into town and back. When we had a footbridge over Libby Creek, it was only about a mile from our house to the bus stop. But spring floods are tough on footbridges.

One mile or two miles made no difference to our brother Earl. He would still have to run to catch the school bus. One morning when we still had a footbridge to cross, we'd left the house as usual well before Earl, and we were now sitting on the bus waiting for him. Suddenly, he burst out of a stand of trees, running just as fast as he could toward us. The bus driver chuckled and said, "Here comes Earl, running across the level, kicking up his heels and running like the devil."

I'm sure our mother was apprehensive about moving us over into Idaho. And I wonder now, writing this, knowing that our loved ones are always with us and do at times let us know they are near, if Dad had given our mother signs that he was still with her, and maybe even letting her know he approved of the move. I hope so. It had to have been a huge step for her. It was hard for us, too, and especially for Larry and Danny because even more than me they missed the land, the creek, and the hills that had all been just outside our door. Our new house was in town, closed in with houses, and in our case, just a small yard between us on one side and a very narrow strip of grass on the other. I know Mom hoped to become more independent by being able to work at a job. However, that never worked out.

The Canadian couple who bought our old place on Libby Creek eventually sold it to the local lumber company, who tore down the house and other buildings and put a road through the property to haul their lumber. The road crossed Libby Creek near the lumber yard, bypassed Trainer Hill, and came out on what is now called the Farm to Market Road and leads to Highway 2. Some years later, that haul road was abandoned, and nature began to reclaim the land. After Ron and I were married, we moved to his hometown in Kansas, but over the years we'd return to visit my siblings and friends and that old home place on Libby Creek. The last time I was there, four years after Ron passed and seventy-one years since I crawled through that barbed-wire fence to learn we were moving to Bonners Ferry, someone had moved onto the land and the road at the top of Trainer Hill was gated off, so I couldn't go down to where our house had been without trespassing. So now, only in memory will I ever go there again.

I don't know if I ever thought about the premonition I had that day climbing through the fence in the spring of 1951 until I was writing this chapter, but I still see it all so clearly. It was just a kind of knowing, but not of exactly what was to happen. Just as I had no memory of exactly what I saw or maybe just "knew" would take our father from us that day he shaved off his mustache.

I may have had other premonitions throughout my growing-up years, but if so, I don't remember them. I do, however, remember a few I had as an adult. On those rare occasions when I've had that sense of knowing ahead of time about an event and it would happen, some were so minor as to make me question why I even had them at all. Like, twice knowing I would win the door prize at a couple of social meetings. The first time, as I was going out the door, the thought, *I'm going to win the door prize tonight*, popped into my head. The other time and place and years apart, I started to pick a number and then it was like my hand stopped and without thought, I moved it over and picked up the winner. I didn't "know" it was the winner, or maybe I did. I just didn't know I knew it. I remembered a vision years ago of a girl from our church packing clothes in a suitcase and looking unhappy, and I thought, *oh, they're moving*. And they did. I have no idea why I got that little minivision, for I was not at all close to the family.

One time though, a premonition may have saved me from an accident—might even have saved my life. I was driving home from Denver when I suddenly "saw" in my head, a big, black bull on the road. I slowed down. A few minutes later, I rounded a curve and saw a big black bull beside the road. Another day, I stepped out the back door of our summer place in Montana and saw for a second or two, a medium-sized taffy-colored dog standing on the patio, looking up at me a few seconds before he vanished. I imagine he'd once lived there.

We had moved to Idaho in August and were settled in our new home in Bonners Ferry, in time for us to start school after Labor Day. I was a freshman in high school, Larry in junior high, and Danny and June in grade school. Sometime my freshman year, I went to work as a live-in for an elderly woman who could walk a little, but was basically wheelchair-bound, and her young collie dog that she treated like a child. I was never comfortable around her. To me she was cranky and demanding. Neither did I bond with her dog. Thinking back, I wonder if it was because she was old, or seemed quite old to me, and I was afraid she'd die on me. I no longer had conscious memory of the people, but my subconscious still did. Anyway, even without the people, conscious or otherwise, being alone with someone who might die is a scary thought for any kid.

I don't remember how long I worked for her. I wasn't at all happy with the job, but I'd have stayed longer if I hadn't learned that the theater was looking for someone to run their popcorn stand. I applied and got the job. The woman I had worked for was also on welfare, so I went to their office at the courthouse to resign. The woman I spoke to said, "Well, you lasted longer than most." Ironically welfare paid me to take care of her, but I have no memory of how much I was paid. I do, however, remember what I was paid for my next two jobs.

I liked my job at the theater, and I also liked the two girl ushers who were my age. Eventually, not that year, but the next, we became friends. I'd had school friends in Libby, but we'd started out together in the first grade. But here, in this school, I was a stranger, and I didn't exactly know how to make friends. At the theater we worked seven nights a week and Saturday afternoons. I don't know about the ushers, but my weekly salary was fourteen dollars.

The owner, a woman probably in her sixties, sat in the ticket booth every night. To the public she appeared hard as nails and cranky to boot, but her manner was deceptive. There was an incident where one Sunday I'd gone with some kids to a neighboring town, and we'd had a flat tire. It caused me to be about fifteen minutes late for work and there had been no way I could let her know. She chewed me out, and normally I would have crept away, but it wasn't really my fault and somehow I got the courage to tell her so. I also added that if she wanted to fire me, then I guess I could find another job.

In standing up for myself that day, I made a friend and from then on, she showed me nothing but affection. She began to bring me a sandwich to have during the Saturday matinees—only me. Because my popcorn stand was in a small add-on building off to the side of the entrance to the theater, the girls who ushered inside the theater never knew, or else they never said anything. She also bought me things, once a nice plaid jacket. That might have been for graduation, I don't really remember now. I worked there all the way through school, leaving only for a full-time job at the variety store when I graduated from high school in the spring of 1955. I am certain my boss had a hand in that, for the man who'd become my new boss came to my popcorn stand to offer me the job. It paid twenty-seven dollars a week.

I still stopped in to see my former boss at her office at the theater now and then, and when Ron and I were married, she gave us a nice set of luggage. Also, after Mom passed and we moved to Ron's hometown in Kansas, she volunteered to handle the sale of the house. We exchanged Christmas cards and always stopped to see her when we were back there on vacation.

An interesting and humorous thing happened while I worked at the theater. It was the spring of '54, my junior year. That year, the Kootenai River, a beautiful, wide blue-green river that flows past the north edge of the downtown section of Bonners Ferry was flooding, as it did to some extent every spring. However, this year it was threatening to inundate the downtown business section and surrounding homes, including our house, with its muddy flood waters, as it had in 1948. My boss's son, who was probably about fifty, lived with his mother and also worked at the theater. He was a jolly, good-natured type.

The town is protected by dikes that had, since the flood in '48, kept the rising waters from spilling over and flooding the whole downtown, but this year the waters kept rising higher and higher and it was feared the dikes were not going to hold. So, the National Guard was called in and many sandbags were filled and layered on top of the dikes. All the downtown businesses, including the theater, two of the schools, the courthouse, and all the homes in that downtown area, including ours, were on alert to be ready to move to higher ground. The downtown was on flat land between two long hills, called the South Hill and the North Hill, so if the town had flooded, as it did in '48, we would all have headed for the hills.

I have no memory of what Mom might have done in preparation should the flood waters spill over the dikes. Our house was a two-story, so I imagine as much as possible was moved upstairs, and Mom was probably to call Earl to come for us if we were given notice to leave.

During that time, our boss's son put on the theater marquee not the title of the next movie, but these words: *Doggone You Kootenai. Stay in Your Own Bed.* We three young girls, the two ushers and me, snickered and shook our heads. *How dumb*, we thought. That is until it appeared in the *Reader's Digest* column, "Life in These United States." Sometimes, opportunity can be under our noses. No, it wasn't a local who had sent it in, but a Canadian passing through town.

The town escaped the flood waters and the river never rose that high again. For some time, plans were being made to construct a large concrete dam on a part of the Kootenai north of Libby. Completed in 1972, it tamed that wild, beautiful river and made its waters, as our boss's son so succinctly put it, stay in their own bed.

I don't know why Mom didn't just move us in to Libby, but I will be forever grateful that she didn't, for in Libby, it's unlikely I would have ever met Ron—except if we were meant to meet then we would have, even there. In that move to Bonners Ferry, I not only found my love, but I also got a name change. Sometime after I started school, someone started calling me *Eunie* instead of Eunice, and the name stuck. I have no idea who or when or where or why, but I loved it! It felt like me! It sounded more modern, and had a lighter, happier sound. I believe that name change was psychologically beneficial for me. From then on, I was Eunie, the name even going with me to Kansas, and all these many years later, I'm still called Eunie. Except when I go back to Montana, then my family and others who knew me back then all call me Eunice.

Ron enlisted in the Air Force in January of 1953. He took his basic training at Pleasanton, California and then was sent to Biloxi, Mississippi for Radar Maintenance School. His assignment, after finishing school, was to the base at Yaak, Montana. Some of the guys had seen his posted orders and told him he was going someplace called Yaak. With a name like that, he thought it must be in Tibet. He was relieved to find it was in Montana. He went home on leave and on January 1, 1954, he left for his new assignment. He took a bus to Denver, flew from there to Spokane, Washington and then took the train to Troy, Montana. At Troy, he was still some sixty miles from the airbase at Yaak. Luckily, he caught a ride with another airman and his family who were headed back to the base.

About twenty miles west of Troy, they turned off on to the Yaak road, then just a one lane gravel road. Still forty miles from the base, it was snow packed between walls of snow shoved up by the snowplows, with turnouts at intervals in case one met an oncoming car or a logging truck, which they soon did. There were no turnouts there, so the guy piled his car off into the snowbank and the logging truck passed, stopped, and the man came back, hooked chains to the car and pulled it back onto the road and they went on to the base without further incident. The base at Yaak was a small radar base, an AC&W (aircraft and warning) site. The town was even smaller, the businesses consisting of a mercantile store and a bar called The Dirty Shame.

The next morning, Ron woke to some yelling and laughter and got up to see a guy run by holding a cotton mattress like a sled, do a belly flop on it, and slide on down the hallway. Ron's roommate, who had been in town, came back early the second morning, and with another guy, walked into the room with a shovel full of snow. The other guy yanked off Ron's covers and the roommate threw in the snow.

Ron loved his time at Yaak and would have even if he hadn't met me. But that, as they say, was icing on the cake.

CHAPTER 11

# SCRAWNY RONNIE AND PUNY EUNIE

RON AND I sort of met in the spring of 1954, my junior year in high school. Ron, then called Bo (a nickname acquired in the Air Force), noticed me first, but I had a good excuse for not noticing him, even though we were in the same place at the same time and in close proximity. We were both at a roller-skating party in the neighboring town of Sandpoint. It was my first time on skates, and I was too busy trying to stay upright to notice anyone, even that really cute guy, and I, wobbling around all over the place, was hard *not* to notice.

The first time I remember seeing him was at a dance sometime that summer of 1954 at a place called Cedar Creek. One of the girls who worked with me at the theater had access to her parents' car, so after work we headed for the dance. The base had furnished a bus for those guys wanting to attend the dance, so there were a lot of Air Force guys there, including Ron.

He asked me to dance and although I don't recall being suddenly enamored, I seemed to always know where he was that night, usually on the dance floor, and of course, I noticed when he and some other girl won a jitterbug contest.

Andy Anderson, Ron's best friend, and I started dating shortly afterward, but in late August, they were both sent on temporary duty to San Antonio for six weeks.

When they returned in early October, Andy and I soon broke

up, and Ron, waiting for just that, arranged a double date with one of his friends who was dating one of my friends. That's all it took. Soon we were a couple, nicknamed by our friends *Scrawny Ronnie and Puny Eunie*.

Ron's story of how he got to San Antonio that summer of 1954 for those six weeks of temporary duty is interesting, so I will share that here.

He was flat broke when he got his orders, usually not a problem as he had a bed and meals and would get paid again. Now, though, he had to get to Spokane, a hundred and sixty miles from the base, to collect his travel pay to get to Texas and his car was at his parents' home in Kansas. The first sixty miles was no problem, as he could ride in an Air Force vehicle into Bonners Ferry. There he looked up the local cop and asked if he could sleep in the jail that night. The cop told him that he wouldn't let anyone sleep in the jail that hadn't been arrested and gave him two dollars for a room in the hotel. Ron then called his dad and asked him to wire twenty dollars to him in Spokane. He then shipped his duffel bag to himself there and used the cop's two dollars to stay overnight in the hotel. When he was back from Texas, Ron tried to pay the cop back, but he wouldn't take it.

The next morning, dressed in his uniform, he went out on the highway and hitched a ride to Spokane. There he got his money from home, so he could get his duffel bag and a taxi to take him to Geiger Field, Spokane's Air Force Base, where he collected his travel pay, and then figured out the cheapest way to get where he had to be in the time allotted. It was a flight to Denver and a train to San Antonio.

Ron always had a perfect sense of direction, except in Bonners Ferry. The base was about eighty miles from Libby to the east and about sixty miles from Bonners Ferry to the west. Bonners Ferry being the closest and also closer to the larger Air Force Base at Spokane was probably why it was chosen for the base post office and for the Liberty Run, a covered vehicle that brought the guys who like Ron were without cars, to town. Eventually, Ron bought an old Hudson, but it was a lemon and totally unreliable. I sold it for twenty-five dollars, as I remember, after we were married, and he was transferred to Canada, where I joined him some six weeks later.

The first time Ron came into town, he rode in the back of that covered vehicle where the only view out was of a long, long winding hill that brought them down into Bonners Ferry. When Ron stepped out of that vehicle, his otherwise great sense of direction was permanently altered in that town. And forever after, for him, in Bonners Ferry, the sun always rose in the west and went down in the east.

My breakup with Ron's best friend didn't even make a hiccup in their friendship and Andy was soon dating another girl and eventually one of my friends, named Marilyn. The two stood up with us when we got married and a month later, they too married. We remained friends throughout the years. The summer of our fiftieth wedding anniversaries, we met in Bonners Ferry, and it so happened that the minister who married us and his wife were back then too. Andy passed in 2007 and Marilyn five years later.

My senior year, I asked Ron to the prom, and when I graduated in the spring with the class of 1955, Ron was there to see me walk across the stage to receive my diploma.

There is a reservation just outside Bonners Ferry, peopled by Native Americans of the Kootenai tribe. And although I often saw adults and small children around town, I never saw those of school age, except one girl a grade or two ahead of me. I never knew her name or anything about her. Not even why she was the only Native American in our school. I don't recall ever seeing her with friends, but I don't know as I ever wondered why. Years later, I would learn that the school-age kids were sent off to Indian boarding schools. Why she wasn't, I never knew.

I became interested in writing in my middle thirties and at one time wrote for a program called Newspapers in Education. One of my stories was about the early day Haskell Indian School in Kansas. It started out as a boarding school for Native American children and was an awful, shameful place. The children were deprived of even the very basics of good care and consideration. They were isolated from any contact with family and stripped of all things Native American, even being renamed with names from the White culture. I'm sure that many of those children were broken and probably very few recovered completely. In any case, they would never be the same. Now a college, Haskell University embraces the Native American culture with pride and dignity.

I don't suppose I ever thought of that girl again until I began doing that research. It was then that I realized how isolated she must have felt, how humiliated, even angry, knowing that this society, in a place that for centuries before had been all theirs, now deemed her inferior. I hated that I knew nothing about her, not even her name.

I started working at the variety store as soon as school was out and for the first time since I was fourteen, had regular working hours and Sundays off. Then on the sixteenth of September 1955, Ron received orders that he was being reassigned to an Air Force base at Beaverlodge, Alberta, Canada. As soon as he got off work, he came to town and that evening he asked me to marry him. I wanted to. I wanted to be with him forever, but this was so sudden. Now I had a decision to make, a life altering one, and I did not trust life at all. My subconscious still harbored my fear of the people and although I'd not had any fainting spells or panic attacks since we'd moved to Idaho, I would again before long.

I was afraid to say yes, even though I wanted to be with him forever. This fear might not have been on a conscious level and not so much a fear of commitment, but of loss—of what could happen if I gave my love and joined my life with his. So, I tried to buy time and suggested he go on ahead and when he could get leave, come back and we could get married then. He said he was afraid that if he left, he might not get back for months and we might lose each other. Well, that was my fear too. I didn't want him to go. What if he didn't come back? What if he found another girl?

So, I fought my fears by leaving an out. I agreed to marry him but added, "Well, I guess if it doesn't work out, we can always get a divorce."

*Poor Ron, what a happy glow those words must have given him.* It's a wonder he didn't back out right then and there.

When I told my boss at the variety store, he asked why we didn't hold off for a while, that I might want to think about college. Ironically, I had once dreamed of college, but a school counselor had assured me, in a very humiliating way, that I had no aptitude for anything, let alone college. I'll write about that experience later. My boss didn't know about that, of course, and now, looking back these many years later, I like to think he saw some potential in me. Then he said we were so young, which was true. I was eighteen, and Ron had just turned twenty-three. I had been fine until he said that, and then anger, unbidden, brought these telling words out of my mouth. "Well then, maybe he won't die on me before the kids are grown!" And, of course, that went back to the pain of losing my father when I was five.

Looking back to 1959 as I write this, two years after moving to Kansas, and Ron and his brother-in-law, Darel Olliff, had just gone into the furniture business, I was brought face-to-face with that fear. Ron was delivering some furniture out of town when the truck caught on fire. He and the delivery boy escaped, but Ron got some minor burns on his hands. The truck was totaled. Someone called me and I took our two-year-old Kathy and went to wait at the funeral home. I was standing in the utility room by the back door waiting when Ron got back from getting his hands treated at the hospital. I felt numb and scared. He was safe, but he could have been killed. *Would he escape the next time?* Even though I had no conscious memory of the people, they were still alive in my subconscious, still a threatening presence, but not to my husband. It was my mom they were still keeping in that bed back in Montana. Even though by then she had been gone for two years. That subconscious fear was probably more about losing my dad, for that was why I'd been afraid to marry Ron.

We were married on October 2, 1955, at 2 p.m. in a simple ceremony in the Trinity Lutheran church, as I'd been attending that church with two of my girlfriends for a couple of years. I had looked for a dress or a suit during my lunch hour in the two stores in Bonners Ferry with women's clothing, but I couldn't find anything suitable or that fit me. I didn't know what to do. I'd only been working at the store four months, and here I was leaving, and it felt wrong to take the day off. I felt guilty too, for flaring up at my boss like I had when he suggested waiting until we were older. But I had to have something to wear for our wedding, so Ron and Andy drove over to Sandpoint (where Ron had first seen me trying to roller-skate) and came back with a light blue suit.

We had a singer at our wedding, but no reception, no cake. Mom, Danny, and June, and Aunt Teddie from my side attended. Ron's family was in Kansas; I'd not meet any of them until nearly two years later. Others attending were our friends, Ron's Air Force buddies, my girlfriends and a few of their mothers, and, of course, Andy and Marilyn, who stood up with us.

We spent a week in Spokane on our honeymoon, Andy loaning us his car. When we left town after the wedding, some of our friends followed us and at the tavern at Deep Creek, about eight miles from Bonners Ferry, they crowded us over with their cars and forced us to stop. Inside, everyone laughing and having something to drink, someone put a quarter in the jukebox and some started dancing. Then one of the guys asked Ron if he could dance with the bride and another stood there and got Ron's attention, while the one who asked me to dance swept me off my feet and carried me out and put me into a waiting car and they took off. A mile up the road, they had a flat tire and Ron pulled up, rescued me, and we went on. A few miles farther up the road, we came to a roadblock, the police looking in all cars before letting them pass. The officer approached us and said to Ron, "You didn't happen to pick up a red-headed hitchhiker back down the road, did you?" Then he noticed the *Just Married* and other writings on the car and said, "No. I guess you wouldn't have," and waved us on. We stayed in small motels, except for the last night when we splurged and spent fifteen dollars to stay at the Ridpath.

After we returned, I went back to my mother's, and Ron left for Canada.

We were married sixty-two years and I feel blessed to have loved him and been loved by him all those years. I miss him more than words can say, but I know he is with me always, and he lets me know it often and in many varied and wonderful ways.

# CHAPTER 12

# MOM'S ILLNESS

**SOON AFTER MOVING** to Idaho, Mom found a job in a restaurant after they closed for the night—washing dishes, mopping floors, and other general cleaning. We lived only a couple of blocks from downtown, so she could walk to work. She was required to report her income to the county welfare office and for every dollar she earned, they deducted that amount from her check, so she could never save up enough to get on her feet. Then on February 2, 1956, she and June were coming home from the movies when she fell and broke her hip, and her working days were over.

Ron left right after our honeymoon for his new assignment in Canada. Apartments were scarce in that little town, but he finally found one on the second floor of a house owned by an older couple and I joined him there on the first day of December.

Mom walked me to the bus depot. We didn't hug, of course, just looked at each other and smiled and said goodbye, but she did write once in those two months before she fell.

I had an overnight layover in Edmonton, so I stayed in a hotel and the next morning took the bus on to Beaverlodge. I remember when the bus came to a stop and I saw Ron standing there waiting, his eyes searching for me, I felt a rise of sudden panic. He looked like a stranger, and I thought, *What have I done?* Although, as soon as I was out of the bus and saw him face-to-face, all doubt vanished.

I don't remember who called to tell us that Mom had broken her hip. Ron got leave and we hurried back to Bonners Ferry. She had to have surgery twice because the first time, the artificial part they'd used was too large.

We knew Mom would need help for a while, so I stayed, and Ron returned to Canada. Larry, Danny, and June were still in school. My older sisters had young families and ranch work. Also, by not living in the same town, it was extremely difficult to impossible for either one to come and care for Mom.

When school was out the first of June, Mom and June went to stay with Aunt Teddie and Blaze, who were living in town by then, and I went back to Ron in Canada. I think Larry worked for the Forest Service that summer and Danny stayed with Mabel and her family on their ranch south of Libby.

That summer, Mom had surgery to remove a tumor and it was discovered that she had colon cancer that had metastasized. Mom had not felt well for a few years and had gone to several doctors, both in Libby and later in Idaho, taking the bus to Sandpoint and maybe even Coeur d'Alene, but none of those doctors had found the cancer. I imagine it was hard to diagnose in those days.

On one of those trips in search of an answer, she brought me back a scarf. I was a high school kid and didn't appreciate it then, but, looking back some years later, I did. I don't remember what she bought the other kids. With cancer, her hip never healed, and she spent the rest of her life in a wheelchair. She passed on April 30, 1957, at the age of fifty-three.

I came back to Mom's again in September with the start of school. I did not care much for the doctor Mom had, as he seemed cold and uncaring, maybe just his mannerism, but I felt she deserved a doctor who at least appeared to care. So, I took her to the other doctor in town and was so pleased with him. He acted as if he cared, and he even made house calls. With Mom in a wheelchair and neither of us having a car (I had not yet learned to drive anyway), that was a huge help.

The welfare office requested I report to them, and there I was told that now that I was home (in essence saying I was another mouth to feed), I could buy groceries in bulk and save money, so they were deducting several dollars from Mom's monthly check, I forgot how many. I probably didn't remember the minute it was out of the woman's mouth, for shame, intimidation, and a touch of anger makes it hard to listen very well. With me home that made four of us, although sometimes Larry was there too. Even I, young as I was, wondered if buying in bulk really made sense. I do think it was just an excuse, a way to save the county money anyway they could. I never did buy in bulk, as I didn't see that it would help and I was a bit overwhelmed as it was, so I just bought in regular amounts and Ron sent me money every payday.

My regret in caring for my mother in those days was in not sharing more of myself with her and not looking for ways to make the life she had left more comfortable. I could have brushed her hair or rubbed her back—maybe had her soak her feet and then rubbed them with lotion, or shared books or magazines or poems with her, or asked her to share stories of her growing-up years with me. I missed a lot by not doing so. Somehow, I seemed to keep my emotional distance from her.

One afternoon Mom was sitting in her wheelchair in the living room when she said to me. "If I were to live my life over again, I would choose the same husband, and I would want all of you kids, but, after your dad passed, I'd like to have always known where the next meal was coming from." I have no idea what I might have said to that or if I said anything at all. My mother was dying. I knew on a conscious level she was dying, but in my subconscious she still lay in that bed in our old house in Montana, and I still stood by her bedside, a five-year-old child, waiting for the people to come and kill her, like they had killed my daddy.

I'm sure she also knew she was dying and probably that I knew it too, but I was too young, and she was my mother. Besides, that doctor we liked so well had told me not to tell her or my siblings. June was fourteen, Danny sixteen, and Larry eighteen. But Mom had to have known. Maybe Aunt Teddie told her, or that doctor in Libby who operated on her and discovered the cancer. I just don't know. Earl and Mabel and Margaret had to have known she was dying, but none of the three had talked to me—that I remember, anyway. I learned after Mom passed that Margaret did tell Larry one time when he was at her house.

Years later, when hospice would come into being, I'd think about how my mother could have benefited—and me too—from hospice care and so lived those months with an open acceptance of her impending death. I wish I'd had some help and guidance in making her more comfortable and maybe even helping us to better communicate with each other.

Oddly enough, I did not have a panic attack or a fainting spell all that time I took care of my mother. Maybe it was because my subconscious believed she was still in that bed in Montana, not there in Idaho, dying of cancer.

When the four years of Ron's enlistment ended on January 27, 1957, he was discharged from the Air Force and came back to Bonners Ferry and got a job at a local lumber mill, a job described as "pulling logs off the chain."

On the last day of April in the afternoon, six days after my twentieth birthday, Ron at work, my siblings at school, Mom called me into her room and asked me to call an ambulance to take her to the hospital. Ron had our car at work, but even if the car was at the house, I still had not learned to drive. Ron would be off at five, so I asked if we could wait until then. She said, no, that she had to go right away. So, I went to the neighbor's house next door and called an ambulance. I think back about how calm she was. I'm sure now that she knew she had little time left and the kids would soon be home from school and she did not want to cause us any anxiety or fear, and she did not want to die with me alone with her or with them here either. No, I'm sure, she figured she'd better not wait for Ron.

I left a note and rode with her in the ambulance. Ron brought the kids out when he got off work. We stayed with her until the dinner hour and then went home to get something to eat. We had left the neighbor's phone number at the desk and were ready to go back to the hospital, when the neighbor came to tell us the doctor had called and wanted us to call him back right away.

Ron and I went uptown to the pay phone outside the telephone office and called. When the doctor came on the phone, he said that he was sorry, but my mother had expired. I knew what that word meant, but I turned to Ron for confirmation or because, even expecting it, it was still a blow. I handed him the phone, and he finished the call.

Poor Danny was blindsided. He sobbed and sobbed. He'd had no idea or would not let himself believe she was dying. I felt so sorry for him, and for June, too. She had been so close to our mother. I don't remember any visual indication of her grief. I think she just stayed silent and withdrawn.

I felt bad that I had not been there for Mom when she passed, but years later, I'd hear of many cases where the dying seem to go when their loved ones aren't present. They may have gone home for a change of clothes or something to eat. Sometimes, they've just stepped out of the room. Ron would pass sixty-one years after Mom, and that time I had just fallen asleep, so I was, in essence, gone too. I'd tried to stay awake, knowing he was leaving me, but I got so tired standing there beside his bed in the hospital, and meant only to sit down and rest just a few minutes, but I fell asleep instead. On Easter morning, the first of April, two months later, he would let me know it was okay and that he had even kissed me goodbye.

Our daughter, Kathy, was ten when Ron's mother, her beloved grandmother, passed and she was devastated. Edith had been ill for some time, but when we knew she was leaving us, we did not tell our kids. It was still believed that children did not grieve as adults, and so they were often not told when a loved one was dying and after the death, they were often shut out of the grieving process or given some explanation that even to a kid, didn't make sense.

Mom's mother died in 1936, a year before I was born. Mom took Earl, Mabel, and Margaret, the three she had then, on the train to Wyoming to attend the funeral. My siblings had never known Mom's mother, so for them there was no actual grieving involved. Still the kids were not told that Grandma had died, but that she was sleeping. Mabel said she wondered what Grandma would do when she woke up and found herself underground, in a box and covered with dirt. Why adults thought *that* was not as sad or as frightening as saying a person had died, is hard to understand. Especially when those who are Christians believe their loved ones go to Heaven.

Ten years before Ron's mother died, and mine was dying, my mother's doctor had told me not to tell my siblings—and they were teenagers. Now, we had three daughters, ten, seven and five, so we didn't tell them either. Hospitals did not allow children younger than fourteen to visit a patient in their rooms, so when their grandmother was brought back to our local hospital, and as I recall, just a few days from passing, we took the kids around to the window of her room to see her, but we did not tell them she would not get well.

Here, I must give special recognition to our Kathy's fourth grade teacher, Mrs. Wava Kaiser. Ron's parents lived just across the street from the grade school, and when Ron's mother was home and feeling well enough (I assume Mrs. Kaiser called first) she'd let Kathy go over during recess to see her.

Edith passed in the early morning hours with her husband and children by her side. Our kids were just out of bed, and I'd just told them about their grandmother, when her doctor came to take them to stay the day with his wife and children. I protested, but he told me in no uncertain terms that my place was with Ron. I believed it was wrong for him to take the girls to his wife, whom they had never even seen before. It wasn't like he was a family friend, although he'd developed a special fondness for Ron's mother. He'd grown up in Norton, where

Edith's parents lived, after moving there from Oakley. His dad, also an MD, had been her doctor when as a young wife and mother, she'd spent a year in the tuberculosis sanatorium at Norton. With this last bout with cancer, she was hospitalized in Colorado Springs for her radiation treatments and his brother-in-law was her doctor there.

I'd always felt guilty for letting the doctor take the girls, for I felt as if I were abandoning them. However, the two older kids have since assured me that they had enjoyed spending the day at his home. Kelly doesn't really remember, but I'm sure if her sisters were okay with it, then she was too. In talking to them while writing this chapter, Kathy said, even as a little girl, she loved Dr. Tom, so whatever he thought was okay by her, except, of course, when she needed to have a shot.

I do know, though, that I should have realized that our Kathy was having a hard time dealing with her loss, for she had adored her grandmother. I wish I'd have known in those days and weeks and months after their grandmother passed that I should have talked to the kids about her. We should have looked at pictures together and I should have encouraged them to talk about her. To share our memories and to cry. We should have visited her grave, brought flowers, or even small mementos to leave on her stone, but in those days, I didn't know any better.

We need our hearts and minds to accept and process our grief and to come to terms with our loss, or it can slip into our subconscious as unresolved grief—and that kind of grief can last a lifetime. So, allow yourself and your children to grieve, to accept, to mourn, but also to laugh, to remember, and to share.

## CHAPTER 13

# WE MOVE TO KANSAS

**I'D HAD NO** panic attacks or fainting spells all that time I took care of my mother, even though my triggers included death and dying—although, they would begin again sometime later. Of course, my conscious memory knew the truth about my mother, knew that although she was sick and dying, there were no evil ones coming for her. Consciously, I knew that. Subconsciously, she was still in that bed in Montana. Even when she died, I felt mostly numb. Ron and Aunt Teddie took care of the arrangements. I did not want to be a part of it.

Up until my mother died, I had not seen a dead body and I was afraid, but Ron talked me into going to the funeral home to see her. I am so glad he did, for she looked so good, all traces of her illness gone, and I did not get panicky, nor did I feel at all faint. I was apprehensive at first, but the minute I saw her, it vanished.

Mom passed on April 30. Her welfare check came the next day. I walked that block from Mom's house to the post office through the back alley and turned it in, telling the man at the window that she had died. I left there and walked back to the house in tears, but in joy too. *My mother was free!* She had to die to do it, but at last she was free!

A few days before the funeral, I saw a former neighbor who, after expressing her condolences, continued to visit awhile. Somehow, she had heard that I was not there when Mom passed and that she had called for me just before she died. Perhaps she did not realize her words were not helpful. Maybe she thought I'd feel better knowing my mother had called for me, as if thoughts of me were her last earthly thoughts and would be comforting. They weren't, for it made me feel that I had let my mother down by not being there. However, knowing what I know now, I'm sure she did not die alone. I'm sure Dad was there, maybe her mother and father, too. Maybe even her baby boy, that healthy-looking little guy who only lived six days, so, I'm sure it was with great joy that she left this earth.

Mom had been raised a Methodist and she did enjoy church, maybe for the hymns as much as anything. In the early years, when the three oldest kids were little, and they lived just about a mile from Libby, she and the kids walked to church, and she even sang in the choir. The move to Libby Creek, seven miles from town, ended that. Our dad did not go to church. He believed in God, but not churches. In Bonners Ferry, I sometimes went to church with my friends. One girl was a Catholic and I didn't understand much of it, as it was then at least partly in Latin. Two other friends went to a Lutheran church, and there I learned that baptism was believed to be a saving grace. I remember years later a young mother who was anxious to get her baby baptized for fear the child would die before the paster could perform what to her was the only way her child could be saved.

Because of going with my friends to that Lutheran church, I worried, when I knew my mother was dying, for fear she had not been baptized and would not go to Heaven. Then somehow, I learned that she had grown up in the Methodist church and they even baptize infants. Oddly enough I never thought about being baptized myself and unless the three older ones were baptized, to my knowledge none of us had. I guess I would have worried if we were all about to die.

Ron's family attended the First Christian (Disciples of Christ) Church, and it was the first I'd heard of baptism by immersion and realized that obviously excluded babies and young children, so, although it was a requirement for church membership, it was not considered a saving grace. Also, I was pleased that communion was served to all, whether one was a church member or not. I was baptized with my sister, June, then fifteen, Ron's little brother, Gary, twelve, and Paula Stubbs, who was engaged to marry Ron's brother, Larry.

I was pregnant, due the end of September, when we left for Kansas in mid-July for Ron's hometown of Phillipsburg. We brought June with us and would have taken Danny, too, but he essentially said we had enough on our plate without adding him. He was only sixteen, but he was always a kind and thoughtful kid, and he grew up to be a kind and thoughtful man. He moved to my sisters' ranch homes, first one and then the other, and eventually moved in with the Schneiders, another ranching family. Their son was a good friend of his and there he found a home.

Larry was out of school and working full time on a ranch south of Libby near the Fisher River when we left for Kansas. A year or so later, he moved to Wyoming and worked for a cousin on our mother's side, and forever after he'd call Wyoming home.

Although we had been married nearly two years, I had never met any of Ron's family, nor had I ever been to Kansas, so it took some adjusting. They welcomed me, this young woman their son had chosen to share his life with, and who would very soon make them grandparents. Ron was their eldest child. Shirley, their second, was married to Darel Olliff, whom Ron would soon join in partnership in the furniture and funeral business. Larry would graduate from high school in the spring, and Gary, at twelve, was their youngest.

That summer of 1957 was hot and dry. Even the winds that swept across that open prairie land were hot. Sometimes I thought the heat and those winds would suffocate me. Eventually, I discovered the park. Even though the small creek that runs through the west edge of the park, next to a hill covered with cottonwood and other deciduous trees, dried up that year, Ron assured me, the water would return in the spring, and if we got rain, even sooner.

Although I believed in God and Jesus, or at least the idea of there being a god and that He had a son, it was some years before I developed enough of a personal relationship with Him that I could pray to Him with the assurance that He heard my pleas and would answer as He saw fit. I often took serious prayers to the park, and after Ron passed, I went there to talk to him as well. I'll write about those times in later chapters.

One of those prayers at the park, many years after I became a Kansan, was answered, but it was not a situation that could be resolved as soon as I had wanted it to. But God let me know that He was aware, and it would be answered in time. That prayer began at home and as I prayed, I heard a voice say. "Go to the park." So, full of hope I hurried to the park, crossed the foot bridge, and walked the west side of the creek, up and down, and prayed and prayed, but nothing happened. Finally, discouraged and very angry, I started back to my car and as I walked along the rail fence on the west side of the road that ran through the park, I said in anger to the voice that had sent me there, "You sent me here and you gave me *nothing!* The least you could have done was send me a butterfly or a bird!" Immediately, a little brown butterfly landed on the top rail of the fence beside me. Surprised, I thought, *If I move close and hold out my hand and it flies up and lands on it, then I'll know that it's from God.* I moved slowly toward it with my hand held out and then just inches away, it flew up and past me, and away toward the east. I turned, my eyes following it until it was lost from sight. Then I heard what I can only describe as a rush of wings from behind me and I turned back to look toward the creek bank, toward where I'd heard the sound. A large white dove flew through the branches of a tall cottonwood that grew in the row of trees that lined the creek. The dove had not flown along the creek that runs from north to south, but from east to west, straight through the branches of one big tree and was gone in seconds. Of course, as the dove flew through that tree, it made no sound. Later, I thought about that "rush of wings" while my eyes followed the butterfly flying east, opposite of the "sound" and I knew it had been just to get my attention, for if the dove was flying then, when I heard the sound, it would have had to be on rewind to fly through that tree again. And, of course, it made no sound as it flew through the tree, and it only took seconds. I knew those two creatures were my answer. They were the Lord's promise that my prayers had been heard and would be answered. In essence, I told the voice, "If you sent me here, then prove it." I even asked for the proof be a butterfly, or a bird, and He gave me both. How perfect! But sometimes our prayers cannot be answered as soon as we'd wish them to be. And that's the way it was in this case.

Time went by and nothing changed with that situation, and I grew impatient, and I asked Him if He'd forgotten. As the years passed and I came to know that I could rely on God, that He would answer my prayers, although sometimes the answer was no. Often I'd turn to the Bible when asking for the Lord's advice or reassurance, by just opening the Bible at random, putting my finger down on one of the two pages and the answer would be there in the scripture—usually. So that's what I did that day, and this was my answer. "There is a time for all things." Ecclesiastes 3:1 The answer was clear, and so I waited.

If the scripture under my finger did not resonate with me, then I'd believe I just needed to wait, and if earlier, He had given me an answer, then I'd know to trust that the answer still holds. A year later, I asked again and got Psalms 56:3-4. "I will trust in the promises of the Lord." A year or two later, I asked again, and my scripture was Isaiah 65:17. "For see I am creating a new heaven and a new earth, so wonderful, no one will even think about the old one anymore." This one I typed out and put in a small worship center I've set up for my nightly prayers. The situation has improved immeasurably, this number of years later, and I know, He has not forgotten, and it looks very much like this scripture from Isaiah has been answered.

Perhaps we need to keep in mind that God doesn't just fix situations overnight. Remember how long it took to "fix" me? Of course, no one asked Him to, not knowing there was something to fix. Although maybe this book is the reason it took forty-three years. Also, sometimes another situation must come to light before the reason for the problem or problems can be solved.

We lived with Ron's parents for a week or so and then rented a duplex where we lived until Katherine Elaine arrived at the end of September. However, by the time Kathy and I were out of the hospital, Ron had moved us from the duplex to a small house on G Street.

June had settled into the high school and seemed to have no trouble making friends and before long got a job in the snack bar at the drive-in theater.

Ron's first job was painting the huge storage tanks at the local refinery. He then got a desk job in the accounting department at the gas company. Two years later, he and Darel bought out the McKinley Furniture Store on the north side of the square from the elderly McKinleys and renamed it Olliff-Boeve Furniture—the grand opening in March of 1959. In 1963, they built a new store on the south side of Highway 36 just west of the city limits.

We moved to the house next door in 1960 and were living there when we welcomed our second child, Kandice Kaye, in April.

Also, that year June graduated from high school and moved to Dodge City, Kansas, where she attended beauty school and met her future husband, Ron Garetson. June was good with numbers and soon found her niche was in accounting and other office work rather than being a beautician. Her husband was in the Navy, and they moved around a lot. They had one son, Shawn, and divorced while living in Jacksonville, Florida. She stayed there and worked as the office manager of a large dealership until she retired. Her memory failing, we moved her back to Phillipsburg in 2014. She spent eight years in assisted living and as of 2022, is in long-term care. Her son, Shawn, lives in Texas.

In April 1961, Ron and I bought a house at 269 West F Street from John Boeve, a distant relative of Ron's, and his wife, Rose. Our other two children were born after we moved there. Kelly Ann, in October 1962 and Ronald Dean, Jr., who arrived on a January day in 1969.

It seemed I had always known I would have four children and

now with three children and my thirty-second birthday just a couple of weeks away, I knew it was time for that fourth child. Ron, although happy with the three we had, let me decide. Soon after I knew I was pregnant, I heard a voice tell me this baby was a boy. The words, unbidden, just out of the blue—why or from whom, I have no idea. I only know I heard the words and the next January we had a baby boy.

We took our first vacation the summer after moving to Kansas. We went to Colorado, taking June and Ron's brother Gary. We left our little Kathy with Ron's mother. Vacations were completely foreign to me, but Ron's parents had taken several and he had fond memories of those times. We were stretched financially, but Ron insisted we go anyway. He said it wasn't that we couldn't afford to go, but that we couldn't afford not to go. He saw it as a time of being together as a family without the stresses of everyday life, especially with two businesses, plus the ambulance service. We pretty much roughed it for a few years, sleeping in the car and tent camping. Eventually, we got a pop-up camper to pull behind the car. About 1965, Darel and Shirley Olliff built a cabin out in the hills west of Denver and were very gracious about us and other family members using it. We went back to Montana and Idaho our second summer in Kansas and tried to make it back about every five years. We were all pretty good campers, except Kathy. Although, since she and her husband, Tom, have retired and are living in Florida and have recently purchased a motorhome, she's found that kind of camping quite enjoyable. One summer we were roughing it in Glacier National Park in the cold and rain and Kathy was not happy. I told her we'd be at Aunt Mabel's tomorrow, and we'd sleep at her house. She breathed a deep sigh of relief and said, "Thank, God!"

Over the years we upgraded until, by retirement, we were into motor homes, but shortly after full retirement, we sold the last motor home and bought a summer place out of Troy, Montana, on Bull Lake's Angel Island. We loved that place and were blessed to be able to spend seventeen summers there.

Darel Olliff's parents had loaned us the money to get started in the businesses, as then we were too broke to get a loan from the bank. We kept our payments up, paying extra when we could, and when that one was paid off, we borrowed from them to buy more shares in the funeral home. Two weeks later, they canceled all the money owed on that note, the note itself to be canceled upon their deaths. Arel also cited in writing the reason they'd decided to do so. He wrote, "Since Ronald D. Boeve helped us acquire and maintain and build up the Olliff-Boeve, Inc. firm, it is only right and just that we give this note to them and canceled upon our deaths."

The Olliffs had come as outsiders to the community in 1945. The town already had a funeral home owned by life-long residents. When Ron joined the firm, business increased substantially, as the Boeves were also life-long residents, well-known and well-liked, with roots in nearby Prairie View. We appreciated the Olliffs forgiving the loan and for acknowledging that Ron had earned it.

Arel liked me and I liked him. He was a good man, kind and gentle. He was not just grandpa to his own two grandsons, but to our kids as well, and they too called him Grandpa Arel. When Ronnie was born, he and Minnie bought me a clothes dryer, and with cloth diapers in January, I did so appreciate their kindness.

Arel passed from cancer in the hospital in Salina in March of 1972. Ron and I were there to see him the day before. He loved to have his hair combed, and he asked me to comb it for him that afternoon.

Darel called our house when his dad passed. Ron was at the funeral home and Darel and Shirley's two boys were staying with us. I was holding three-year-old Ronnie in my arms when I answered the phone. The kids, knowing that Grandpa Arel was dying, started crying when they understood by my words and tone of voice that he was gone.

Then I no longer heard Darel's voice on the phone, nor was I conscious of my child in my arms, or our three girls and Darel and Shirley's two boys crying, nor was I even in my house. Instead, I stood at the top of a beautiful, grassy green meadow dotted with yellow flowers that sloped down toward a wide blue river. Arel, his back to me, was running and leaping with joyous abandon down that beautiful meadow toward that wide, blue river, pumping his arms upward toward a clear blue sky. When he reached the river, the scene vanished and I was back in the house, still on the phone with Darel, Ronnie still in my arms, the other kids still crying. Darel had noticed nothing amiss, even though we were still on the phone. It was as if, for that glimpse into that beautiful world Arel had entered—so joyous, so happy, so free—time had stood still.

When we moved to Kansas that summer of 1957 and I joined Ron's family's church, I got a broader view of religion. The Disciples were a more liberal church then the ones I'd gone to with my friends. When the church relaxed the ancient biblical view that women should not usurp the men's role in church leadership and serve as elders or pastors, I was elected the first woman elder. Not a job I really wanted, but one I believed in wholeheartedly. One family left the church over that, but a few years later, the husband told me it wasn't because of me, but because the Bible says women are not to be elders.

I don't of course know what our Lord does about us sinners, but I believe He gathers us all in, regardless of our sins and our church's requirements and the rules therein, all different, in some way, it seems, from our fellow churches, even though we use the same Bible and have the same God.

I believe that even nonbelievers, the second they slip through that thin veil and see God face-to-face, become instant believers. Maybe they were raised by nonbelievers and never saw the inside of a church or maybe raised in the church but suffered cruelty and shame from the hands of church leaders or their own church-going parents. I believe God knew us before we were born and knows the road we traveled through life and being the ultimate father, when we (like the prodigal son) come back to Him, He gathers us to Him.

We may have some work to do when we get there, not because of our church, if any, or the rules therein, but because of how we treated others. But for me, knowing the great love our Lord has for us, I'm sure we aren't turned away, despite our sins, for God sees what we, with our human eyes, see only dimly, if at all. I know I'm supposed to believe that the Devil was an angel turned rogue who thumbed his nose at God and created his own kingdom—a hellish place of torture and damnation—and started grabbing up the souls of us sinners to fill it. We are also to believe that God could do nothing to stop him, or wouldn't, which to me is unthinkable. For I believe God reigns supreme, *and there is no power greater than Him, or no greater love.* We are His children—made in His likeness. Even when we are bad, He never abandons us. Human fathers, and mothers too, have abandoned their children, but not God. I'm sure He will show us how we hurt others and how we became who we are by the road we traveled on earth, and we may have to make some kind of restitution. But cast us into a place of eternal damnation, ruled by an evil god equal in strength to the Lord? Our own Father? For me, it just doesn't add up.

CHAPTER 14

# RON'S GROWING-UP YEARS

**WHEN I MET** Ron, he was called Bo, a nickname he had acquired in the Air Force, and I called him that until we moved to his hometown in Kansas. There he was called Ronnie and so I made the switch and then again, when gradually, as the years passed, he became Ron to the community and to me too, especially after we had our own little Ronnie. However, all through the years he remained Bo to our Montana and Idaho family and friends.

Ron and his sister Shirley were born on a farm near Prairie View to Louis and Edith (Bogart) Boeve—Ron in 1932, Shirley in 1934. Those were Depression years and that, coupled with the dust storms, made it next to impossible to survive on a farm, so they moved to Phillipsburg when Ron was three and Shirley a little over a year. They moved into an elderly man's home where Edith took care of him in exchange for a place to live, and Lou looked for work. In those early years, Lou worked several jobs, mostly manual labor, and was at one time a substitute rural mail carrier. Eventually he went into business with another man in a café called the Horseshoe and at some point, owned and operated a filling station he named Boeve's Super Service. I have no time frame for either transaction, except that Ron said he waited on customers at the café when he was fourteen, and as a little boy of maybe eight or ten, he liked being at his dad's gas station, where the locals gathered to rehash the news of the town and country, as well as world news brought in by radio and newspapers.

The station was also ripe for a goodly amount of bantering, jokes, and stories, although maybe not all were suitable for young ears.

Ron said he always got a kick out of one joke his dad played on any unsuspecting fellow who came in and sat on the corner of his office desk. He had the desk wired, a button on the wall a few feet away to deliver the shock. A few minutes after the man was seated, Lou would stroll over to the button that would send the man leaping from the desk with a yelp and most likely a few choice words, amid grins and laughter from the audience.

On occasion, one who'd been shocked became the bait to lure in another, by sitting there and when that innocent fellow walked in, he'd slide off and offer him the seat. That tickled little Ronnie and he'd have to work at holding in his laughter as the "sacrificial lamb" accepted that kind gesture.

That is until one day, the sheriff walked in and the guy sitting on the desk slid off and offered it to him. Ron said his heart gave a leap of fear and he looked to his dad. *He wouldn't, would he? Not the sheriff!* But, after a few minutes, his dad casually strolled over to the wall and Ronnie started for the door, ready to run home and tell his mother what his dad had done, for surely, he'd be arrested and carted off to a jail cell. Then, his dad pushed the button, and the sheriff gave a yelp and leaped off the desk. Ronnie was halfway out the door when he heard the laughter. Everyone was laughing, even the sheriff.

As I recall, Ron said he was fourteen when, for reasons no one knew, his dad began to drink and eventually became addicted. He lost everything he'd worked so hard for, even their brand-new home. Ron said his dad told him years later when he had recovered and was again successful, this time as the county sheriff, that when he was young, he was told by a loved one that he would never amount to anything. He believed those words had triggered his downfall. Why? We can only speculate, but we'll never know the circumstances that led to those words, or how often they were spoken. Could they have slipped into his subconscious mind like "the people" had hidden away in mine when I was in the second grade and eventually left me with panic attacks and fainting spells?

For years I've had a quote from an unknown source tacked up on a wall in my office. I love it and wanted to use it in this book, but I've searched the Internet for the author of those words of wisdom, but no luck. It speaks of those of us with old stories, old beliefs, that might not have been true in the first place and how those beliefs dominate our lives and will continue to influence our thoughts and actions unless we can acknowledge them and make an effort to change them, to let go of those old beliefs and create new ones with new thoughts.

Some might think that's ridiculous, but I *know* from experience that grief, unresolved, whatever its source, lives on in the subconscious, and without our knowledge dictates our thoughts and actions. Just as the opposite also dictates our subconscious behavior, but for good, instead of ill. Proverbs 23:7 says, "As he thinketh in his heart, so is he." Norman Vincent Peale in his book, *Positive Imaging,* mentions that scripture and adds, "In other words, as you see yourself, so you are."

If, for whatever reason, Ron's dad had been told, in essence, he'd be a failure, even if the words were not intentionally meant to harm, they did, especially if from a loved one. Maybe he was a kind of surrogate for another and so was tarnished with the same brush. At any rate those words had to have wounded him deeply, as they would have any one of us, for they are shaming words and not easy to live with. It's likely that they eventually sunk into his subconscious mind, and so they were for many years no longer a conscious memory. However, the subconscious can be a powerful force, and as mine did with me, his had to have also ruled him unknowingly. Then something brought those words to light, and now fully cognizant of those words and why, he could then fight the demon and win. Perhaps in therapy for his addiction, Lou came to terms with that old shaming story, those words possibly the catalyst that had led to him becoming addicted.

Also, it is to be noted that his father passed that year and more than likely was a contributing factor. It may seem an insurmountable task, but many, like Ron's dad, eventually, through therapy, grim determination, or in some other way, come to the realization that they have been victims of an old story and old belief that wasn't even true in the first place. With that realization, they can change that old recording of the past and begin to create a new story with new thoughts and so break the chains of the past and set themselves free. Many, like Lou, will once again rise to the top.

Lou was elected county sheriff at age fifty-five and served ten years in that capacity, where he earned the admiration and respect of many for his kindness, his fairness, and his "not always by the book" mentality. He judged with sympathy and understanding when dealing with those who needed a break, an extra shot at coming to believe they weren't losers.

One Christmas he'd had to put a young man, hardly more than a boy, in jail, but he brought him home for our family's Christmas dinner. Once, neighbors reported that Mrs. Brown's boys were shooting off guns where they lived at the edge of town, so he went to see the woman. When she opened the door, he told her he'd heard a report of some boys firing guns, but he couldn't hear anything. Then he turned and went back to his car.

An envelope came to his office at the courthouse in 1971, unsigned, and postmarked, Kearney, Nebraska. Inside was a poem titled "One Kindly Deed." The poem starts with these words: "If I can do one kindly deed for someone else on earth... I shall consider that my life has carried out its worth." It goes on with words expressing how the writer would befriend and help his fellow man in every way he could. At the bottom, the sender wrote: "Lou, I would like you to have this poem by James Metcalfe. It's your philosophy."

Lou, as you might guess from the "wired" office desk, had a great sense of humor and his sons all inherited that same fun-loving attitude. He passed on Super Bowl Sunday, January 22, 1984, which his three sons, smiling through tears, said he probably did on purpose and was up there in Heaven just grinning big time for ruining their Super Bowl.

Even if he could, I'm sure he wouldn't have done that. Or maybe he would have, knowing in their grief that it would be a relief to laugh, to smile, and tell others about their ornery dad. Although he was a bit ornery, for he was as human as the rest of us, he dearly loved his family, and even came to Sunday coffee at least once after he passed.

We always met at the folks' home every Sunday after church for coffee, a tradition that went back to Lou's parents and grandparents—"A Dutch thing," a friend once said. After Edith passed and Lou married Blanche, whom he'd known in their teen years, they carried on the tradition, and when Lou passed, Blanche kept it up. One Sunday in September, after Lou had passed in January, Ron and I left church a little early, as he needed to go to the funeral home and wanted to be back in time for coffee. He dropped me off at Blanche's and I went in to wait for everyone else to get out of church. I sat in Lou's chair at the head of the table facing the kitchen door to wait for the others. The door had a window large enough that one could see the top half of any adult who came to the door. As I sat there, I suddenly saw Lou standing at the door and saw the doorknob turn. Then Lou's image began breaking up into pieces, like pixels on a TV screen when one image morphs into another, and then Ron was there, opening the door and coming inside.

One time I was driving to the bakery but was still some distance away, when I saw Lou's car parked at the curb in front of the bakery. Then "in my head" I saw Lou back his car out away from the curb and hit the oncoming car. Then seconds later, it happened exactly as I'd "seen" it.

Among the grandkids' memories of their grandpa, was getting five chocolate stars (at a time) from Grandpa at those Sunday morning coffees, eating donuts with him on Saturdays at his office, and once he took them up on the roof of the courthouse to survey the whole town. They also remember being put in a jail cell one Saturday. Of course, he was playing with them, and, of course, that day the cells were empty, so they were his only prisoners.

Sometimes at meetings in the grown-up world, the participants are asked, as an ice breaker, to name three things about themselves, two truths and one lie, and the rest are to guess which one is the lie. Several times Kandy has used the fact that she spent time in the county jail as a juvenile. Most, of course, think that's the lie.

Ron and his siblings were greatly influenced by a strong, loving mother. As mentioned earlier, she contracted tuberculosis when Ron and Shirley were six and four and spent a year in the sanatorium at Norton, thirty miles away. During that time, Ron and Shirley lived with their dad's parents at Prairie View. Some sixteen years later, Edith would survive a bout with breast cancer and then, some ten years later, finally, succumb to another onslaught of the disease and pass from this earth at age fifty-seven. She was a loving, hands-on mother who supported her children in all ways and praised them for efforts made, successful or not. She even got up out of bed when her kids came home from a party or a date and cooked them something to eat. She went to all her sons' games that she possibly could and was, I'm sure, the most enthusiastic supporter and cheered the loudest of any parent in the stands. She was loved by her community as well, and those many months she endured her cancer treatments, several businesses put get-well boxes on their counters for people to leave cards and other messages of support. Every week they were gathered up and given to Lou to take to her. One year, the only year our church, the First Christian (Disciples of Christ), ever bestowed this honor on one of our mothers in the congregation, they named her Christian Mother of the Year.

Early on, Edith kept the books for her husband's filing station. Later she worked in a greenhouse and flower shop and until her final illness, kept the books for Darel and Ron's furniture store.

Sometime after Edith passed, I dreamed she came back to us. It was a beautiful dream, and we were all so excited, so happy to see her again and to have her back with us. Then she told us she could not stay. We pleaded with her not to go, but she told us she had to go back, unless we chose someone to go in her place. Of course, she knew we could not exchange one loved one for another, and as she saw us come to that realization, she smiled and disappeared. It was just a dream, I think.

Ron was a doer, and an achiever. He worked to be the best he could be all his life. In school, although small and skinny, he played every sport from grade school on. In a write-up in the local newspaper about a football game the junior high boys played, wrestling the win from a neighboring town, the article described the positions and plays and named each boy who had individually triumphed in those plays, but the writer prefaced Ron's name with a word that might have meant size, but it is also an endearing term: "Little Ronnie Boeve put on one of the best downfield blocks we've seen this year. He played his end position with a finesse that the high school boys could well remember." Not just Ronnie Boeve, but *Little Ronnie Boeve*.

Besides playing sports, he was in the school plays, and at fourteen began working summers as a waiter in the Horseshoe Café. He had other part-time jobs, and eventually became the janitor at the post office. Each morning he'd run up the flag and get about half of the cleaning done before school and at 11 a.m. he'd get a pass to go back to the post office and finish the cleaning. After school he'd have ball practice or a game. I assume he also cleaned on Saturdays. I just learned from Kandy, who is our family genealogist, that the 1950 census has her dad listed as Ronnie Boeve, age seventeen, and his occupation as janitor at the post office.

For Christmas in 1941, a prominent businessman gave the then nine-year-old Ron a Bible in which he'd written, "Dear Ronnie, I wish you a Merry Christmas. I hear you are quite the honorable young man." (He also gave him a token worth one dollar off on tires.) I don't now remember what Ron said about it or how the man came to know him. The inscription seems personal, as if he'd had an occasion to admire that young boy. Also, even though Ron was just a kid in high school, when he went to see the banker at the First National Bank for help to buy his class ring, the man did not hesitate to give him a loan.

He was the president of his class of 1950, a member of the National Honor Society, and was chosen to attend Sunflower Boys State in Wichita. He had really bad teeth and at the age of seventeen had to have false teeth. He was probably the only kid in the school with false teeth. However, as recorded in his high school yearbook of 1950, in the section on the Senior Class Will, where each senior willed something of theirs to an underclassman, Ron willed his false teeth. To me that shows so much of his character. He knew how to take lemons and make lemonade. He told me years later that when we first started dating that he was afraid that when I found out he had false teeth, I wouldn't like him anymore. I don't remember when I found out, but it made no difference at all to me, for I'd never dated a guy who kissed as good as he did. After graduation he worked at Quanz Floral and the Sanford Hatchery and then joined the Air Force.

In the Air Force he made staff sergeant, as high as you go in four years as an enlisted man. As mentioned earlier, he was a partner in the furniture store and funeral home. Later they purchased the funeral home at Logan and sometime later bought out their Phillipsburg competitor, Miles Funeral Home. Over time they even purchased a funeral home in Hays and bought and sold one in Topeka and another in Arizona.

Ron served on the city council and as mayor. He was president of the local Rotary club, district governor of Rotary and led a Rotary group study team to India for six weeks. He was also district chairman of Rotary's Polio Plus campaign to eradicate polio in those countries still suffering. He was an Eagle Scout leader for some years and managed a youth baseball team. He served the church as deacon and elder, board chairman, and was on several committees in the church.

He was well-liked and respected in the community. Our kids and I held an open house for him on his seventieth birthday and two men from the complete opposite ends of our local society gave him a gift. I don't believe men ordinarily give other men gifts and those were the only ones he received. One of the men gave him two special coins from his collection, and the other man also gave him a special collectors coin plus a padlock used on the Rock Island, the train that ran through Phillipsburg in earlier days.

I've heard stories from those he served in the funeral business of his kindness, his loving care, and sympathy. One told me of losing their baby and how he was so kind, so gentle. He expressed his sympathy, his sorrow for their loss and when he took her from them, he picked her up in his arms and held her to him, as gently as if she were a living child. The daughters of a man who died in his bed at home told me that when Ron came into the room, he offered his condolences and talked about their dad, how he was so good-natured and how he loved to tease. Then as he walked around the foot of the bed, he gently squeezed their dad's blanket-covered toes and said, "We're going to take good care of you, old friend." As the other nodded in agreement, one of the daughters said, "Those words and that simple gesture really touched us."

Those girls' dad and Ron and Darel had often bantered back and forth over the years. One time, their dad had gone on and on to them about wanting the fanciest of funerals, the priciest casket and so on. Either Ron or Darel, I can't remember which, told him, they weren't going to ask his family to spend that kind of money on the likes of him, so when he passed, they'd just "kick the shit" out of him and bury him in a shoe box.

When Ron passed, a family member on my side living in Montana told me that when she called our local flower shop to order flowers for his service, the woman who answered said, "For Ron Boeve? He was such a good guy. We'll fix you something really nice."

## CHAPTER 15

# I BEGIN WRITING

**LIKE MY MOTHER,** I've always loved to read, and like my father, I seem to have a bent toward writing. As a kid, I loved to curl up with a good book, to imagine the lives I'd read about in those stories. Our mother often read to us in the evenings and not only did I love those stories but also the atmosphere that encased those evening hours. *Our mother sitting in a chair by the old library table in the living room, reading by the light of the kerosene lamp, my siblings and I gathered close, listening to her voice, our minds painting pictures.*

In the sixth grade, the teacher had us all write a poem. The details of it have escaped me, but I wrote about a cat asleep in the sun, curled up on the windowsill of a white church with a tall steeple. The teacher liked it so well, she urged me to send it to the *Weekly Reader*, a little magazine in a newspaper format used in grade schools. She even helped me get it ready to mail. It slipped through the mail slot, never to be seen again.

In the eighth grade, we were each assigned to write an essay. I don't remember what mine was about, but the teacher praised it and had me read it to the class. I'm sure I was pleased and happy and maybe even a bit proud, but I doubt that I came home bursting with either one of those success stories, for I pretty much kept things to myself. Anyway, the signs were there that my bent was toward the written word.

I loved my English and literature classes, especially my sophomore year when we did a section on Shakespeare. A lot of the kids moaned and groaned at having to learn Hamlet's soliloquy: "What dreams may come when we have shuffled off this mortal coil." And Mark Antony's speech at Caesar's burial: "Friends, Romans, Countrymen, lend me your ears." I loved it and even now can still recite parts of both. I took journalism my junior year and I loved that, too. Sometime that spring, our teacher drove three or four of us girls to the University of Idaho at Moscow, where we visited the journalism classes and stayed in the dorms. I loved it and dreamed of college and a career in journalism.

It was a pipe dream, of course, but I dreamed that impossible dream for a while and then the school gave us IQ and aptitude tests. The results for me? *I had no aptitude for anything.* Then the counselor added that since I was a girl, manual labor was out, so I'd have to be a housewife. He then said, "At least you have a normal IQ." *At least?* Yes, those were his words, but it was the disdain in his voice that spoke even louder than his words, for I heard; *But a fat lot of good that's going to do you.*

I was so ashamed. Of course, it wasn't the normal IQ that shamed me, but the way he'd spoke of it. I never told my mother. If the school sent her reports of my IQ and zero aptitude, she never said anything to me.

I know that society then expected girls to become housewives and mothers, although some would also become teachers and nurses. So, it wasn't so odd that he found the role of a housewife the most suitable occupation for me, and I imagine most of the other girls as well, but I hope he didn't speak to any of them like he did to me, or to the boys either.

In sharing with Kelly, many years later, she wondered if the man knew I was a welfare recipient. I have no clue. Maybe it was in my records. If so, and he saw us as sponges on society, then his tone of voice made sense. Although maybe he was just a bully who had issues in his own life and had picked up on my insecurities.

I don't think the man was a member of the faculty, for I'd never seen him before, that I remember. He may have traveled from school to school. I don't recall his physical size, but he was obviously a small man—small in human kindness and generosity of spirit. He might not have been good at his job either.

As in all walks of life we humans tread while earning our keep, some of us are not all that competent in our job and, of course, that includes school counselors as well. There are several stories about kids receiving poor information from their high school counselors, but despite that, go on to succeed admirably in their chosen careers.

However, for me, if any dream of college remained, it dissolved when my Ron, my love, came into my life.

Although it was journalism that had first excited me, I believe it was more about writing than about journalism, for it was fiction, especially historical fiction, that drew me and was often the genre I chose to read. Eventually, it would also be my choice to write about. This book, of course, is the exception.

I was thirty-two years old and sitting in the chapel at the funeral home attending a service for a member of our church, when the writing bug bit me again. Yes, I could attend a funeral without getting panicky and passing out—if I had to. Usually I could find a good excuse not to go, but this was one I felt I had to attend. I didn't view the body and I came late enough to sit in the back and left immediately thereafter.

Perhaps I was meant to go to this one, for shortly after I was seated, my thoughts were drawn to a woman who came into my head with a story she wanted me to write. She kept me engaged throughout the funeral service and afterward went home with me. She stayed for some time. How long? I have no idea. Maybe a week, maybe two. I just don't remember. She never had a name. I guess I was to give her one. She lived on a farm during the Alaskan gold rush, her husband gone to the gold fields. She had some children. I once knew how many. I never wrote any of it down and one day, she just wasn't there anymore. She did, however, leave me with an interest in writing fiction, and very soon afterward I began to collect books on writing and subscribed to *Writer's Digest*.

Eventually, I took a correspondence course on writing for children. I enjoyed the course and began to build some confidence as I received good reports on my assignments. Sometime after I finished the course, I wrote and sold three children's stories: "Alone on the Mountain" to *Boy's Life*, "Tommy and the Bookcase," to A Nazarene Church publication, and "The Apartment Horse" to *Wee Wisdom*. They were published in 1977.

Then, one day I decided to try writing articles, so I wrote one about my dad when he packed horses for the Forest Service and submitted it to *Montana* magazine. The story ran in the Mar/Apr 1982 issue, and I was delighted.

With that bit of success, I decided to try to write a book for the middle grades, but afraid I couldn't invent a whole book-length story, I looked for a girl who had once lived and had a story to tell. I was deep into my research about the girl's life and her story, when my brother Danny called. He had read my story in *Montana* magazine about our dad and wondered why I had mentioned three of our siblings who lived in other states, but not the other three, including himself, who still lived in Montana. I snatched up my copy and soon saw the reason for his question. The magazine had accidentally dropped from the article one sentence—the sentence that named those three. I was devastated! Totally sick! It ruined the whole piece for me. I called them and they issued an apology in the next magazine, but it brought little if any comfort. In fact, I was so sick at heart, I shelved my research on the girl and vowed never to write anything ever again.

It took ten years for the pain to subside enough so I could return to my research on that girl's life. However, after a few years passed, I did write several more stories. I'd send them out, but even when I received encouragement, I didn't follow through. One literary agent I'd submitted a middle grade story to even called me. She was interested, but the manuscript was way too long. However, if I'd cut down the number of words, she would like to see it again. So, did I reduce the number of words? Yes. Did I send it back to her, or to anyone else? No.

I know it seems odd that one can receive encouragement and then reject it, but that's what I did. I also wrote two adult short stories, but I never submitted them anywhere. However, I did submit one children's short story. It was rejected but the editor enclosed an encouraging note letting me know it was a good story, just not the right one for his publishing company. Did I resubmit it to another? No. Why didn't I try again? I know it was because of that article, printed by *Montana* magazine, where half of my siblings had been deleted from the story. Even if the magazine had dropped out the other three as well, it would have helped, but by leaving them in and dropping the others out, the wound went too deep. Even though it's been many years and two of my siblings have passed, a scar remains. Although I didn't know it then, the worst was yet to come.

After those ten years passed and I returned to my research on the girl, I wrote the story and after a few tries, sold it to a top publisher and I was delighted, but I got kicked in the stomach again. This well-known publishing company was in the process of selling out. The publisher might have been retiring, or maybe had passed. I don't know as I ever knew. The buyer was a newcomer to the business. The short version of this long and agonizing story of getting this book published began with a few errors in the first printing. I was upset, but I could live with it. Then it was selected as a Kansas Reading Circle book, and my delight turned to horror. A librarian in southwest Kansas wrote to the publisher, pointing out those "few" errors. So, he set out to make those corrections himself, without notifying me or even running it by me afterward and printed a second copy.

When I got my copy of this second printing, I was horrified, mad, totally sick, and ashamed. This second printing contained the same original errors and a bunch more, fifty all told of every kind. I called him, but he brushed me off and we ended up in a heated exchange.

He believed he was right, and I was wrong, and that's all there was to it. I went through the book and highlighted all those errors in yellow and wrote the errors on paper and why they were errors and sent both the book and the papers to him, saving a copy of each, in anticipation of a "war of words." He did not respond. Eventually, I went back east and visited him at his publishing house, but all I did was make an enemy. I sent the second copy to the librarian who had stirred up this hornet's nest and this was her reply: "Well, it's a vast improvement over that first one." I couldn't believe it! I felt as if I had fallen into a world as crazy as Alice's Wonderland. Then someone else pointed those errors out to him and he reprinted the book with most of the errors corrected, although I wouldn't know it until I got the third printing. It took three more printings and several years before the rest of the errors were corrected. Even after all these years, I try not to *think* about that second printing out there somewhere in the world.

I talked to a local lawyer about suing him. He contacted another, who had worked with authors and publishers, and this is basically what he said: "Forget it. You're the author of one small book and he is a big publisher. It's doubtful you'll win, especially if the judge is not well-versed in literature."

So, I paid both lawyers and tried to move on.

The third copy wasn't too bad, so I ordered some to sell at book talks and author's book sales, always explaining the error problems, but when I'd order copies for those functions, directly from him, he'd never send them. So, I started ordering through the secretary. Once in need of some books, I called, and he answered. I ordered them anyway, as I thought it would just make matters worse. However, I did ask about the secretary, and he told me she was out of the office for a couple of weeks.

Did I get those books? No! When I thought she'd be back in the office, I called and reordered them. I told her about ordering from him and as before I had not received them. She said, "Eunice! Eunice! Eunice! When will you ever learn?"

Because he had the right of first refusal I had to send him my second manuscript. Twice I checked with him to see if it had been printed. Twice, he said it had been, and twice I set up a book signing and then discovered, both times through the secretary—and thankfully before the signing—it had not been printed at all. In two years, the contract up, the book still not in print, I took it back and got it published by another publisher.

Despite this horrible experience, I continued to write, ending up with nine historical fiction novels: seven middle grade and two for adults. I also wrote a few articles, even another one for *Montana* magazine and from 2010 to 2017, a yearly chapter series for Newspapers in Education.

My books have earned several awards. Two received the Kansas Author's Coffin Award, one became a Kansas Notable Book, and two were Kansas Reading Circle books. In 2005, following Hurricane Katrina, a library in New Orleans, damaged in the flood waters, contacted the governors of each state and asked them to choose, sign, and send a book to help restock their library. Our then Kansas governor, Kathleen Sebelius, chose my *Maggie Rose and Sass* book. Our town has a replica of an old fort named Fort Bissell where our local history is preserved along with other buildings reminiscent of the early days of our town's past. For the past several years they have selected a local resident to recognize for their work and named them Fort Bissell Person of the Year. I was selected in 2016 for my writing.

Ron's health beginning to fail, I thought I had written my last book in 2017. Titled *A Home in America*, it's a story of a Volga German family who leave Russia for a new life in Kansas. Then Ron passed through that thin veil between us on January 25, 2018, at 1:46 a.m. and before daylight, had let our eldest granddaughter know that he still lived, was still with us, and before noon had sent a sign to her sister, who knew immediately it was from her papa. I got the third sign the next day. Four months later and nine more messages and signs from him, he would give me a dream of our life together, that would eventually lead to me writing this memoir. I call it the Big Dream and will share it and all the other ways he has let me, and our family know that not only is he alive and well and loves us dearly, but also that I should spread the word that there is but a thin veil between us who are earthbound and our departed loved ones.

# CHAPTER 16

# I AM SET FREE!

**IN NOVEMBER OF** 1977, with one girl in college and two more soon to follow, I decided I needed to help with finances. So, I started working at a school for special needs children as a speech paraprofessional, as we nonprofessionals were called. I was trained and monitored by the speech therapist in Phillipsburg and would work at the school for eight years. The school was started in the former grade school at Glade. Those children were now bused into the Phillipsburg grade school and the Glade school was renamed Glade Training Center. The students, ages five to twenty-one, were bused in from surrounding towns.

Four years later, Ron, knowing I had once wanted to go to college, asked if I'd still like to go. He said I could quit my job when school let out in the spring and start classes in the fall. There were several from here attending college at Hays, just sixty miles from us, who carpooled, and I could join them. I was excited and delighted, but also a bit apprehensive. There weren't many career options available for a forty-four-year-old in a small town, and I decided my best bet was to aim for a degree in teaching. I thought I could take a lot of history and literature courses and teach high school, for nothing else appealed to me at all and with my affliction I sure wouldn't be able to handle nursing.

Then at about six thirty the morning of February 7, 1981, I had a dream, and woke immediately when the dream ended with a woman saying to me, "Things are not always as they appear." I knew I needed to write down the dream while it was still fresh in my mind, so I got up, wrote it down, and went back to bed.

The next night, just as I was about to drop off to sleep, my eyes snapped open, for I suddenly knew that dream was telling me something. So, I got up and read what I had written the night before. The dream was in symbols, but in reading it that night, I knew the meaning. It was about me going to college. In a nutshell, what the dream told me was that every choice elicits a change, and sometimes instead of a gain, it's a loss. So be sure before you choose.

In the dream, we lived by a river, which I interpreted as symbolizing the rhythm of life, the same waters never returning, ever flowing onward, like the passing years of our lives. The trees and grass were green, and I knew that although it was summer, it was late summer, the light fading, representative of fall approaching. I took that to mean that I have now and only now to decide my fall and winter life. Then Kathy and Kandy, our two oldest daughters disappeared, and I couldn't find them anywhere. I searched and searched, and I was heartbroken. I felt, reading those words, that losing the girls could be symbolic of maybe spreading myself too thin and losing precious moments with my children and perhaps my husband too. Ron was there in my dream, but a shadowy figure, which I took to mean that this was my decision and mine alone. But whatever decision I made would affect him too. With Ron so busy with work and me busy running back and forth, attending college sixty miles away, would we lose this bond between us? It seemed unbreakable, but would it stay that way, if we didn't have time for each other? And our children? Although Ronnie didn't appear in my dream, he was only twelve, he needed me, and I needed time with him as well.

Then I was in what appeared to be an old European village, in a shop that sold clocks. I asked the man in the shop a question, but, then I couldn't remember what I asked. He looked at me and frowned. Then I heard these words inside my head, "Get your act together.

Decide and get on with it." I knew, of course, that the man and his shop represented time, and it was time to decide. Something about the man reminded me of Blaze, my uncle whom we never called *uncle*, and I thought about how he was always telling us kids stories, mostly just fun stories that made us laugh, and I wondered if he represented my desire to write. Was my idea of college just a dream of the past and no longer true? Did I really want to be a teacher? I thought of this older woman I'd known who had told me that her parents had forbidden her to marry because he was Catholic, so she married another. Years later, her mother asked her if she wasn't just as happy in this marriage. She said she told her mother that she loved her husband, but it wasn't the same. I thought then that the answer was no.

I loved my husband and my children—they were my first choice. If I chose to add this, a college degree and then a full-time teaching job, it would have a great effect on my life and theirs. Would I still love my life, but only as that woman had loved her husband? She knew she had made the wrong choice, and that even though she loved him, it wasn't the same. I knew then without a doubt that if I chose college, I'd be taking time and energy away from those I loved the most. She had chosen to obey her parents instead of listening to her heart and knew she had made the wrong choice.

I felt like my dream was saying, *choose carefully*. And, as if to add to my fear of losing something precious, Kelly, our youngest daughter, then disappeared. I searched and searched, but I could not find her and then I knew she and her sisters had all three drowned in that river near my home—that river of time, ever flowing onward. They were gone and I knew in the dream that I would never see them again.

Then three women appeared by that river of time. They'd been picking strawberries, and one showed me a small strawberry in her hand and asked if it was a real strawberry. I told her that yes it was real, but different from the usual berry we find in the stores or the garden, for I saw it as the berry that grew wild where we lived when I was a kid back in Montana. Those strawberries were tiny, but sweeter than the large, domesticated berries. I wondered if that berry in the woman's hand represented the fruits of our labors. Maybe it wasn't the big things I thought I wanted, like going to college, but the smaller, sweeter things, like more time with my family and maybe even writing again. The woman looked at me and said that she had not been sure, because not all things are as they appear. Those were the words I'd heard as I woke from my dream.

After reading that account of the dream symbols I knew that I would not be going to college. In fact, I no longer even wanted to go and I knew, too, I had absolutely no desire to be a teacher. I'm sure I knew all of this subconsciously and that was why I'd had the dream. The dream gave me the tools to know on a conscious level that that ship had sailed, probably a long, long time ago.

We had come to Kansas with no job, no money, and we had borrowed every cent to go into the two businesses. Although we made our payments and always paid extra when we could, we still had a ways to go. With the girls in college, it would really be a financial burden for me to go too, for not only the cost I'd incur, but I'd also have to quit my job at the school and lose that additional source of income. And yet Ron was willing to go that extra mile for me. *Gotta love that man!* I thanked God for that dream, and I bet Ron thanked Him for it too, and quite profusely.

I continued to work at Glade four more years. Then I had that out-of-body experience and learned why I'd been plagued with panic attacks and fainting spells for forty-three years. It happened in September when my sister Mabel and her husband John, who lived on a ranch in Montana, came to visit us. Ron often joined a group of guys at a local café for coffee and that morning he took John along. Mabel and I were sitting in our dining room having coffee when she began to talk about when our dad died. Immediately, I started to panic, my vision clouding, and I half rose from my chair, ready to head for the bathroom, my usual escape route. Then Mabel said, "You know when Mom had that breakdown, if she hadn't had June,

I think she would have lost her mind."

Her words startled me and stayed my flight, my panic subsiding. I was puzzled. "What!" I said. "What breakdown? Our *mother*! I don't remember a breakdown."

Then she told me what I had lost all conscious memory of and suddenly I was back in our old home in Montana, and I was again a little girl of five standing by my mother's bedside where she lay sleeping, baby June beside her. The shadows of the coming night were darkening the room and I looked at my mother and then at the window and then back at her and again at the window, and I knew I was waiting for the people, waiting for my mother to start mumbling words, and then I would sense the people and know they had come for my mother, and I was absolutely terrified! Then I was back at the table with Mabel and somehow, I "knew," absolutely knew that this was the source of my panic attacks and fainting spells. I simply knew it!

Of course, as an adult, I knew that people didn't roam the world peering into windows for their next victim to kill—aside from maybe serial killers—and that those who come to the dying, are loved ones who have passed and have come to welcome them to their new home. But that terrified five-year old, who had lived all those years in my subconscious, didn't know that. I'm so thankful for that out-of-body experience, that moment in time that took me back to the child I once was, so I could see and understand the source of my panic attacks and fainting spells. That "visit" to my mother's bedside had brought me face-to-face with the fear I'd carried so long in my subconscious memory. That "journey" back in time had taken me back to see what it really was, a childhood fear that was never consciously resolved.

Mabel had not been aware of my absence for my physical body, of course, had stayed behind. I suppose I was only gone seconds, although those episodes seem like they last a much longer time. But I sure don't know how that all works. I did not tell Mabel about my experience, for I didn't speak of my oddities then and only now, with this book, am I sharing it all with the world. No more hiding. In fact I should let her know that she was the instrument that put into action that out-of-body experience that set me free. I never thought of this before, but I owed her big time, so I need to tell her as soon as possible.

That journey back to my mother's bedside completely resolved that grief and fear I'd carried for so long and it brought to light those other times I feared the people, like when I had my tonsils out, and especially that terrible fear that they had killed my daddy, and as an adult I understood what I could not understand as a child.

I never again had another panic attack or fainting spell. If that out-of-body experience left any lingering of unresolved grief, it completely dissolved that December when Ron and I attended a week-long seminar in Denver for those in the funeral business. Called Life Appreciation, one part of the week was intended to give funeral home people insight into how best to serve the grieving, the other part to work with those in the business who have issues relating to their own personal unresolved grief.

We were given individual attention most in our guest rooms, but one of the men and I shared the big conference room, me at one end, he at the other. We were separated by the width of that large room and hidden from each other by panels set up like walls surrounding us. We had seen each other on entering the room, so I knew the other person was a man from Oklahoma. At one point I heard a sudden outburst of agonized crying. I would never know that man's story, but I heard his pain loud and clear in that terrible harsh sobbing. I hope he found what he needed, and if not resolved there, that he continued therapy back home.

I was extremely lucky to have had that out-of-body experience before attending the seminar, so I could tell the therapist the whole story and how that experience had set me free. I shared it all and let the healing tears flow.

I also talked about that year and a half I stayed with Mom when she was dying, and how I felt I had failed her. The therapist had me write a letter to her, although by then she'd been in Heaven twenty-eight years. I unburdened myself, easing my guilt for those times I felt I had failed her.

On the last day of the seminar, I was put through a kind of ritual of disposing of past grief. I was given a large piece of white cloth, one of the hotel's napkins, and told to put all my pain, fear, and grief into that napkin, along with the letter I had written to my mother, the only physical item inside, and then to fold it over and over, until all that grief and fear and sorrow along with the letter was secure inside the napkin and could not escape. Then six others in the group, three on a side, like actual pall bearers—perhaps intended to be symbolic—lifted me up off my feet and stretched me out flat on my back, full length, their arms supporting me. Then the therapist picked up the folded napkin with all my pain and fear and grief, and Mom's letter, secure inside, put it on my stomach and placed my hands over it. Then they carried me to the window that someone had opened, and set me up on my feet, my hands clinging to the napkin. My support group, those who had carried me to the window, now stayed close, their hands still touching or lightly holding on to me. The therapist then had me step up to the window and throw out the napkin. I looked down then, those two or three stories, and saw it there, next to the building in a patch of dirt and melting snow. It's a scene I used to see in my mind, quite often. I hadn't thought of that seminar for a long time, but now as I write these words, I look out that window, down to the ground, and there it is, that napkin with all my grief and fear and sorrow and Mom's letter inside, still lying in that patch of dirt and melting snow.

I don't know if any others were put through that ritual. Ron wasn't, and he had not helped carry anyone either. I hope that the man in the other side of the room and via another window, had thrown his own napkin full of grief and pain and sorrow down into that patch of dirt and melting snow.

I finished that year of being a para at the school, and that spring, when school was out, and now free of panic attacks and fainting spells, I quit and took on a job I would come to love—a job at the funeral home—a job I would probably have missed if I'd gone to college and become a teacher. Again I thanked God for the dream that had stopped me from pursuing a life I didn't really want.

CHAPTER 17

# THE FUNERAL HOME

**I BEGAN WORKING** at our funeral home in May of 1985. At that time, we did the book work in ledgers by hand, and typed obituaries and all other needed paperwork on a typewriter. A few years later, we bought our first computer. This was not one for general use, but especially for funeral homes. I'm not sure when we got regular computers, or even the year I got one at home. I know I used a word processor to write my stories in 1993 and found it a vast improvement over the typewriter. Of course, the computer beat that one all to pieces.

Darel and Ron no longer had the ambulance service by the time I came on board, as our county government had taken it over at midnight on January 1, 1974. They were no longer in the furniture store, either, having sold it in 1983 to Ron's brother Larry and two other men.

Ron's youngest brother Gary graduated from mortuary school in 1967 and joined Darel and Ron at the funeral home. In 1978, they purchased Brocks North Hill Chapel, a funeral home in Hays, and Gary became the manager. He and two partners bought the business in 1990. Gary retired in 2007 and he and his wife, Saunie, moved to Oklahoma.

One time, back when they still had the ambulance and the furniture store, Ron and Darel were the only ones in the store one day when they got an ambulance call. Ron called me to run over and stay until they got back. I was a full-time homemaker then and we lived just a block away. Shortly after they left, I had a customer. She was interested in replacing her kitchen floor with new linoleum. Well, about all I knew about the linoleum in the store was that it was downstairs, but I couldn't give her prices or anything else. I apologized, explaining about the ambulance run and asked if one of them could call her when they got back. She told me no, that she would just come back another time. A week, maybe two, went by and the guys, again alone in the store, got an ambulance call and called me. I was only there a few minutes, when that same woman stepped through the door, stopped dead still and said, "Oh, no! Not you again!"

Some years later, after the guys were out of the ambulance business, Darel was invited by some organization to speak about those days of running the ambulance. He began his talk by saying they had started out with just a vehicle and a cot and got their oxygen bottles filled at the refinery. "We had minimal equipment," he said. Then he grinned and added, "For instance, our Jaws of Life was a crowbar."

We attended a program in 1987 about how emergency personnel, the first responders on the scene of an accident or other tragedy, can give emotional support to those survivors on the scene. It was called First Faith, and basically, it's giving those survivors the truth, rather than glossing it over with a kind of hope that will blindside them later. Afterward, I discussed this with Darel, and he told me about a time, years before, when they had taken the ambulance to a train vs. car wreck in which the mother of a nine-year-old girl had been killed. He said, "I went over to her, and she looked up at me and said, 'My mother is not a bit good, is she?' I told her, 'No, honey, your mother is not a bit good.' The girl then said, 'She's dead, isn't she?'" He told her that yes, her mother was dead. He told me he agonized over that for a long time, wondering if that had been the right thing to say, and of course it was. He had been her "first faith contact" and in him, in that terrifying place, she had found someone to trust, and that was a measure of comfort. He didn't lie to her, and not only did he give her the dignity of the truth, but he let her lead him to what she wanted to know. What she, in this case, already knew but needed confirmation. Even in regular deaths, children are not always given the truth. Remember, my sister was told that Grandma was sleeping, and she wondered what Grandma would do when she woke up in a box underground with dirt piled on top of it.

There is this lighter side to the funeral business, for even in death, it's not all sadness and gloom. There were these two old buddies, I'll call them, Carl and Joe, both pretty much soused all the time, and one rarely, if ever, seen without the other. Then Joe passed. When he was in his casket ready for public viewing, Carl staggered in, and when he reached the casket, he grabbed Joe's arm and yelled, "Get up, Joe! Get up!"

One time when we were extra busy and four bodies were lying in state, a woman came in, marched up to look first at one and then at another and on until she had viewed all four, then she turned to Darel, and said, "My, my! What are you boys going to do with all your money?"

One elderly woman's family told this story about when they went to the nursing home to tell her that her sister had passed, and that she would need to go with them to make the funeral arrangements. She looked at them, frowned, and said, "Why do we need to get the funeral home involved? Why can't we just throw her over the crick bank?"

One story I'll have to tell on Ron was when his funeral family had pulled into the cemetery for the committal service, and he went over and after getting them all out of their cars so he could lead them as a group to the grave site, he said, "Follow me," turned and fell over a low headstone. They all burst out laughing and when Ron was back on his feet, one of them said, "Do we have to do that too?" He said they teased him about that for years.

I got a firsthand experience of being in a dust storm while working at the funeral home that helped me when I wrote *The Summer of the Crow*, which was set in Kansas during the Dust Bowl days. Ron and I had gone to Colorado Springs to pick up a man who had died in a hospital there. On the way home, we were near the Colorado Kansas border, Ron driving, when we were suddenly encased in a world of dust. The dust was so thick, we couldn't even see the front end of the van. We inched along, fearing at any moment we'd run into someone ahead of us or be run into by someone from behind. The dust seemed to shift into every nook and cranny until it was absolutely suffocating. We finally crawled into Goodland, Kansas where, thankfully, the storm had ceased. Exhausted, we got a motel for the night. The people at the motel were surprised to see us, as the road had been closed. We must have been just ahead of the closure. Otherwise, how could we have missed it? It was an awful experience, but it really came in handy when I wrote my dust bowl story.

I also used one of Ron's family stories in that book. When Ron and his sister, Shirley, were little, they lived on a farm a few miles out of Prairie View. One day they were coming home from town with a wagon and team of horses when a dust storm blew up. Their dad stopped at the house to let them out before taking the horses on to the barn. He hurried to unharness the team, but by then the dust was so thick that he could no longer even see the house. But dust storms create static electricity and flashes of light were bouncing off the metal blades of the windmill and knowing where the house was in relation to the windmill, he made his way back to the house and as he got closer, he caught the dim light of the lamp Edith had set in the window to guide him. In my book, the main character Brady and his dad seek shelter in the barn, and they also use those flashes of light from the windmill to get to the house.

Our son Ronnie joined the business after graduating from mortuary school in 1989. Darel and Shirley's son, Kenton, had finished his schooling a few years earlier and the two boys purchased the business from their dads in January 1997.

Later, Kenton decided to change careers and Chris Hugunin bought into the business. In January 2022, Chris's son Conlee, a recent graduate of mortuary school, became the new man on board, and I imagine he will eventually buy out his dad and Ronnie when they're ready to retire.

Ronnie's kids were more cognizant of their dad's occupation than our kids were of Ron's. Probably because of me, who lived in fear of having one of my attacks. After that open house the kids and I held for Ron on his seventieth birthday (Chapter 14) the grandkids—Kelly's two and Ronnie's three—held an impromptu funeral service. There was a piano at the center and Jordyn, the eldest, although only nine and probably having never touched a keyboard, was the pianist. At first Elizabeth, age three, played the role of the deceased, lying there on the floor, clad in the nice dress she had worn for Papa's party, her hands folded across her chest. However, that was soon so terribly, terribly boring and she sat up and complained. So, Ally, age six, also in a pretty dress, took over the role of the deceased. Emily, age seven, preached the service. Johnny was only a few weeks old at the time, so he pretty much slept through it all.

One time out at the cemetery where I'd taken Ronnie's kids, Jordyn and Ally, after school to see their mother's step-grandfather's grave, Ally climbed up on a nearby stone and sat there, legs dangling. "I can do this," she said proudly, "cause I'm a funeral director's daughter."

Ronnie brought the kids' pet rabbit to Johnny's day care for show and tell one day and one of the kids thought he knew Ronnie but had mistaken him for another man. Johnny immediately corrected him. "He's the funeral director," he said. "And that's weird."

My mother's name was among those many errors in that terrible fiasco of getting my first book published, an error that continued through three more publications. I'd dedicated the book in memory of my parents, and Mom's name, Hazel, was spelled *Haxel* through those first three printings. Our daughter Kathy suggested that since it didn't appear they were ever going to get it right, why didn't I just change it on her headstone.

One year, shortly before Memorial Day, Ron and I were out checking in all the cemeteries to be sure the monument company had the new stones set and had engraved on the existing stones information on the recent deaths. Our daughters, Kathy and Kelly, were home from college that day and went with us. We were at a rural cemetery north of town, and as we walked among the headstones, Kelly saw one with the inscription, *Gone but not Forgotten.* She thought those were such sad words and said she hoped no one would ever put those words on her headstone. "Don't worry," her sister quipped. "On yours we'll put, *Out of Sight, Out of Mind.*"

One day when Ronnie got a death call, Johnny, then about five, said, "Don't call anyone, Dad, just give me some gloves and I'll go with you." His dad told him that maybe he could go when he was a little older. He also said to Ronnie one day, his face all screwed up in a frown, "Dad, who's the funeral coach?"

I was keeping our first grandchild, Jordyn, then three, while her parents were on a trip. There were two funerals that day both in churches, and a man lying in state in the chapel. So she stayed with me there. She was very interested in that man in the casket, so I picked her up and carried her into the chapel to look at him. First, she asked if he was sleeping. I told her that he was dead. I thought she might ask more about being dead, but she didn't. She was silent for a bit and then said, "Does he have hair in his nose?" I told her that, yes, I did see that he had some hair in his nose. Then, she looked at me and asked if I had hair in my nose, but after looking, decided I didn't. Then she asked if the man was God. I told her that no, he was just a man. Then she was done looking and we went back into the living quarters, and she took a nap.

Working at the funeral home was a job with variety. Besides book work and other duties, Shirley and I registered those attending the services, and afterward, one of us stood out in the middle of highway 183 with a stop sign so the funeral procession could pull out onto the highway unimpeded and start its way to the cemetery.

I started a small library in the funeral home for the grieving and for those who wanted to comfort and support the grieving. I read those books, so I would know enough to help them select one that would resonate with them in their situation.

I especially wanted to have books for parents where they could read accounts of how children who were not allowed to grieve, or even to know what was going on at times when they most needed to know and how they could feel isolated and more fearful. Society was slowly moving out of that mindset that children were to be kept from knowing a loved one was dying or had died, and the belief that children did not really mourn—that they'd soon forget and would go back to their play. I know I was super sensitive to that situation, so I also provided children's books on that topic as well.

I remember one little girl who was with her family gathered in the chapel to view the child's grandmother, when one of the adults said to the child, "Your dear grandmother is in Heaven now." The little girl replied with a frown, "No, she isn't. She's over there in that box."

When Blanche, Ron's stepmother, passed and after the committal service at the cemetery and we were going back to our cars, our granddaughter, Elizabeth, age three, looked up at her parents and said, "Why'd they put Grandma in that box?"

Another little girl I met in the chapel with her grandmother viewing a deceased relative, looked at me with a questioning look when her grandmother told her the woman was sleeping. I smiled and she smiled back at me as if we shared a secret. Now, knowing so much more about how deceased loved ones can interact with the living, and that children are particularly sensitive to their presence, I wonder if the woman was there, perhaps smiling and in some way communicating with the little girl.

Among the books in our small library was Dr. Raymond Moody's *Life After Life*, published in 1975 on near-death experiences. A philosopher, psychologist, and physician, he was a skeptic and an atheist when he began his study on NDEs in 1968. His studies convinced him that we survive the death experience, and he became a believer. His book was a bestseller and woke the world to the fact or belief, depending on one's take, that there is a continuation of life after death. My take is that life after death is an indisputable fact.

Elizabeth Kubler Ross was a world renowned expert on death and dying. She often compared the shedding of our bodies in death to the butterfly shedding its cocoon. The analogy is perfect, for as the butterfly is now free to fly in its new world, so do we, when free of our earthly body, "fly" away to that new world awaiting us.

Kubler-Ross's uses of the butterfly from the cocoooon is now often used to illustrate the passage of life from this world. However, one needs to be careful about using that illustration with children. One Sunday School teacher had just given that "butterfly from the cocoon" version of passing into Heaven when one little boy raised his hand and said, "I saw a dead butterfly once."

Over the years, through my own experiences and in reading those books about death and dying as I built up the funeral home library, I began to share with individuals and receive stories in return; stories some had never shared, or only with a select few. Now, since Ron passed and has kept in contact with us and in such a variety of ways, I am certain our loved ones are never far from us, in that place we Christians call Heaven. It's Gan Eden for Judaism, Vicenta for Hinduism, and of course others have their own names, except for atheists. One doesn't name what one doesn't know exists, but one day, I believe, they'll get a big surprise.

# CHAPTER 18

# A NEAR-DEATH EXPERIENCE

IN 1987, I heard about Mary, who lived in a neighboring town and who I was told had died, visited Heaven, and then returned to her earthly life. An event called a near-death experience, or NDE for short.

My own experiences are minor compared to an NDE, but odd enough to have kept me from sharing too readily until now. The many ways that Ron has contacted me and our family since his passing, and the feeling that I should write this book, has loosened my tongue and I've begun to share and not worry if I'm believed or not. Although, I've discovered in sharing my "experiences," that there are a lot of us who have had contact in some form with a passed loved one or know someone who has had such an experience. Some have shared with a select few, but many aren't comfortable sharing at all.

I think that many, like I used to be, were unaware that there is a proliferation of stories and experiences such as ours, but we don't hear about them, for few share their experiences. For a long time, I didn't even tell Ron, and then not everything—but I wish I had. Of course, he knows all my secrets now, and is giving me all kinds of messages and signs, more than I ever thought possible, and urging me with this book to tell it all.

Those stories, mine and those I've heard from others who have received a sign or message, visual or otherwise, from a passed loved one, confirms, at least for me, that we do not have just life after death, but we will be aware of those loves ones who still live on earth's plane and will have the ability to connect with them in some way. However, not all of those still earthbound can pick up on their loved one's messages. But just to know others can and have done so can be a comfort.

Those contacts from loved ones can come immediately after a loved one passes, or years later. My mother had been gone fifty-one years when she appeared to me in full form for a few seconds, as I recounted in chapter five. Whereas my brother, Danny, who you will read about in the next chapter, appeared to me in full form, just a month and a half after he passed. Some of us have received multiple signs or contacts while others only a few, or only one, and others have had none. I believe some of us are born with that sort of extra perception that makes it easier to pick up on the messages from loved ones, although in varying degrees, some more, some less. There are also some who have discovered by another's experience that what they thought was their imagination wasn't at all.

By the time I visited with Mary about her NDE, I'd read a lot of books on death and dying, including Dr. Raymond Moody's *Life After Life*. I was also actively involved in our local hospice that provides end-of-life care. I wrote their monthly newsletter and a short weekly piece for the local newspapers, and on occasion gave talks at hospice meetings, all of which furthered my education on the subject.

I did love my job at the funeral home. I loved working every day with Ron, and I loved the variety of my work. Well, not keeping the books so much. Shirley was better at that than I was. I did like helping with funerals and all that entailed and getting involved with hospice was perfect for me. I also saw how Ron and Darel served those families with the kind of loving compassion all funeral directors should, but don't always, and I was proud to be a member of the team.

I ran across an old talk I gave in 1986 to Compassionate Friends, a bereavement program for those who had lost children, a year after I'd started working at the funeral home, and nearly two years since my sister, Mabel, had spoken those words that had sent me "back" to my mother's bedside in Montana.

In that talk, I touched lightly on my own problems as a child dealing with death, but I mostly cited stories culled from those books I'd gathered for the funeral home library. My primary aim was the one closest to my heart, which was about children and grief and that they should be told truths, not euphemisms.

I must have been forty, fifty years old when I took my cat to the vet to be euthanized, as she was suffering from cancer. He took her away to another room to administer the injection and when he brought her back to me said, "She's asleep now." A little startled, I said, "You mean she's dead?" He said, "Yes." So even to a grown-up and about a pet, the vet didn't feel comfortable using the word *dead*. Although, since Ron "died" I use the word *passed* because I know that only his body died. He simply passed from his world into the next, and that is what will happen to the rest of us.

I told one group I was speaking to about my dad appearing to speak to someone I could not see the night he passed. I did not tell them that I had sensed the people, that I knew they were there. I let them think he had a fever, which he likely did, leaving it at that, for in those days, telling them I had known the people were there, wasn't something I was yet brave enough to share completely.

Now, knowing that children seem to be closer to the spiritual world than adults usually are, I wonder if there had been one or more in attendance, who in those last days or hours of their child's earthly life, were given evidence that he or she had seen a passed loved one, even Jesus, or an angel. I was such a novice then—so totally ignorant of the fact that there is but a thin veil between us.

Collectively, we are all reluctant to speak of our experiences such as visions, out-of-body experiences, and seeing passed loved ones as solid in form as they looked in their earthly life, although if only for a second or two. However, if someone shares with us, then we are generally quite eager to share our stories. When I told that group about my sister Mabel's words about Mom's breakdown, words that sent me back to my mother's bedside, a five-year-old again, I called it a memory instead of an out-of-body experience. I didn't know the term yet or even know that it happened to other people—so I sure as heck wasn't going to risk being seen as some kind of a nut who made up crazy stories. I hadn't even shared it with Ron.

I did, however, tell them about the seminar Ron and I had attended in Denver and sang its praises, for it had been a wonderful experience. I didn't need it as far as the panic and fainting issues were concerned, for the out-of-body experience had fixed that, but it resolved my guilt over not having been the best caregiver for my mom when she was dying.

The day I went to Mary's home to hear her near-death experience, I was excited and a bit anxious as I had never met her before, but she soon put me at ease and willingly shared her story. Mary was in her middle years then. Her NDE had happened four years before while she was in the hospital for what was to be routine surgery. But the experience was as fresh to her as if it had happened yesterday. She smiled when she told me that she had not wanted to be resuscitated, should something go wrong, but she wasn't allowed to sign the paper and her husband wouldn't. Apparently at that time, patients weren't allowed to sign those papers for themselves.

"Little did I know then," she said, "that had my husband signed that paper, I might have missed the greatest adventure of my life." She paused, then added with a grin, "Well, no, I guess not. I'd have made it to Heaven all right, but if he'd signed that paper, I might not have been able to come back and talk about it." Again, she paused and with another smile, added, "Well, I'm sure that if God wanted me to come back, maybe even to share this experience with you, a piece of paper wouldn't have stopped Him."

She was in surgery when she suffered what they thought was a heart attack. She said the sudden pain was excruciating, and then it was gone, and she found herself up near the ceiling looking down on herself on the table, the doctor trying to revive her. She saw the doctor use the paddles to start her heart, and the first time she went briefly back into her body and then out and back up near the ceiling again. With the second use of the paddles, she said, "The walls of the hospital just peeled away, and I was in the most beautiful country with lush green grass, abundant flowers and trees, flowing streams, and on the hillsides and in the open, unfenced meadows and pastures, sheep and cattle were grazing."

She said the colors were so vivid, so rich, and over it all was a beautiful, bright, luminous light, but it did not hurt her eyes. She said that when she looked around, it was as if she were looking at the whole world and it was unending.

"I could look at a place and I'd be there," she said, "It was so beautiful, so peaceful, and I had no worries at all." Then her family appeared and came toward her, with her mother at the head of the group. Among those family members were two teenage boys and she remembered when they had passed. She grinned then and added, "Even my ex-husband was there. However, he did not crowd up close as the others had but stayed out a little way away from the group." Then she added, with that same grin and a twinkle in her eyes, "I think he thought I might still be mad at him."

She'd wanted to stay, but her mother told her she had to go back. Then she was back in the hospital with family members by her bedside and immediately, she began to share her experience with them. She said she had most, maybe all of the story told, when a nurse came in and, hearing her talk about Heaven, thought she was hallucinating and gave her a shot that put her out.

"Every morning," she said, "I'm compelled to open my drapes and look out, a hope in me, that I will see that beautiful country again. I know I won't, but I am still compelled to look."

Mary shared her story at a hospice meeting and at my church's adult Sunday School class and, although we didn't see each other very often, we remained friends. She died at her home sixteen years later. Her daughter called me when her mother was in her final days, so I got to see her once again. The family told me later that the day before she passed, she spoke to someone the family knew who had passed a few years before. Then, she looked at them and said, "I won't go today, but I will tomorrow." And she did.

I've read a lot of near-death experiences and hers was typical, except instead of going through a tunnel-like passageway, as most of them seem to do, the hospital walls had simply opened for her to step into that beautiful world. She saw members of her family as most do, and she mentioned the light, as most do. A common phrase among those who witness the light, and Mary said it too, was "But it didn't hurt my eyes." One woman added, "and I have sensitive eyes."

Mary's mother had told her she had to go back. She didn't want to, but her mother told her that it wasn't her time. In some of the cases I've read about, they are given the choice. I thought it was interesting that the ex-husband came with the others to greet her. Some might wonder about eternal life with an ex-spouse. Of course, there has to be a lot of them who share Heaven, but Heaven is, in Mary's words, unending. Also, we surely lose our human frailties and see the whole picture and can grasp concepts our earthly minds and eyes saw only dimly, if at all, and ex-spouses would no longer be a problem.

An Asian friend told me about an NDE she'd had when she was a young woman back in her homeland. She said she suddenly found herself in a beautiful country and described it pretty much as Mary had. I asked if it looked like her homeland, and she said, "No. Not really, but it was the most beautiful place I'd ever seen." In those years, she was a Buddhist, and in that NDE, she saw Buddha. He told her she was not to be there yet, that she had to go back. Then he summoned an angel to carry her back and she came out of a three-day coma in her bed at home.

I've yet to hear in those NDEs of a hell, at least not with that Satan fellow and his pit of fire and brimstone. However, I have read of a few NDEs where they felt they were in a less-than desirable place, but they didn't call it hell. Maybe God has a kind of hell where those who created a lot of hell on earth are given a taste of what they had put others through, or He lets them see and so understand how their life experiences had shaped them. How what had happened to them, perhaps in their formative years, had formed who they'd become. Some who have had a NDE speak of a life review, and that could be a bit of hell. I imagine that even the human version of the "junkyard dog" would come back through that thin veil and start right off walking the straight and narrow. I wonder if those who had taken a life or lives were to have a NDE and get a life review if it would include meeting their victim(s) and being forced to hear their stories.

As I stated in chapter 13, I don't believe in hell, but neither do I presume to be the expert on the matter. I know many people do believe in that evil kingdom, but I just can't. Well, I do believe in *a* hell, but it is right here on earth, and the cruelty, the evil, is manmade, a lot of it inflicted on children. As the early eighteenth-century poet Alexander Pope wrote: "As the twig is bent, so grows the tree." I also believe that we can rise above whatever horrors we've endured by changing our way of thinking—although that's not an easy task and would most likely require some therapy, although an out-of-body or near-death experience could unravel that mystery in seconds.

Melvin Morse, in his book, *Closer to the Light,* tells of an early Egyptian named Osiris who was captured by his enemies and sealed in a box for a short period of time. When they let him out, he described a NDE. This so astounded them that they declared him a god-king and made him the ruler over them. All the god-kings that followed Osiris were sealed in a box and when it was opened, if they were still alive and if they spoke of a NDE they became the next king. It was believed that each one was a direct reincarnation of Osiris.

Morse states in his book that the nearly 2,000 years the pharaohs ruled in Egypt, that it was a kinder, gentler place due to the practice of subjecting each new king to a NDE. For when he returned to his earthly body, he was a kinder, gentler, humbler person, and so he ruled his people with kindness, which led to the people being kinder to each other.

Perhaps, if it became common knowledge that we all survive death and that we will, in our new place of residence, be able to know how our earthbound loved ones are living their lives, and how we were once seen from that same vantage point, we might all become a little kinder and gentler while we trod earth's plane.

In all the years I've recited the Lord's Prayer, I've always said this part, "And lead us not into temptation." Then I read the book, *Forty Years a Medium*, by Estelle Roberts, about this passage. According to her, theologians have debated these words for years. Those opposed to the part we all recite "and lead us not into temptation," say that God would never lead us into temptation, and so it should be changed to "and leave us not when in temptation." So that's what I say now.

CHAPTER 19

# RON'S MYASTHENIA GRAVIS AND DANNY

**WE BEGAN PART-TIME** retirement in 1994 and in 1995, we sold the motor home and purchased our Montana vacation home on an island called Angel Island, on Bull Lake, fifteen miles from Troy. We did so enjoy those summers on the island with visits from family and friends from home, my family in the area, and those from my school years in Bonners Ferry. Every summer we hosted a gathering of my Goyen family in the Island's community center.

We enjoyed all those who visited us, but we especially enjoyed the kids and grandkids. Everyone loved the place, the mountains, the lake, and the rivers, especially the Kootenai River with the falls and the swinging bridge. With Canada right next door, we often took our kids, grandkids, and friends to Banff, Lake Louise, and places in between. We enjoyed riding the ferries in Canada and those in Washington that took us to Canada's Vancouver Island and Washington's San Juan Islands.

The summer of 2010, Ron broke his leg just before we were to leave for Montana and had to spend his time there in a wheelchair. Perhaps then he saw the writing on the wall, for he talked of selling our Angel Island place and buying something on a lake back home. So, we listed it in September of the next year, 2011.

Ron began having trouble with his eyes in April of 2012 and in

May, he was diagnosed with the auto immune disease myasthenia gravis, or MG for short. The disease affects the involuntary muscles, in his case, the muscles of his eyelids. They would not lift on their own, so to see, he had to lift and hold them with his fingers. Often, he saw double and could no longer see well enough to read or watch TV, so he spent time listening to books on tape. Eventually, with huge doses of prednisone, his eyelid muscles began working again and his eyesight improved so he could at least read some and watch TV. Although he struggled with this disease, I don't remember him ever complaining.

Our Angel Island place now on the market for eight months and no takers, Ron was beginning to worry. So, on May 2, 2012, I went to the city park and asked God for a buyer. I crossed the creek on the footbridge and sat on a fallen log, in the shade of the trees. A slight breeze ruffling the leaves overhead, I talked to God about our Angel Island place. I told him that Ron was worried about it, and if there was no reason for it not to sell, would He please find a buyer just as soon as possible. I whispered an Amen and then a voice from among the leaves and branches in the tall tree overhead, said, "Consider it done."

On June 1, the realtor called. We had a buyer. We left for Montana on June 7 to close the deal, clear out our things, and say goodbye.

We carried away a lot of memories of those seventeen summers, especially of the grandchildren, and for me, a special one of my mom. It was in this kitchen on July 21, 2008, that Mom appeared before me those few seconds, smiling at me with love and pride in her eyes.

Kathy also saw my mother in a daytime vison that year. In the vision, her grandmother was sitting at a table in the kitchen of our old house on Libby Creek. Although Kathy had never seen my mother or the house, she knew who she was and where she was. (Mom passed in April before Kathy was born in September.)

Ron's youngest brother Gary passed on February 26, 2014. By then, Ron was again taking large doses of prednisone and his face and body were so swollen from the medication that his regular clothes no longer fit him. The only suit I could find for him to wear to the funeral didn't fit just great, being slightly too large, but it worked, and I slit the back of his shirt so it would button in front. I'm sure he didn't feel very comfortable in that suit, especially when he had to pull up the pants every now and then, but he bore it all with dignity and grace.

Eventually, the disease backed off again and the prednisone was reduced to a maintenance level, and he did quite well all through 2015–16. In July 2016, Ronnie and Michele rented a place on Angel Island just across the road from where we'd had our place, so Ron and I went for a week. The buyers had replaced our modest dwelling with a brand-new structure reminiscent of a mountain chalet.

We enjoyed our time with the kids, and I visited my sisters, Mabel and Margaret, at their homes, and my brother Earl, in the nursing home at Libby. We also spent a day in Bonners Ferry. On the way home we stopped to see my brother, Larry, in Wyoming. It was Ron's last trip to that country he so loved.

My brother Earl, passed in September, so I went back to Montana for the funeral, but Ron didn't feel well enough to go with me. Earl had failed a lot in the past few years, and when I had left him in July to go home, I knew I'd not see him again this side of Heaven. For several years before he started failing, Earl would visit us in late fall and each time he'd bring us a Montana Christmas tree. We saw him quite a lot those years we summered on Angel Island. Once, when he was visiting us there, he told me about one time when he was eighteen and driving his truck down a mountain road, he heard a loud, commanding voice yell three times in quick succession, "Slow down! Slow down! Slow down!"

He obeyed the voice, slowing way down, and as he rounded a curve just ahead, he saw that a rockslide had come down off the mountain and on to the road. Without that warning, it's doubtful he would have grown any older. He passed in his eighty-seventh year.

Our daughter Kelly is a speech pathologist and worked in a school before retiring. One day, coming home from work, a truck pulled out in front of her. She slammed on the brakes, but she knew she was going to hit it. She said then everything seemed to go into slow motion and the next thing she knew, she was in front of the truck and going on down the road.

I was telling a minister about how God had to have intervened to save Kelly, and he told me a similar story about being saved by that same kind of divine intervention. That day, to avoid hitting a car that was passing another, he took to the ditch, and for him too, everything seemed to go into slow motion. Then he saw inside his car in front of him a pair of hands folded as if, he said, in peace and protection, and he came out on the road again safe and sound. He said he knew that road and there is a culvert there that ordinarily he would have hit, and it would have wrecked him.

Perhaps we all have a preset time and maybe even the method in which we will pass. If so, then sometimes we'd have to be stopped if it appears we are about to end our lives prematurely. That voice kept Earl earthbound for sixty-nine more years. In Kelly's case, there was no time for a voice to save her, so did God or an angel take over and carry her car around and past the truck? So, if we have a preset time and it looks like, through no fault of our own, as in Kelly and the minister's case, we're about to end it, then God must either step in and work a miracle or alter our life plan.

We must consider too, that we have choices—free will—and the choices we make, large and small, determine the course of our lives. Of course, Kelly and the minister had no choice, but Earl did, and he slowed down. Sometimes, though, when we are warned, we refuse to heed the warning, choosing instead to keep barreling on down the road.

After Ron's mother passed, his dad married Blanche. The two had dated in their early years, but both had married others. Ron's dad and mother had remained here, but Blanche and her husband had moved to Washington state. Now, both Ron's mother and Blanche's husband had passed so Blanche moved back to Kansas and she and

Ron's dad soon married. One day, Blanche told me that she came back specifically to look up Ron's dad, now that he was single too. One day trying to decide whether she should go or not, she asked God, and He replied in a clearly audible voice, "No!" I was surprised and I wondered what He might have had planned for the two of them, had she obeyed instead of barreling on down the road.

My brother Danny passed in 2006, at age sixty-five, a sudden, unexpected passing. He died in his sleep in his bed in the early morning hours, his wife unaware until she went to wake him for breakfast.

We had left our summer place in Montana earlier than usual, so we were at home when Danny passed. We left the next day for his funeral. We were in Nebraska, near the Wyoming line, when I asked Danny to give me a sign that he was okay, and very soon afterward, he did.

We always change drivers every hundred miles, and I was driving on Wyoming's interstate, when I found myself in Danny's bedroom in Montana. I was at the head of his bed, perhaps suspended a little, for I was looking down on him. However, I was not aware of my body. (Of course, it was still back in the car.) He had been lying on his side but turned over on his back as I looked down on him. He opened his eyes and looked around and then closed them again. There was a kind of sepia-toned light around him and his side of the bed, so I could see that part clearly, but the rest of the room was dark, including the side of the bed where his wife still slept, unaware. Then I saw Dad and Mom standing by the bed and I heard them say, "Danny." He opened his eyes and turned his head to look at them. They held out their hands and said, "Come, son." He got up off the bed and standing, he took their hands in his. Then he looked back to where Lindy lay sleeping. They said, "She'll be all right." I keep saying "they" for it seems as if they spoke as one. With those words, Danny turned back to them, and I was once again conscious of driving on the interstate in Wyoming.

I had known nothing of driving while I was away, and apparently

Ron, who was in the passenger seat noticed nothing unusual while I was gone. So, in some way, time must be suspended. Also, this was the day after Danny passed, so his body was not actually in his bed, but in the funeral home at Libby. I believe he sent me that vision of how he had passed in answer to my query. One thing I now know is that they do think outside the box, and free of their earthly restraints, they can do amazing things. I loved that Danny let me see that he's with our dad and mom.

I never told Ron about that vision or out-of-body experience. I was afraid of sharing this odd side of me for fear he would think less of me. I wish I had. Ron had lost his brother Larry in February, just six months before I lost Danny. Larry and Danny were the same age, both good, kind, selfless men. How comforting it might have been for Ron to hear about my parents coming for Danny. I'm sure he believed his parents had come for his brother, but I had actually seen mine in that out-of-body vision. I know now, he would have loved to have heard that story, but what would he have thought? How does that make sense? I'm seeing Danny in his bed, but he's not there. I see Mom and Dad, but they're in Heaven. And not only that, it happened while I was driving the car on the interstate.

Now I know there would have been no risk in telling him. He would have believed me and loved me just the same. Now, too, I think he may have had some "experiences" of his own. He did share one with me, many years after the fact, about his first time as a newly elected elder in our church. He was really nervous that Sunday morning, but as he rose to step into the pulpit and deliver the offertory and communion mediations, he looked down and saw the face of Jesus in the carpet.

I had my own experience with seeing Jesus one morning in church. Like Ron's, it was some years ago and I'd forgotten it, but I'd written it in my diary, and I ran across it one day while searching for another entry. I never told Ron that story either.

That Sunday morning the elder, in his communion meditation,

told a story I had heard from him a few days before, but this time he embellished it way out of proportion to the real event and I silently scoffed. Immediately I heard Jesus laugh and for an instant I saw His face. Somehow, it didn't seem so out of the ordinary then and I laughed inside at being chastised by our Lord Jesus. Every time I'd remember, I'd have to smile. I knew He was saying to me, "So that's how he chooses to tell it, silly woman. It doesn't matter if the story is embellished, or even made up completely. That's not the point." And of course, it wasn't. I loved it!

Just as it was some years later that Ron shared that story with me, I wonder now how many other experiences he kept to himself. Not that I blame him. I certainly have no room to talk. It's hard to share these "stories" so out of the mainstream of our culture, for fear of not being believed, of having the other person say it had to be a dream or your imagination, or who knows what else. And if you are sharing with someone you dearly love, you do not want to risk appearing too crazy. Still, one day I did tell him about hearing a voice that told me to "Go look in the Bible."

This is the story. Some years before, I had come through a bad time in which I felt I was to blame, even though I really wasn't, for I hadn't known any better. I was lying in bed, mentally beating myself up, my tears shed in silence as Ron slept beside me. Then a voice up near the ceiling said, "Go look in the Bible." I answered with a disdainful, "Oh, sure." The voice repeated the words, this time in the voice of a parent disciplining a child. "Oh, all right!" I said, still in that same irritated tone of voice, "but you keep him asleep!" (meaning Ron, of course). Although I could not see anything on that wall near the ceiling, I "saw" a downward movement, like a nod, and I knew Ron would stay asleep. I went downstairs and got the Bible, and I just opened it, put my finger on one of the pages, looked down and read, "Not everything that happens is your fault." Wow! What wonderful words! What freeing words! With a truly grateful heart, I thanked the voice, went back to bed, and fell into a deep and restful sleep. Some years later I would begin to use that random way of getting answers from the Bible. I'd just open it, put my finger on a page, then read the scripture under my finger. Most of the time I would get what I needed.

Ron was delighted with the story and thought it was perfect for *Guidepost* magazine, and so I submitted it. They sent a man to interview me, but I never heard anything from him or the magazine. For a long time I believed the man didn't find me credible and considered me unworthy of a reply. But just now, writing this all these years later, it dawned on me that maybe the reason *Guidepost* didn't get back to me was because those words I told him I saw in the Bible, looking like all the other words on that page, aren't there. I hadn't figured it out by then or I would have told the man who interviewed me. That might have made all the difference.

As I recall, I went looking one day for that particular scripture, and when I couldn't find it, I asked several ministers, although not why. Many years later, I checked it out on the computer, and it wasn't there either. I was innocent when I said I read those words in the Bible, for I really did, but those words were just for me, for that moment in time, a direct message from a higher power, maybe God, maybe an angel or Jesus, but the *Guidepost* editors didn't know that.

My next contact with Danny was the morning of the tenth of September, about two months after he passed. I woke that Sunday morning from a wonderful dream of being with him. I call it a dream, but it was too real to have been just a dream. I believe it was an actual visit from Danny that happened while I was sleeping. Danny was sixty-five when he passed in July, and he had not looked well when we saw him earlier that summer in Montana. But in this dream visit he looked wonderful! He looked at least thirty years younger and just radiated health and happiness. I remember we had a wonderful conversation, and we laughed a lot, but I don't remember what we talked about, except these words, spoken just seconds before I woke up. "Danny," I said, "tell me about Jesus." He laughed and said, "Oh, I'll tell you about Him another time."

The next morning in church, as we stood to sing the opening hymn, which happened to be "Amazing Grace," the song I chose for his funeral service at his wife Lindy's request, Danny stood up right beside me. He was looking at me with dancing eyes and just grinning all over himself. Then in seconds, he vanished. Ron never mentioned him, so he must not have seen him, and being so reticent about sharing this with him, or anyone, I never told him.

Lindy had chosen taped music for Danny's funeral, and the CD played at the service was ours, a part of a two-disc set from the artist George Jones. On March 4, 2007, I was driving to an author's event and was listening to that CD. As I neared the exit, I pulled the CD out and laid it on the passenger's seat and as I turned off the highway, it slid off the seat. I parked the car and leaned over to retrieve the disc, but I couldn't find it, so I got out and scoured that van, but it was nowhere to be found. The next day, I had the van serviced and asked them to keep an eye out for the CD. They always vacuum when they service a vehicle, and they did that day as well and no CD was found. Because I love that song, I bought another copy exactly like the one I'd had, so now I have that new set and the # 2 disc from the original set.

Then one day coming home from a trip, Ron driving, he asked me to play the George Jones CD. I opened the case and the #1 disc, the one with the song, "Amazing Grace," in this second CD was gone. The #2 disc was still in the case, but #1was gone.

We laughed and talked about Danny. Was he stealing those discs with the "Amazing Grace" song? It was sort of a joke, but I kept wondering. So, one day I asked Danny if he was stealing those discs, and if I bought his Lindy a copy, would he leave ours alone. I didn't get an answer, but I bought one for her exactly like the other two. I meant to get us another one too, but there were no more of those two-disc sets left. So, I settled for the one-disc CD that featured other artists and their songs, along with George Jones's "Amazing Grace." A year passed and we still had that third one. On Dec. 23, 2008, just on a spur of the moment, I called a Libby flower shop and had a poinsettia delivered to Danny's Lindy.

The next afternoon, getting things ready for our Christmas Eve with our kids and grandkids, I got out a tape of Christmas songs to listen to, but the tape player wouldn't work. (Later it would.) So, I got out the CD player and opened the drawer where I kept the CDs and on top of a case was one loose disc. It was disc #1 the Amazing Grace CD by George Jones, either the one that had slid off the car seat, or the second one that had disappeared from the car. A week or so later the second one showed up in the car, in its case.

I never expected to get them at all, let alone both. Maybe the poinsettia cinched the deal. I think he was saying thanks. Just getting one of them was surprising, but both? Wow! Of, course he'd have no use for them. Any song he wants to hear, I'm sure he can just ask the universe for, kind of like us asking Siri or Alexa.

What has so far turned out to be my last contact from Danny happened after Lindy called me one day, depressed and missing her Danny so very much. We talked for over an hour and afterward, I went uptown. As I walked across the parking lot back to my car, I saw two pennies. I picked them up, looked at the dates and saw one was a 2006, the year Danny passed. The other was dated 2008, the current year, and I "knew" those pennies were for Lindy. At home, I secured them to a small card and wrote: *To Lindy from Danny "Pennies from Heaven,"* and I sent the card, along with a *Guidepost* magazine with a story about a young boy who sends his mother pennies from Heaven. Then I called Lindy and told her that I knew Danny was telling her that he knew how hard she was grieving, and in this way, he was sending his love. Lindy keeps the card with the pennies on her kitchen windowsill.

CHAPTER 20

# RON'S BATTLE WITH MYASTHENIA GRAVIS

**RON'S HEALTH BEGAN** to decline more and more as we moved through 2016. Ron and I had learned to play golf in our retirement years, but myasthenia gravis had ended that early on, so we'd given away our clubs and golf cart. But one day Ron decided he was doing well enough to get another golf cart to drive around, but before long he had to give that one away, too.

Eventually he started sleeping in a recliner, as he could no longer sleep in a bed, and that led to a lift chair. He developed A-fib, sleep apnea, and began having trouble with balance, falling several times. Once we discovered he'd been walking with a torn Achilles tendon and I took him to Kearney, Nebraska, for surgery. A couple of his falls landed him in the ER, and once they sent him to the hospital at Hays for a few days. Other problems plagued him, even the shingles, and more medications were prescribed.

In February of 2017, his brother-in-law and old partner in the furniture and funeral business, Darel Olliff, passed. In June, our daughter, Kelly, began treatment for cancer, and he worried so about her. A couple of times through the spring and summer months, he made it to Rotary and in the fall insisted on going to the football games.

We were sitting in the living room on the evening of November 9, 2017, when he began to talk as if he were working on a funeral in the Logan Funeral Home. He talked to Max and Mary Lou Donahey, who used to live in the Logan Funeral Home and helped with funerals, as if they were still there. Max had passed some years before and Mary Lou had moved to where their sons lived. He also saw his sister, Shirley, and my sister, June, sitting in the same chair across the room from where he was sitting. It scared me, and I called Ronnie to help me get him to the emergency room at the hospital, where, by the time we arrived, he was back in present time and thinking clearly again.

He was diagnosed as having had a mini stroke, and I took him to the hospital in Kearney, Nebraska for a heart cath. The findings were a 50 percent blockage of the main artery. On the way home he had a few bouts of short-term confusion, and when we entered Phillipsburg's city limits, he thought Gary (the brother who had passed three years before) was driving and I was in the back seat. He talked to both of us in the positions where he saw us. Thankfully that soon passed, and he was okay again, and there were no more episodes like that.

On November 16, he was feeling good, exceptionally so, I thought, and he decided to go to Rotary. He even drove himself. Ronnie was at Rotary, too, and was so pleased to see his dad looking and acting so much better, and he was hopeful.

The next day, November 17, was a Friday, a football night, this time between Phillipsburg and Marysville, a neighboring high school. They were playing for the championship, and I would have had to tie Ron to his chair for him to have missed that game, or any game where his grandson, Johnny, was playing. They lost, but it was still a good evening, until he got out of the car at home. While I was getting his wheelchair out of the back of the van, he fell on the driveway. I called Ronnie, and he and Michele got him up and into the house.

The next few days, his hip bothered him a lot and he needed help getting in and out of his chair and walking. He didn't seem to be improving, so I called the ambulance to take him to the emergency room. There a CT scan showed a fracture and on Wednesday, November 22, the day before Thanksgiving, he entered the hospital.

The idea was that a month of no pressure on the hip would allow the fracture to heal. But it was the beginning of the end. He would leave us and take up residence with loved ones in Heaven on January 25, 2018, at 1:46 a.m., but he never really left us, thanks to that thin veil between us.

Nancy, a physician's assistant who was then commuting from her home in Wichita, was working the ER the day I brought Ron into the emergency room. While we waited for the surgeon to tell us about the x-rays, Nancy and I stood on either side of Ron's ER bed and we three carried on a small bit of conversation. Then a woman I knew came into the ER and I went over to speak to her. Nancy told me later that as I stepped away, Ron said, his eyes following me, "Isn't she beautiful?" I am so thankful she told me, for those words are for me a priceless treasure.

On Thanksgiving Day, Ronnie and Michele brought Ron's dinner out to the hospital, and also one for Nancy, as she was also away from home.

We had asked for a reclining chair in place of a bed, and he slept well in the chair until the night of November 29, when he somehow tipped his chair over backward. The hospital staff was so good to him, often interacting with him in a fun and teasing way. He loved it and teased them back. One nurse said about him tipping his chair over, "We came in and there you were, your legs sticking straight up in the air."

Roxie was one he loved to engage in light banter and one time she had a week off and when she returned, he asked in a mock, demanding voice, where in the heck she'd been. She told him that she'd had the week off, and during that week, she shopped and ate dinner out and had run out of money. "So," she said, "I robbed the bank downtown." Then she leaned in close to him, and with a dark frown, her eyes narrowed and squinting, like she really meant business, she said in an exaggerated whisper "And I left your fingerprints all over it."

A few days later, Ron's longtime friend and fellow Rotarian came to see him. Ron told me afterward that Curt had told him they had not had Rotary because it was Christmas Eve. I said I didn't know it was Christmas Eve and he said, "Oh, well, maybe it was New Year's Eve, they are both on the same day anyway."

That day, when I was leaving to go home for lunch and let the dog out, he called me back as he thought I'd turned in the wrong direction to be leaving to go home. So now even his sense of direction was messed up, the first since he'd ridden into Bonners Ferry in the back of that Air Force vehicle back in 1954.

November 30. That evening Ron was feeling good, both mentally and physically. Mike and Kelly came from Hays and joined Ronnie and Michele, their dad and I in his room and we laughed and talked, Ron actively joining in the conversation. He seemed to enjoy it as much as we did.

On December 7 Mandy, the daughter of a good friend of Ron's, was tending to Ron and he kept her laughing with stories about her dad, who had passed a few years before. She was from Logan, where Ron and Darel also owned and operated the funeral home. Ron worked most of those funerals, and over the years, he and her dad had become good friends.

On December 15 Ronnie asked the manager of the retirement center if she would take his dad in their van to see his grandson Johnny play a basketball game at the high school. Ron sat in his wheelchair on the stage, and I sat beside him, so we had a good view of the game. Ron was so pleased to watch the boy he so loved play that night. It would be the last game he'd get to see him play, as far as we know. But I'd not be surprised if I were to learn that after that January 25 morning, he showed up at all of Johnny's games—and didn't need a wheelchair anymore.

The day after the ballgame, Ron was put on oxygen. It perked him up, so he felt better, and he was beginning to get anxious for Christmas and for his other daughters, Kathy and Kandy, both of whom lived in Omaha, to come home. He was diagnosed with pneumonia the next day and had a restless night. He was better by morning.

On December 18, the physical therapist brought her children to Ron's room, and they entertained him with Christmas carols and presented him with a gift of a Kansas Jayhawks T-shirt and a plate of homemade cookies. I took pictures of the event and those pictures captured Ron's enjoyment of the evening.

The next day, Ron was restless. He wouldn't eat and he imagined things. They moved him to another room with more light, hoping that would help, but it didn't. I stayed until 11:30 that night. Now I noticed his skin seemed to have taken on a yellowish tinge and his liver function was tested. He still wouldn't eat but a bite or two, and a sonogram showed his gall bladder needed to be removed. He was taken by ambulance to the hospital at Kearney, Nebraska, where he had laparoscopic surgery.

On Christmas Day, an ambulance brought him back to this hospital, and that evening, we had our Christmas in the outpatients' room, which the hospital graciously offered us. They set up tables and even covered them with bright red tablecloths.

Ron has always given the grandkids silly gifts for Christmas and insisted that this year be no different. Recruiting my help, he came up with a large cup with a monkey on it, the handle the monkey's tail. The cup was filled with plastic bags of "monkey poop" (teriyaki flavored jerky pieces) and an 8x10 photo of just their Papa's butt clad in bright green boxer shorts with a picture of the Grinch and *Happy Holidays* written in large print across it. His granddaughters Emily and Elizabeth (Kelly and Mike's daughters) had given him the shorts some years ago and I'd taken that picture of his butt clad in those shorts that same Christmas. He remembered that photo and had me get five enlarged copies for each of the grandkids. Then he sent me to the bank to get them each a brand-new one-hundred-dollar bill. It would be his last gift to them.

The grandkids had enjoyed their goofy gifts from their papa so much that as they got older, they began giving him goofy gifts in return, hence the Grinch shorts. He began the silly gift giving when Jordyn, the oldest grandchild, was three. That year he gave her a bean sandwich and wrapped as a gift. It did so tickle her and giggling, she grabbed my hand and pulled me into the kitchen to help her make one for him. And so it went, each year a new silly gift and more grandchildren arriving, until there were five.

In 2015, sometime before Christmas, Ron had confessed to Ally that he couldn't think of anything for his "special" gift for her, Jordyn, and Johnny, and their cousins, Emily and Elizabeth. She suggested a referee whistle. When the kids stayed overnight and it was time to get up, or we were taking them someplace, he'd get out the old silver referee whistle he used when he refereed high school home games, blow on it and yell, "Everybody out of the pool!" So that was what he gave them that year. He had them open their gift all together and, as if on cue, they all blew on their whistle and yelled "Everybody out of the pool!"

A week or so before that Christmas of 2015, Johnny, the youngest Boeve grandkid, asked me to help him give his papa something to show how much he and his sisters and their cousins loved those silly gifts that Papa had given them over the years. He thought about a T-shirt with pictures all over it of past Christmases of them getting those silly gifts from Papa. Finally deciding there were too many photos for one shirt, he settled for only a few photos and these words: *Ron Boeve, Sr. The Best Papa Ever*. Johnny generously shared his ideas with his sisters and two cousins and, so, along with the shirt, they came up with a notebook with a group photo of him and the kids on the cover and inside the story of all those silly gifts and copies of the pictures taken those many Christmas Eve nights. They presented it to him that Christmas Eve of 2015 and he loved it! In fact, he was so touched by his gift of "Past Christmases," that a few tears accompanied his smiles.

This Christmas night of 2017, celebrated in the hospital outpatient room, he ate a good dinner, and his mind was clear, although he was, I knew, quite tired. I was hopeful then and dared to think that he could come home before long.

The next night, after I went home, he fell and they called me back, as he was in a lot of pain. I stayed all night, so thankful they'd called me. They had given him Tylenol, instead of the oxycontin he'd been taking, and that didn't cut it, but he couldn't take the oxycontin until the Tylenol wore off. It was so upsetting, watching him suffer those four hours. Whoever had given him the Tylenol hadn't realized he needed stronger stuff.

On December 27 he had pneumonia again. Also, a CT scan showed a fractured vertebrae from the fall. I so admired this man who, with reason after reason to be down and discouraged, (and he was at times, but rarely and not for long), and who, despite it all, could still make a joke of things. When the man who cleaned the rooms came in to do Ron's the day after he fell and fractured his vertebrae, Ron told him he knew he did a really good job because when he fell, and he lifted a hand to measure about an inch width with his thumb and forefinger, "My nose was about this far from the floor and that floor was spotless."

One afternoon, when his sister Shirley was out visiting him, a newly hired therapist stopped in to introduce herself to him. Ron then introduced her to Shirley. He then turned to me and said, "And this is my wife, Eunie. I picked her out back when I was still drinking." I loved it! I nearly fell off my chair laughing, and it still makes me smile. It's another treasured memory.

## CHAPTER 21

# RON'S LAST EARTHBOUND DAYS

**AN X-RAY OF** Ron's hip showed it was healing, but he was still in pain. Thankfully, oxycontin killed the pain. He was often confused, seeing things that weren't there and sometimes seemed to be someplace besides the hospital—once in our church.

Sometimes when I couldn't understand what he was telling me, he would get agitated and upset with me, but often his words were just mumbles of sound. I felt that hope was gone, and the next stop would be the nursing home. Although I knew that he was leaving me, I still clung to a little more time even as I knew there was none.

On January 1 the kids and I decided on our own to get their dad up more and out of the room. We took him for rides up and down the hallways in his wheelchair and in the evenings, Ronnie and Michele brought him homecooked food and we ate together in the dining room after the staff had left. Jordyn, Brandyn, Ally, and John often joined us. I was sad for Kathy and Kandy, with jobs in Omaha, and Kelly, in Hays, who was working, as well as undergoing cancer treatments. Those three rarely got to be with their dad. They called every day, and he often talked about them, so I knew he missed them.

January 14 Ron was awake all night and restless. He had been given a pill that morning and he'd slept all day. They woke him to take his pills and change his clothes, but he never fully came awake until near midnight and again he was awake and restless all night.

Now, too, his lungs were filling with fluid. Michele and I took him to Hays to have the fluid drawn off his lungs. For some reason, the person who was at the door to meet us did not know how to get him out of our van and into a wheelchair. And, if Michele hadn't stepped in and grabbed Ron, he would have fallen on the cement entryway. She grabbed him just in time and held on tight. She staggered some, but she held on. After we got back to this hospital, Michele ran home and fixed him tomato soup and a toasted cheese sandwich. He'd not had any food all day, as he wouldn't eat, and by then he was starved. Although he rarely ate more than a bite or two or three, he ate most of the soup and sandwich.

On January 15 the heart doctor said Ron's heart was only pumping at about a 30 percent capacity, and his blood pressure wasn't at all stable. His veins weren't good enough now for the antibiotics they were giving him, so they put in a PICC line. That evening Jordyn brought a crockpot of soup for our dinner together in the dining room. That night Ron talked to Ronnie about his casket.

Two days later I walked into Ron's room at eight o'clock in the morning, and after giving him a kiss and a hug, I started to sit in my chair beside him. "Oh," he said, "You can't sit there, Larry is sitting there now." Larry, his brother who passed on February 1, 2006. Then he said, "Oh, but he said, he'd get up and let you sit there." I said, "No Larry, you stay seated, I can sit over here." I could not see Larry. Perhaps, because he wasn't there for me, but for his big brother. Neither did I know when he left.

On January 18 Ron was having another one of those now rare, good days, and Jordyn had come out to visit him. They were talking when her papa leaned forward a little and, looking out his open door into the hallway, said, "Well, hi, Larry." She had heard about Uncle Larry visiting her papa the day before, and she said she nearly jumped out of her skin. Then the man stuck his head in the doorway, and she saw he was a different Larry who'd been visiting his wife in a room across from her papa's.

I don't have a time frame for this next event, but it was after his brother Larry had been to see him, for we wondered how he could possibly know this, unless Larry had told him. Perhaps time is much more fluid in the spirit world, and the future is not hidden from them as it is from us. Maybe Larry was even in the hospital hallway that day and had egged his brother on. So, this is the story. The physical therapist was pushing Ron in his wheelchair up the hallway when Ronnie came out to see his dad. He took over the wheelchair just as a woman came down the hall. She stopped in front of them and said to Ron, "You look so familiar. Are you Ron Boeve?" Ronnie said, his dad gave a little chuckle and said, "No. I'm Rob Boeve." Then he gave that little laugh again and said, "No. I'm Ron Boeve." Ronnie said he had no idea where that could have come from, but his dad seemed to have his wits about him and so he surely hadn't forgotten his name. Besides, his dad acted like it was a joke. Later, when he told me, I had no idea either. It was indeed a mystery, but not for long. After Ron passed, the Hays paper printed a death notice. They'd printed his name correctly throughout the body of the notice, but the headline read, *Rob Boeve*.

Our Kelly was upset when she saw that their Hays paper had her dad's name wrong. But when she called and told me, the proverbial light bulb lit up for me and I told her about him telling the woman he was "Rob Boeve." She wasn't upset after that.

I've wondered about that incident. Did Ron use that seemingly odd exchange between the woman and himself, so Ronnie would know and bear witness to the rest of us, that even on the verge of passing from this world, he was very much aware of the next and had no fear of the transition. In fact, he could even joke about it. Anyway, I am sure it was not a coincidence.

On January 19, our dog, Muffin, passed. A brown dachshund, she'd been suffering with heart and kidney failure. Ronnie called Arnie, who opens the graves and sets the tents for the interments for the funeral home. He has buried pets for others where he lives. It's a lovely place, even in January with thick grass and trees.

Ron had wanted to go to church that day. He had told me he wanted to take this special someone he'd been praying for to the altar, but I couldn't take him, not by myself, and Ronnie had a funeral to work. A little later he said he wanted to talk to me, but he didn't want to in his hospital room. I suggested the hospital's family room, which would be private, and so we went there. He sat there in his wheelchair in silence for a few minutes, head bowed, and then he looked at me and said, "I think I will be leaving soon."

I said, "Yes. It looks that way." Looking back the words seem emotionless and I think they were. I heard my words, but they were just words. I couldn't let myself believe it was so, even though I knew we had come to the end of our lives together. Then I told him I loved him dearly and would miss him so much. *And oh, I certainly do—so much.* He told me he loved me, too, so very much, and put extra emphasis on the "so very much." We talked about how lucky we were to have found each other, and how slim the odds had been that we would. We talked about how blessed our lives together had been, how blessed we were to have kids to be proud of, and wonderful grandkids.

We talked a while about our kids and grandkids. He asked then about our finances, and I told him what we had in savings and that I'd be selling the rentals and putting that away too. When I finished he said, "Gee, I wish I could stay and help you spend it." I kissed him then, a long, deep kiss, trying to put all the love I had in it. When I drew back, he looked at me and said, "I guess you do love me." When we got back to the room, he went to sleep and slept all afternoon and evening, and all night long, a deep, quiet sleep.

On the morning of January 20, Ron was still wanting to go to the church, to the altar, and so our nephew Kenton Olliff came out and helped Ronnie get him there and into the church. Kenton's wife Carol and his mom (Ron's sister Shirley) and I went out in another car. Ronnie wheeled his dad into the sanctuary, and I followed. The rest waited in the foyer.

I stayed at the back of the sanctuary in the choir loft and watched while Ronnie took his dad in his wheelchair to the front of the sanctuary and left him sitting before the communion table, the cross that hangs from the baptistry before him. Ronnie had started back up the aisle to wait in the foyer with the others when he turned and with his cell phone took a picture of his dad. I treasure that photo of my love sitting there in his wheelchair, the oxygen bottle attached, a woolen cap covering his head, a blanket draped around his shoulders. As I sat there that day, my eyes on my love, his head bowed, and almost palpable silence filling the room, the words, "prayer warrior" came to mind, and that's what I think of when I see that picture.

I sat in the back in the choir loft until he began to look around, so I knew he was finished with his visit with God. I went to the door and got Ronnie. We walked down the aisle to his dad, and Ronnie asked if he could serve us communion. His dad nodded and Ronnie went into the back room and brought out the sacraments.

Kathy and Kandy arrived from Omaha about noon, Kelly, from Hays, soon after. Ron looked and acted like he felt good, and he was clearheaded, so he and his girls had a good visit. Jordyn and Brandyn brought out dinner and we ate together in the dining room. John came too, as well as Michele's Kylie, Kevin, and Kynlie.

After the kids left about ten o'clock, Ron asked if he had to die tomorrow and I told him no, that I thought we had a little while longer to be together. He told me he saw his death certificate and I was the informant (the one who signs the certificate confirming the information is correct). Of course, as an old funeral director, he'd know I'd be the one to sign it. He had asked if he had to die tomorrow, so he must not have seen his date of death.

The next day the nurses told me Ron had been awake most of the night and had fallen asleep a little while before I arrived at eight. He dozed off and on all day, sometimes when he was awake, but not seeming to really be there, he'd mumble and sometimes laugh and sometimes he'd smile. I wondered if he was seeing his brothers, Larry and Gary, and maybe his parents, or Darel Olliff, his old partner in the furniture and funeral businesses who had passed the previous February, nearly a year ago. Perhaps any or all were there giving Ron the lowdown on Heaven. When I was leaving that night, he said, "We have a little more time together, don't we?" I told him I thought we did. Once that day, he'd started talking about he and Darel buying out the McKinley Furniture Store to start their own business and when he bought into the funeral home. Then he said, "That should be enough, shouldn't it?" I knew he was thinking about his obituary, so at home that night, I wrote up a rough draft in case he asked me about it, but he didn't.

The next morning, January 22, Ron was awake when I arrived at my usual time and the minute I walked in the door, he told me that the sister of his old friend who'd grown up in Phillipsburg, but now lived in Colorado, had passed. I asked how he knew, and he paused for a second, then he told me that George, another old friend who lived here had told him. I had been there until after ten the night before and now at eight o'clock in the morning, it hardly seemed possible that he would have had a visitor.

I looked toward the nurse who was in the room, and she looked at me with what I perceived as a "knowing" look and said in a low voice, "He's not had any visitors." Later, I would ask his friend. No, he hadn't even known about her passing until later that morning. So, I wondered how Ron had known. Perhaps, the woman herself had come to tell him. Or maybe he had done a little time travel and had gone to see his old friend in Colorado, although his friend would not have known that, or he would have told me. Likely, his brother Larry had slipped back in to give him the news. I was also intrigued by the expression on the nurse's face. She was middle aged, so she had probably been around enough of the dying to have seen evidence of that thin veil between us.

He slept a lot that day and talked in his sleep. Now even awake, he didn't seem totally conscious. That afternoon, Ronnie stayed with his dad while Kathy, Kandy, Kelly and I went to Pizza Hut. When we got back, Ronnie told us that their dad, in the midst of his mumbling and incoherent talk, suddenly had said, just as clear as could be, "Thank you, Father, for this day."

Then, Ronnie put into words what we all knew. "Don't you think it's time we let him go?" The girls and I agreed. His quality of life had deteriorated so much that it wasn't fair to him for us to keep him here any longer. The kids no longer brought food out, as he had grown too sick to join us. He wouldn't eat that night when they brought his food, but when Jordyn, Ally, and John come out to see him, he ate a cookie and a little ice cream.

Kathy and Kandy left for Omaha the next morning. Ron told them to drive safely. It's the only clear sentence he would say all day. Kelly left a little later. She's had a long, hard struggle battling cancer. Thankfully, she had finished her last treatment ten days before. I was so sad for our girls, for they knew they would never see their dad again this side of Heaven.

Ronnie and Michele and I met with Ron's doctor and two hospital staff members about moving him to the former hospice room. He'd be taken off his meds except for the ones that would keep the fluid off his heart and lungs and the morphine to keep him comfortable. I went home at eleven that night and Ronnie stayed all night with him.

On the morning of January 24, I arrived at seven. He'd been unresponsive all night, and he stayed that way all day. Family and friends came to be with us, which helped. That evening, Ronnie stayed with his dad while I went home for a while as I planned to stay with Ron all night. While I was home, I called my sister Mabel in Montana to tell her that he wouldn't be with us much longer. Mabel had wanted to call me all day about a dream she'd had of Ron but was afraid it would not be a good time.

She had awakened from the dream of him that morning. "It was so real," she said. I can't believe it was just a dream." Then she told me her dream. She was in some town, not her town of Libby, or mine of Phillipsburg, when she noticed a man standing up the street waving to her. So, she went to see who he was and as she got closer, she saw it was Ron. She said he looked just wonderful, years younger and so happy, so healthy. Mabel had visited us in October, just a little over a month before he went into the hospital, so she definitely knew the difference. She said they talked and laughed, and although she could not recall a word they said, it had been a wonderful conversation. She said they then hugged each other goodbye and as she turned away, she woke up. "I lay there," she said, "totally amazed. It had been so *real*. I could not believe it had been just a dream. That I had not actually been with him."

Actually, I believe she had. I believe Ron came to her in what I call a dream visitation. It was so much like the dream I'd had with my brother Danny after he died. The thing was, Ron had not yet passed—not completely, but I think, in those last few days, he was in and out of our world and the world awaiting him.

Although he might have appeared in a coma-like state, I'm sure he was not completely tethered to his body. I think, too, that he had nudged me that night to call Mabel. I'd not given thought to calling her and then suddenly I decide to call—just her. Not my other siblings, just Mabel, and she happened to have a fantastic story to tell me about Ron. I believe he wanted me to know that he had been there—that it had been more than a dream. I believe he wanted me to know that he had been with Mabel, just as he would always be with me and his family of loved ones on earth.

Mabel's husband John had died in 2013. The day after he passed, I was sitting in the living room when I suddenly caught a strong smell of pine, like the pine trees that grow abundantly in northwest Montana. Both Ron and I have mentioned that when we first arrive in that country, we are acutely aware of the scent of those pine trees. I just knew John was there and I said aloud, "Is that you, John?" Immediately, the smell was gone.

Three years later I was back in the Northwest visiting friends and family. I'd just left the ranch where Mabel still lived, and we had talked of many things. Then for a second or two, I saw John in the passenger seat of my car. His body was in a hazy blue mist, but his face was as clear as it would be if he were still earthbound, and his expression was one of approval. I think he came to me, knowing I'd let her know, that he was still with her, still loved her.

After talking to Mabel, I went back to stay all night with Ron, feeling certain he would leave us very soon, perhaps in the night or early morning and I wanted to be with him when he passed.

Ronnie had a hard time leaving, but he knew I wanted to be alone with his dad, or he would have stayed. I knew that some of Ron's loved ones, "his people" like those who had come for my dad, would come for him, and I hoped I would be able to see them or at the very least sense their presence. That night I stood by his bedside and talked to him. Although he appeared unresponsive, his breathing raspy and labored, I knew it was possible he could hear my words. I told him how much I loved him, and that it was all right to go now and that I'd join him one day. I told him his mom and dad and Larry and Gary and other loved ones were waiting for him. Sometime after midnight, I got so very tired I could hardly stand up, and so I sat down for just a few minutes, just to rest a little, and immediately fell asleep. I woke with the nurse on duty kneeling beside me. He had taken my hand to wake me, and softly, gently, he told me that Ron was gone. I remember hearing the time as 1:46 a.m. His death certificate lists the time as 2 a.m.

I have missed him so much. I know I will always miss him. These words from Joan Didion's book, *The Year of Magical Thinking*, published by Knopf Publishing Group 2005, describes so well my loss. "We cannot know the heart of the difference between grief as we imagine it and grief as it is: that unending absence that follows the loss of the one we so love."

CHAPTER 22

# WONDERFUL EVIDENCE

**WHEN JORDYN GOT** up that morning and learned that her papa had passed, she said through tears, "Papa came to see me in the night. I know it was him. He came to tell me goodbye." Then she told us how she woke up in the night and sensed a presence in the room. Then it faded and she fell back into a deep sleep. At noon that day, Ally drove over to her mother's to pick up her brother, as everyone was eating at my house. As she sat in the car waiting for John, a flock of small black birds and a large white dove flew over and lit on the wires overhead where she had a clear view of them. She said she knew immediately that they were from her papa, and she took a picture on her cell phone to show us. It was amazing how those birds were sitting on that wire: three small black birds on each side of the large white dove. So, within hours of his passing, he'd let us know through those two granddaughters that he was still around, still with us.

And that was just the beginning.

The casket Ronnie wanted for his dad could not be found in the sources in Kansas or nearby states. Finally, he found one in Boston that could be shipped out immediately. Because of having to wait on the casket, Ronnie took me to see his dad in the preparation room. When I looked at him, lying there on the table, dressed in his suit and tie, I felt a sudden rush of something like joy, for he looked wonderful! All signs of sickness were gone, and even his eighty-five years looked ten, fifteen, or more years younger, and his mustache was perfect!

A few days before, I'd trimmed his mustache and had not done the best job, as it was a bit uneven. I felt bad about it and was so pleased to see it looking perfect. I thanked Chris, Ronnie's partner in the funeral home who had taken care of Ron for fixing it, but he looked puzzled and said he hadn't touched it, as it had looked perfect to him. So, had Ron called on some angelic help, or did he fix it himself? Either way, it made me so very happy, as I'm sure Ron knew it would, for he had to know that I felt bad about it. Besides, he was soon going to be lying in state in that casket that had to come all the way from Boston, and he wanted to look his best for all of us.

Ron's funeral service, held on January 29, 2018 at the Huck Boyd Center, was very well attended as he had made many friends in his sojourn on earth. Now I began what someone had coined "the new normal."

I've heard of several cases where the deceased attended their own funeral, but if Ron did, he kept a low profile.

Martha, the mother of a friend of mine, told me that her husband had passed from severe diabetes. His legs had been amputated in hopes of extending his life, but it was not to be, and she was devastated. "I started crying at the funeral and could not stop," she told me. "Then I heard him say, "Don't cry. I'm fine. I can even run now.""

I thought of Martha's message from her husband when Stephen Hawking, who was completely paralyzed most of his adult life by ALS, (amyotrophic lateral sclerosis a.k.a. Lou Gehrig's Disease) passed in March of 2018. In an interview for the 2011 Guardian Review he spoke of his belief that there is no afterlife, that the brain is much like a computer that stops working when its components fail. He called belief in the afterlife, a fairy tale. Wow! What a wonderful surprise when his components failed and his soul, his spirit, not only lived on, but his new place of residence was vastly superior to the old, and what a delight, what a thrill, to be able to walk and even to run now.

A very good friend told me that at her sister's wake, her young daughter later told her that she had seen her aunt standing by the casket when members of the family spoke of her. This aunt was a Catholic nun and although she was not dressed in the traditional habit in the casket, that young girl said, that was what she was wearing as she stood there listening to those family members share memories of her life.

I was told about Bill, who was estranged from his wife, and at the funeral she saw for a few seconds a golden glow over the casket and heard words to the effect that everything would be all right.

I am sure that this sampling of a loved one's presence at their own funeral is duplicated in some way time and again at thousands of other funerals.

Ron and I had been together sixty-three years—one year of courtship and sixty-two in marriage. Now that his earthly life had ended and I'd been set adrift, it was for me like trying to cross a huge body of rough water in a canoe without paddles. But I had no choice, I had to go on.

Jordyn and Ally had received the first and second signs from their papa, that wonderful evidence that he was still with us. The fixing of his mustache was the third. In the next four months, I would receive eight more signs and on May 28, he sent me a dream symbolizing our life together and showing me that I needed to go on—that I had more work to do. Soon, I would come to know that "my work," with Ron's continued help, was to write this memoir.

A few days after the funeral, I was driving to the grocery store, and as I turned on the street just north of the post office, a man in a pickup pulled away from the outside mail drop-box, and seeing my vehicle approach, braked and waited for me to pass. His window was down and as I drove by, I saw his face clearly. *It was Ron's.* I was startled for a moment, but soon passed it off as my imagination, for how could that be possible? A year and a half later, I would see him again as I saw him then, this time in full form, superimposed over another man, and I would come to know that this is one of the ways our loved ones come to us. It's called doubling, and I knew then that when I saw Ron's face that day at the outside mailbox, that he had used that method to appear to me, to let me know he loved me and would always be with me.

The next message from Ron was on February 2, although I wouldn't "get it" until a year and a half later, and only then because I had written it in my diary and came across it accidentally (or maybe not) while looking for another entry.

That day, February 2, I went with Ronnie and Michele out of town to attend Johnny's game, and while I was gone, a dear friend of mine stopped by the house. She called me the next day to tell me that she had come by to see me and had been so surprised to see one lone daffodil in bloom right by my front door. Just a day or so before I'd noticed that the daffodils that grow along the front of my house were coming up a bit early, due to some extra warm, sunny weather, but they were nowhere near ready to bloom. When I hung up the phone, I looked out the front door, but there was no daffodil in bloom there or anywhere along that row of green stalks and leaves pushing up out of the ground. I was sort of in a fog those days, and with no energy to figure that one out, I shrugged it off and soon forgot about it, but thankfully, I did record it in my diary.

For several years this friend, who is an artist, has hosted a group of other friends and me at her home twice a month. All are true artists, but me. I can sketch well enough by looking at a picture, but I have no interest in art. I just use it as an excuse to be there to enjoy their friendship. In late afternoon, we always end our sessions with refreshments, and for some months, maybe a year before Ron entered the hospital for that last long stay that led to his passing, this friend started sending home with me a serving of whatever we'd had that day for Ron. He was so pleased and looked forward to those twice monthly Wednesday afternoon treats. So, when I saw that diary entry two-and-a-half years later and now knew that in Heaven nothing was beyond Ron's capabilities, I knew he had caused that daffodil to bloom for her. A thank you for all those desserts she'd sent to him.

Sometimes in the spring, when the daffodils were blooming, Ron would stop and pick one for me as he came in from work. In addition to the traditional roses and cards and candy on special days, he would on occasion give me a handwritten or illustrated "love" note, not only for special occasions, but "just because." Sometimes he'd put a little spin on those gifts he'd give me. One year for Valentine's Day, he had hidden those little valentines that kids usually give out at school that come in packages of a couple dozen or more, all over the house and when I found them all, he gave me a big valentine.

I think he thought when he had that daffodil bloom for my friend that I would know it was from him and take comfort in knowing he was nearby. I'm sure he knew I had not picked up on his doubling with the man at the mailbox, and now I had also failed to grasp the meaning of this flower for my friend.

Of course, he knew that I knew he was still with us. He had fixed his own mustache, Jordyn and Ally had received his messages, but I had not picked up on these last two signs. The first because I had not yet heard of doubling and the other perhaps because I did not yet know the extent of Ron's ability to make himself known in so many varied and wonderful ways.

I think how appropriate that flower in bloom on a winter day was for my friend, whose backyard is a beautiful garden of flowers and shrubs and trees in season. I called her immediately the day I read the diary and had figured it out. She was surprised and I hope pleased and didn't just wonder about my sanity. However, I'm sure it pleased Ron that I finally "got" it. Some months later, maybe a year after the daffodil bloomed for my friend, another friend told me how her husband, who also passed in the winter, had a flower bloom for her—in the snow!

The morning of February 7, was what I then believed was my first contact with Ron (excluding the mustache), as I didn't then believe I'd actually seen his face in that pickup at the mailbox or that a daffodil had bloomed for my friend.

I was standing at the sink washing a few dishes when I heard a soft kind of swish sound. I thought someone had come into the kitchen, but when I turned to look, no one was there. Except, someone was, for as I turned back to the sink, I felt arms from behind come around my waist and hug me for just a second or two.

Later that afternoon, I was standing at the end of the dining room table looking at lists and deciding what to do next when I heard that soft swish sound again, and looking up, saw a faint blue mist at the height of where, if Ron was there and I knew he was, his head would be. Immediately it dissipated. I believe he'd tried to show himself to me, but maybe, being so new to the process, or maybe because he had used too much energy hugging me earlier in the day, the blue mist was all he could manage. But I knew he was there.

For many evenings after Ron passed, instead of watching TV in the family room, I sat in his room, the bedroom we had converted into a room for him when he could no longer sleep in a bed, using a lift chair both day and night. We had taken his *Man Cave* sign from his office in the basement and put it on the door and plastered the walls with family photos.

We had a safe in a corner of that room and when Ron moved in, he'd set the lamp he'd inherited when his dad passed on top of it. The lamp had been a gift to Lou when he retired as county sheriff. It's a caricature of an old-time Western sheriff. It's about two feet tall, in boots and hat, holstered pistol, and on his vest, a big shiny "officer of the law" star.

Ron never used the lamp, as he had an end table and another lamp. However, when I gave away his lift chair and moved in a twin-sized hide-a-bed, I also gave away his end table and lamp and used the safe for an end table and Lou's sheriff lamp for a light. For several weeks, I sat there every night and stared at the TV before finally crawling into bed and trying to sleep.

It had begun three nights earlier, on the seventh of March. I was sitting on that small hide-a-bed watching TV when the light in the sheriff lamp went off. As I got up to get a new bulb, it came back on, so I sat back down, and the light went off again. This time I checked the outlet, although it was a new one that we'd had put in for the lift chair. By then the light was back on again. It went off and then on again and then stayed on. The next evening as I sat watching TV, it happened again, the light going off then on, then off and on again and then stayed on. The next night it was the same story. I figured the lamp had a short in it, so I planned to get a new lamp the next day. That night in bed I'd started reading the book, *Hello from Heaven*, by Bill Guggenheim and Judy Guggenheim, about after-death communication, called ADC. It's about the various ways our loved ones who have passed use to contact us and one way is with electricity. They use lights, TVs, phones, and radios as signs that they are still with us.

*So, then I knew!* That night, I waited, and when the light went off, I laughed and said, "Is that you, Ron?" It came back on and then off and on again, just blink, blink, blink, and then stayed on. I talked to him then, feeling happy, even joyful, but I cried some, too. I thanked him for giving me that hug while I stood at the kitchen sink, and for trying to let me see him as I stood by the dining room table, but all I could make out was the blue mist. Then the light went off again and stayed off. I waited and then reached up and touched the base of the lamp and it came back on. In a few minutes, it went off again. I touched it and it came back on and stayed on. The lamp worked perfectly fine from then on.

As March turned to April, Ronnie helped me trade off my van for a Jeep Cherokee and I had him put deer whistles on it, as Ron had always put them on our cars. Although there are now plenty of deer in Kansas, unless it had been a really tough winter, Montana has always had a proliferation of deer, and those seventeen summers we spent in our place in Montana, we saw our share of them, sometimes in our yard. We also saw moose, usually by the lake, but a couple of times they appeared in our back yard. Once we had friends visiting us from Kansas when the wife said as she looked out the window, "Do you know you have a bear in your back yard?" One evening as I took the dog out before going to bed, I saw a mountain lion in our driveway. We came right back in and later my brave husband took the dog out.

When Ronnie had attached the deer whistles, he'd looked at me and said, "Do you think these things really work?" I told him about one time in Montana when we saw a deer, some distance away, grazing in a grassy meadow. She raised her head as we came near and watched as we drove on by. "Anyway," I'd added, "They can't hurt."

On Easter Sunday I was driving to Logan, twenty miles away, to attend church with my sister, June, who lived in an assisted living facility there. I was just a few miles out of Logan, when I saw a deer off in a field to my left running flat out and going in the same direction I was. I slowed way down and watched her swerve toward the highway, jump a fence, and cross the highway in front of me and out into the field on my right. Because I had slowed way down, I was back far enough to be safe and to enjoy the sight. Now in the field on my right, she abruptly stopped, turned broadside to the road, and stood still, head up, and watched with her full attention as I drove on by. I could hardly wait to tell Ronnie, so when I got to Logan, I called him on my cell. "So why do you think that deer stopped and looked at my car as I drove by?" I asked.

"The deer whistles," he said.

June and I were invited to Mike and Kelly's home in Hays for Easter dinner, and I told the story at the dinner table. Right away, Kelly said, "I bet Dad did that to show Ronnie those whistles work." As soon as she said that I knew! I couldn't believe I'd not realized it before. It was so Ron, who so loved to "stick the fool" on someone, as his Grandma Boeve used to say, and happening the very next day. Of course, it was Ron!

The whole setup had been so perfect, the deer in that "sweet spot" not so close as to scare me, or put me at risk, but close enough that I slowed down and that allowed her to be in the other field in time to hear my whistles as I approached and drove on by. As I said later to Ronnie, even a Hollywood director couldn't have staged the scene any better.

I had thought it was a neat experience, but without Kelly's special insight, I might still believe it was just a deer running across the road for her own purposes, whatever that might be. In other words, at first I thought it was just a deer, but with her words I knew, without question, it was Ron herding that deer where he wanted it to go.

I might have come to that realization sometime later, but I might not have, too, which is why we need to share these kinds of contacts from passed loved ones. I'm sure there are many who do miss signs from their loved ones. I've since read where deer are among the more common animal signs used by our loved ones behind that thin veil.

Although I received much more from Ron that Easter Sunday, I did not share it that day at the dinner table. I did eventually, but I just couldn't that day.

# CHAPTER 23

# A KISS GOODBYE, MY BIRTHDAY, AND THE BIG DREAM

**EASTER SUNDAY, 2018,** continued. In the church in Logan where June lives in assisted living and where I often attend with her, the minister rarely if ever uses the pulpit, preferring to stand down on the floor in front of the two rows of pews, even when delivering the sermon.

That Sunday, I was sitting there in the pew with June listening to the pastor when I happened to look up at the pulpit and Ron was standing there. He was in shadow form, but I could clearly see his smile and the expression of love on his face as he looked at me. Then he vanished.

Sometime later when we stood to sing one of the hymns, I held the open book and mouthed the words, but I was too filled with emotion to sing. Then I was no longer in the church, but in the hospital in Phillipsburg, standing in the doorway of the room where Ron had passed last January.

I had wanted to be awake for him when he left, but I had also hoped to see or at least sense the presence of those who would come for him. But as I stood by his bed in that early morning hour, I got so sleepy, so tired, that I sat down in the chair on the other side of his bed, intending to rest for just a moment and fell asleep, and he passed while I was sleeping.

Now, from my vantage point in the doorway of the hospital

room, I could see Ron in the hospital bed and me sitting straight up in the chair on the other side of his bed asleep, my head drooping.

Then I saw Ron sit up and slip off the bed and onto the floor and I saw that his hospital gown was still on the bed, and he was clothed in what appeared to be a bodysuit of a light golden color. Later going back over that time, I realized that although it had not registered with me, his physical body would still be clothed in that gown and what I was seeing was his spiritual body, which radiated a kind of golden light. (I'd been confused, but later, telling Ronnie about it, he had pointed that out to me.) Later, too I'd realize that when he sat up and slipped off that bed, it was with the grace and agility of a young man.

I watched as he walked around the foot of the bed and came to where I saw myself sitting. Then he leaned over and kissed me on the top of my head. Then he straightened up and looked up at the wall behind me, up toward the ceiling, and I knew that he was looking for whoever was coming for him.

Then, I was back in the church in Logan, the congregation still singing, and I sat there and struggled to hold back my tears.

Later, I smiled thinking about that early morning hour back in January when I had been determined to stay awake and had hoped, when he passed, to know who had come for him. Then I almost got a second chance. It was right up to that very moment and then I got sent back to the church. I bet Ron did that on purpose, grinning as I disappeared.

I turned eighty-one on April 24, and Ron remembered. The day before I had begun reading *It's a Wonderful Life* by Kristi Robinett. It's about how those who have passed from this life to the next have access to what's going on in our lives, a portal, so to speak, that our loved ones can use to let us know they are still close to us, still love us. Just as Ron has been doing for us ever since he passed. She also wrote that among other ways of letting us know that they are cognizant of the course of our daily lives, they may on our birthday, an anniversary, or other special event, do something that will resonate with us. Perhaps a butterfly to light on our shoulder, maybe a bird to peck at our window, maybe a coin that has some significance, like the pennies Danny had me find for his Lindy. Or we'll find a feather or hear a special song. In my case, it was a feather.

I slept in that morning and didn't shower until after I'd eaten breakfast and read the paper. So, it was late morning when, just out of the shower and drying off, I heard a knock on the front door and with that knock, I remembered I had heard that doorbell a minute or two before! *Why had it not registered then?* Now, I heard the door open, and I threw on my robe and hurried to the living room just as the door closed behind whoever had been in my house and I saw on the end table between the two recliners, an arrangement of yellow roses. I looked toward the living room window and saw Brenda from the flower shop getting into her car, so I went to the window to wave a "thanks," as she backed out of the driveway.

It was raining, a gentle, long-needed rain, and as I stood at the window admiring it, I looked down and there on the sidewalk by the front door was a feather, a black feather. Immediately, I thought it might be from Ron, and I went out in the rain and picked it up. As I came back inside, I thought, *well, Ron, if this is from you and I'm sure it is, then, how about a bluebird or a hummingbird feather (none that are native to Kansas) instead of a common crow's feather.* Then, I knew! It was because of my book, *The Summer of the Crow.* My book that I'd set in Kansas. The main character, a young boy named Brady, whose friend, Eddie, has a pet crow. How perfect!

Like the deer whistle event, finding the feather was also so perfectly choreographed. For instance, when Brenda brought the flowers, a birthday gift from Kandy and Kathy and Tom, my kids in Omaha, she rang the doorbell, and somehow Ron kept me from realizing it until she knocked. I didn't have the TV on, nor am I hard of hearing, so maybe he put his hands over my ears. *That thought makes me smile.* And by me not hearing the doorbell, I didn't answer it, and she thinking I wasn't home had knocked just in case before coming inside and leaving the flowers. By the time I was in my robe and in the living room, she was closing the door behind her. I saw the flowers then and went to the window to wave a thanks as she got into her car, saw the rain and then that single black feather.

Later, I would think about how Ron had to have perfectly orchestrated that event for me. It had required minute precision, for if I had heard the doorbell and received the flowers in hand, I would have thanked Brenda then, probably chatted a few minutes, maybe even commented on the rain, and then she would have gone back to her car, and I'd have gone back to the bedroom to get dressed without ever seeing that feather.

Ronnie and Michele had asked me to go to lunch with them on their lunch break, so I took the feather back to the bedroom and got dressed. Then my sister Margaret called from Idaho with birthday wishes. We talked until I saw Ronnie and Michele pull up in the driveway and so, telling my sister I had to go, I grabbed up my jacket and hurried out into the rain. If Ron had not arranged it so I'd already have the feather, would I have seen it then as I hurried to their car? And, if so, would I have thought anything about it? The timing, so exact, so perfect, is to me as amazing as the actual finding of the feather. Also, the feather, although it was out in the rain, wasn't wet at all.

When I called the kids to thank them for the flowers and told them about the feather and how the florist when she didn't get an answer to the doorbell, knocked just in case, and then came on into the house. Kandy said, "Only in a small town."

The day after the crow feather, I was in my office and had been at the computer a while checking email. When I finished, I turned my swivel chair around, ready to stand up and go downstairs, and there before me stood our last three dogs, all deceased, and all looking up at me. Muffin, our last dog, a brown dachshund of thirteen years who'd passed a week before Ron, stood in the lead and at her right flank was Heidi, a tiny black dachshund, who died in 2006 at age fifteen. Up close to her and behind Muffin, was Pe Chi, a brown male Pekingese, who died in 1991 at age fifteen. Then in seconds, they vanished. I believe Ron sent them to me, so I'd know they were with him in Heaven.

We had two other dogs in our marriage, and I can understand why our first dog, a male boxer named Rocky wasn't there. We'd brought him with us from Idaho, but we didn't have him long, for he was a drifter who moved from home to home, and that's how he had come to us.

But I'm surprised that our second dog, Tootsie, a small mixed-breed female, white with some black markings, wasn't there. We got her as a puppy a few years before Ronnie was born and she lived with us for twelve years. There is an explanation I am sure, but I don't know what it is. The day she left us, she was hit by a car and killed. Because it was a Sunday and the city office closed, the cop had removed her tags before disposing of her body. When he checked the next day at the city office, he took the tags to Ron at the furniture store. For some time after she was gone, I'd hear the jingle of those tags that had been attached to her collar.

On April 26 I received a request for a death certificate for Ron from his cancer insurance, which thankfully, he'd never needed. We both had cancer policies, and I had canceled Ron's in February and was quite sure I'd sent a certified copy of the death certificate. So, although I was sure I had sent one, I sent another, and it was then that it dawned on me that it had been a while since I'd had a mammogram. So, I checked. It had been six years, so I figured I'd better get one. I did and I had early-stage breast cancer, healed with the removal of the growth, a few lymph nodes, and six weeks of radiation. I am as positive as I can be that Ron had orchestrated that whole thing about his death certificate. I don't think canceling the policy even required one. It just makes sense considering his other interactions with me, and it appears he knows everything, so he knew where I was headed. Without that reminder, I probably would not have thought of getting a mammogram for some time, maybe several more years, and then it might have been too late, or the treatment much, much more extensive.

Kelly discovered she had cancer when one day at the school where she was a speech pathologist, she stepped out of her classroom and into some water someone had spilled just outside her door and fell, hurting her shoulder. The school sent her to have the shoulder checked and in reviewing her medical history, discovered she had not had a mammogram for several years so, she had one that day and it showed she had cancer. As noted in a previous chapter, she finished her treatments just a few weeks before her dad passed. I credit Ron with alerting me to my cancer, she credits God for her wake-up call. She said when she went out into the hallway and stepped in that water, He pushed her down.

I don't remember dreaming at all after Ron passed, until the morning of May 28. Then I dreamed an amazing, detailed dream that would eventually lead me to writing this memoir. I call it the Big Dream.

I woke up tired and lethargic, and after breakfast and the paper read, both of which I now do in Ron's recliner instead of my own, I tipped back with my feet up, and lying there, fell asleep. Although I didn't realize it then, I began to dream. Ronnie called me sometime later on my landline, so I went into the kitchen to answer it. He just wondered how I was doing, and we only talked a few minutes. Then I went back to Ron's chair, intending to sleep some more.

It was then, as I tipped back, ready to doze off again, that I remembered the dream, and I knew immediately it was from Ron, and lying there in his chair, I closed my eyes and went over the dream several times. Then knowing I'd have to write it down, as I did not want to forget any part of it, I went to the computer to type and save it.

The dream began with Ron and I down along the Kootenai River north of Libby, Montana, directly across from the place where I was born, then called the Boothman place. My parents rented it just before buying the place over on Libby Creek. Others were with us, all familiar, but none I could identify in my waking state. My memory sees them as shadowy figures who I knew in the dream were members of both of our families, mine there in Montana and Idaho, and Ron's too. Although in reality, they were back in Kansas. I would not meet them until two years after we were married and had moved there. We mingled with our families, laughing and talking, some of us wading at the water's edge. No one was swimming, for evidently, even in a dream, we knew of the river's treacherous undertows.

Then Ron and I left our families and walked away from the river and up onto the road, which was really Highway 37, but in the dream, just an unpaved gravel road, and we were very happy. At one point, I reached for his hand, and it felt warm and solid, as real as if this were not a dream, but real life. I believe this symbolized our marriage, our joining of hands. Also, when we were dating, our song was "Hold My Hand" by Don Cornell. So, happily, we walked along and then I looked down and saw that I was barefoot. I had left my shoes—in the dream they were sandals—back by the river's edge where we'd left our families. I knew I would need those sandals to continue on with Ron, so I told him I would run back and get them, that it wasn't so far back, and I would soon catch up to him. Ron agreed and said he would just go on ahead.

Of course, this symbolized his passing—his going on ahead. But I needed to go back and get my sandals, a symbol that I had more living to do. So, I turned back and that once smooth, level road now rose straight up before me, high and rough and strewn with rocks and brush. This, of course, symbolizes those first rough days and weeks and months of mourning: the funeral and those long days and nights when one feels set adrift and numb to life around them. I started the climb. It was hard, but I made it to the top and now the road was straight down and as rough and rocky and brushy as it had been coming up, with the added feature of a deep, dark pool on the right at the bottom of this steep, steep hill. I knew if I made a misstep, I would fall into that pool and drown. (Later, in analyzing the dream, I think this represented the pool of prolonged and unresolved grief—a grief that can last a lifetime.) I was afraid of that pool, but I had to get down that hill. I had to get my sandals, for I could not get back to Ron without them.

I knew if I went down the left side of this steep, steep hill, it would lessen my chances of falling into that deep, dark pool. So, I looked to my left and saw a tree limb overhead hanging low and stretching out long enough that I believed I could use it, going hand over hand, to get to the left side of this hill. I reached up and grabbed the tree branch, then the phone rang, waking me.

Ronnie had called at the exact moment to wake me, for I was at that moment reaching for the tree branch, preparing to work my way over to the left and down this steep, steep hill, the best way to avoid falling into the deep, dark pool. But I am only now at the top; I've a long way yet to go. It would be on January 4, 2019, a few weeks shy of a year since Ron passed, that I would come to realize the full significance of this dream and what getting my sandals would entail. It was then that I would think about writing this book and over time, I'd begin to understand that those sandals were a metaphor for that job. In essence, what I needed to do to finish my life's work before I could rejoin Ron on that road we had traveled together and from where there will be no parting.

All of these wonderful gifts he continues to give me as evidence that he is alive and well and very much aware of my life here on earth and that he continues to love me as dearly as before, I will come to know that I need to share. Although there is no scientific evidence, for at this point there is no "lab-tested" evidence of the afterlife, there are many passed loved ones, like Ron, who are sending overwhelming anecdotal evidence that there is a place beyond our earthly existence for us when we have shed our physical bodies. And, as many of our loved ones who have passed, like Ron, have proven, they are exactly who they were, and very aware of our existence on this lower plane and still love us. To that end they try to communicate with us, for they want us to know there is but a thin veil between us earthbound ones and those who have passed into the next life. And because I seem to have a natural bent toward writing, what better way to spread the word than with a book.

Like the deer whistle and the crow feather for my birthday, this dream was also so perfectly choreographed. I love that Ron used the Kootenai River as the setting for this Big Dream. This river comes down from Canada and flows by the north edge of Libby and on to where I was born, just across the road from where the dream began. From there it flows west to Bonners Ferry, where we met and were married. It then turns back north and goes on into Canada, where Ron was stationed after we were married. The symbolism was all so perfect.

CHAPTER 24

# THE HEART CHAKRA AND MORE

**I BEGAN READING** about chakras used in some types of metaphysical healing in June of 2018, around five months after Ron passed. According to what I've read, there are seven of them in the human body, located as follows: the base of the spine, slightly below the navel, the base of the sternum, the throat, the center of the forehead, just above the crown of the skull, and the heart chakra, located in the center of the chest. The book also gave information as to how to ask for a dream visit from a loved one who has passed, so I thought I'd give it a try. It involves a small ritual with a photo or memento, a light, and a verbal request. It is said that those dream visits are short and sweet, but very real and very clear. It seemed a strange thing to do, but I'd already had so many "gifts" from Ron, so detailed, so extraordinary, that I thought this simple request would be no trouble at all for him. I don't know why I thought he might not want to, but to be sure this would be something he would want to do, I asked him for a sign, and I asked that the sign be a cardinal.

Although we used to have a lot of cardinals in our yard, I hadn't seen one or heard their songs all year, or maybe even longer. I'd put out water and kept our bird feeders filled, and had seen lots of birds, but no cardinals. Ron's sister Shirley, who lives maybe a quarter to a half mile from me, as the crow (or cardinal) flies, always had a pair at her feeders, so I wondered what had happened to ours.

The morning after asking Ron for the cardinal sign, I looked out the window from my office upstairs, the room that used to be our bedroom, and saw, sitting side by side in the hackberry tree in our backyard, a pair of cardinals, a male and a female. Not just one cardinal, but two! A pair! What *we* are—a pair and always will be, despite what we earthbound call death. His answer had to be a definite yes. The two sat there for a few minutes as if being sure I got the message, and then flew away.

I set up the dream visit for that night. I followed the instructions to the letter and climbed into bed. I had just dropped off to sleep when I saw Ron, not distinctly, not clearly, but in shadow form lean over me and kiss me on what I knew to be the heart chakra, which is in the center of the chest. It jolted me awake and I wondered, *Did it really happen or was it just my imagination?* I was wearing pajamas and had covers over me, but I felt no lifting of my pajama top nor was I aware of the covers being disturbed in any way. Still, I saw him bend over me and I felt his kiss on my bare skin. *On the heart charka.* I lay there a long time, amazed and happy.

I can see how this could be seen as just a dream or my imagination. I might think so, too, except that I felt the kiss and it was so real. I also saw him leaning over me. If it were simply my imagination, I think the kiss would have been on my lips, maybe my forehead, or my cheek, even on my hand—any part of me uncovered, since I'd felt no lifting of my pajama top or the covers. Also, I had asked for a cardinal as a sign, and he sent me a pair. Not just one, but a pair, double the sign. A kiss on the heart chakra, not the cheeks, the forehead, the lips, for me further demonstrates his love for me and how aware he is of everything I do or think about. According to the books on the chakras, the heart chakra is the seat of unconditional love. I don't think it gets any better than that. One day I may ask for another dream visit, but for now I'm content with the one I got. Maybe because it was so perfect in every way, I have no need to ask again. I might someday, but not now.

My next interaction with Ron came on July 7, and I think this time, he was teasing me. Kelly and I were coming home from Omaha having spent the weekend with Kathy and Tom and Kandy when we stopped for gas. While Kelly was filling her car, I went inside for a snack. My psoriasis diet calls for low sugar and low carbs, which is hard to find in snacks. I was still looking when Kelly came in, got a coffee, and was ready to go. So, I grabbed up a package of pistachio nuts, telling Kelly as I did that her dad really liked them, but I'd thought for years that I didn't, until one day I tasted one from a package of his. For some time afterward, when we'd get some, he'd remind me with a grin that I didn't like them. Back in the car, I opened the package, took out a nut, popped it into my mouth, and just as fast, spit it out. I had picked up a package laced with chili seasoning. Kelly laughed and said, "Do you suppose Dad did that?" I looked at her like I thought she'd lost her mind and she said, "You just told me that Dad used to tease you about not liking them. So maybe he guided your hand, so you'd pick up that package he knew you wouldn't like." I knew it would be just like him, and I could almost see him grinning at me. Later, I thought that even the chili seasoning pointed to Ron's hand in it, for he was famous for his chili. Well, in our family, anyway, for he was the chili maker for us, and for years he made the chili for our church's annual fall festival and got rave reviews.

August 16 started as a bad day. I had not slept well the previous night, and I was tired, depressed, and anxious. And although I miss Ron every day, this day my longing for him seemed all consuming. I'd gone to the family room to watch TV early that evening, watching some sitcoms and then a movie. It was a good movie, the acting so natural, so real, as if the actors were really in love. Although I loved it, I wept all the way through it, for it made me miss Ron even more. After the movie, I watched some home videos of family Christmases and vacations. But that hadn't cheered me either. I was really bummed when I decided to just go to bed.

The overhead light switch is at the top of the three steps that lead to the basement, and I needed its light to make my way upstairs to the living room, so on bare feet, I crossed the floor, stepped down on to the first step leading into the basement, and felt something brush my foot. I looked down, and there, by my bare foot, was a baby toad no bigger than a mouse. I got a waste basket and herded it inside, took it upstairs and turned it loose in the yard.

I was mystified as to how that baby toad could have even made it into the house, much less get down to those basement steps. In fact I was sure that with steps at both outside entrances and the doors closed to the hot August air, that little baby toad could not have even made it into the house, much less down those steps to the family room and then more steps to the basement. Unless it had help. Then I remembered that evening, just a few weeks shy of sixteen years before when our grandson Johnny was born, and I suddenly knew Ron had sent that baby toad.

Johnny was born in the evening in the hospital in Alma, Nebraska, and Ron and I had kept his sisters, Jordyn and Ally, then nine and six, at our home. When we got the news from Ronnie, we jumped in the car and headed for Nebraska to see this new little guy. It was getting dark when we arrived and as we walked up to the front door of the hospital, the two little girls, so excited about seeing their new little baby brother, suddenly weren't interested in him at all. A bunch of toads of all sizes, drawn by the lights at the front door and the possibility of some tasty bugs, were hopping all around, and the girls wanted to stay out and play with them—which we let them do for a little while. I smiled at the memory of that happy time and thanked Ron for jolting me out of my sadness and for using a baby toad instead of a big, ol' adult one.

Some months later, I watched a video of that day Johnny was born and smiled to watch those little girls outside the hospital, Ally holding a baby toad in her hands, and Jordyn yelling, "There's another big one!"

We gathered together on September 7 this day to honor the

memory of our beloved husband, father, and grandfather for what would have been his eighty-sixth birthday. We had his favorite foods: pork chops, mashed potatoes and gravy, creamed corn, and watermelon. We topped it off with a chocolate cake with fudge frosting. I always baked him that cake for his birthday (as his mother had done before me) and as a nod to Montana and Angel Island where we'd had our summer home, and the moose we often saw in and around the lake, and twice in our back yard, "moose tracks" ice cream.

The next morning Ronnie and Michele took their two little grandsons to the bakery for donuts. The boys soon spied the vending machines that would, for a quarter, give out a little toy or trinket of one kind or another. Neither Ronnie nor Michele had any quarters, so Ronnie gave the boys a dollar bill to take to the counter and exchange for quarters. They came back with four brand-new shiny Montana quarters.

Ronnie told me later that those coins did startle him, and he wondered, but then decided it was probably just a coincidence. That is until the boys tried them in the machines and not even one would work. He said, "I knew this was Dad having a little fun with me."

I loved it! *Loved it for Ronnie and for me, too.* This was another sign that he is with us and even knows when we go out for donuts.

Some would be skeptical, but the odds that it was a coincidence is a huge stretch for me. Here in Kansas, how likely are we to get a Montana quarter, let alone four brand-new shiny ones? Besides, this was Ron, who so loved Montana, and who so loved to tease, and who had already sent us evidence of his presence in such a wide variety of ways, some, I'm sure, much harder to orchestrate then giving those two little boys four Montana quarters to surprise Ronnie. I thought I should check the computer in case the new Montana quarters were being recalled because they wouldn't work in vending machines, but I never did. Anyway, even if it were so, Ron would have known and have used it to his advantage.

Some would say that my next experience was just a memory

reawakened, but I say it was Ron there with me in the present time. It's odd that it didn't bring the welling of tears, but a comforting feeling of his presence, of his enduring love. The girls, who had been home for what would have been their dad's birthday, had left early on Sunday morning, so I went to church. Our regular pastor was gone and so an elder gave the sermon. In his sermon, he talked about various forms of communication, saying one form, between those in love, is a kiss. When he said, "kiss," I felt a sudden, swift, light sensation on my lips, like a quick kiss. My mind wasn't actively taking in the words of the sermon, as I was in a meditative mode, hearing his words, but not actively listening, and when I heard the word *kiss* and felt the kiss, it was almost in a dream-like state. Perhaps in that sort of mindlessness, I was open to receive his kiss. My heart filled with joy, knowing Ron was here in the church with me.

I saw Ron again in the Logan church pulpit on Sunday morning, September 30. Ron's sister Shirley and I had gone to Logan to go with June to her church, and the services were well underway when I suddenly saw Ron in the pulpit. His form was shadowy, as before, his body shape more outline than substance, and even though his features were not distinct, I still clearly saw that he was smiling and looking at me with love. All through the rest of the service, I could see him there, looking at me and smiling. Then, as we stood to sing the last song, he disappeared.

Several years after Ron bought into the funeral home at Phillipsburg, he and Darel purchased the Logan home. However, Ron was usually the one who worked the services there, and he developed a love for the community as he guided those families through those important rituals of planning and carrying out the funeral service and burial of their loved ones. On occasion throughout those years, in the absence of the minister, Ron had also served the community as a guest speaker in this church.

# CHAPTER 25

# JAX'S BIRTH

**ON NOVEMBER 14,** 2018, Jordyn and Brandyn gave us little Jaxtyn Michael Tweedy, our first great-grandchild. I had gone to bed at midnight, knowing Jordyn was in the Smith Center hospital and the baby would soon be arriving. I was excited, not only because we'd have this new little one in our lives, but also because I felt certain that Ron would find some way to share the good news with me. He did, and in a way I could never have imagined.

I soon fell asleep and at some point, I dreamed that a man just literally walked into my dream. In full form, he was no one I knew, and of no particular age. Then Ron walked in behind him, also in full form, and he was looking at me and smiling a beaming, loving smile. I woke then, cried a little and yet felt strangely comforted and I soon fell back into a deep and dreamless sleep.

The next time I woke, it was three o'clock. I went right back to sleep and woke again at seven with Ronnie calling to tell me that he was now a grandpa. The baby had arrived at 1:49 a.m. all six pounds, five ounces of him, and all was well. Then I remembered my dream of Ron and the other man and so I "knew," or believed anyway, that Ron had come into my dreams to share with me this great-grandson's birth. I knew the dream had been between midnight and 3 a.m., so I was sure that Ron and that other guy, whoever he was, had come into my dream at the exact time of the birth. For, on earth, Ron believed in being punctual. I doubt if he'd be any different in the spirit world.

I was pleased and so happy that Ron had come to me to let me know he knew about the baby. I still wondered why that first man had come into my dream, but I do know that Ron had come to celebrate with me the birth of our first great-grandchild. It was, I knew, what my Ron would do.

Three days later, I was on the phone with Kelly, telling her about the dream and that other man. She said, "Maybe that other man was Jax as a soul, but in the form of the man he would become, and Dad was telling you that he knew him there in the spirit world."

Wow! I got goosebumps. Maybe one day I would have come to that conclusion, but probably not on my own. Kelly's words prompted me to search for an answer and I discovered a book in my own library that substantiated her words.

The book is by Bob Olsen and titled, *Answers to the Afterlife.* In one section, Olsen answers a woman who had written him about having just had a baby and she wondered if her father, who had passed, was aware of this little one.

Olsen answers that her father knew her son before she did, because they were in the spirit world together before her son was born and that they knew each other as grandfather and grandson. He also added that her father was also fully aware of the child's birth because he's aware of everything in her life.

I had to laugh when I told Kandy what her sister said about the guy who walked into my dream ahead of their dad on the night Jax was born. She expressed amazement, maybe even awe, and then said, "I never would have thought of that. I would have thought that other man just got into the wrong dream by mistake."

A friend told me that one day she was watching her now adult grandson, then three years old, sitting on the floor playing with his toys, when he suddenly looked up from his play and seemed to be thinking about something. Then he turned and looking up at her, said, "You know, Grandma, I knew you before I was born."

Another friend told me an almost identical story about when

her now adult daughter was about three years old and was shown a picture of her grandfather, my friend's father. He had passed before her child was born, and she was so surprised when her daughter said, "I know him. I remember him."

This next story I heard second hand (the mother told another, who told me). She said that when her son, Randy, was born, he had some health issues and needed to be kept in the hospital for some time after she was discharged. Randy had been named after his mother's brother who had passed eleven months before Randy was born. One day when he was about three, his mother showed him a picture of her brother, his Uncle Randy. "I know him," he said, "When I was a baby, he came to the hospital to see me."

That is just a sampling of the many stories that have come from the mouths of the little ones. I need to move on with this, but I will add just one more, as it is quite unusual. My friend's little daughter was just three when she said to her, "I saw you when I was in Heaven, and I chose you to be my mom." My friend encouraged her little girl to tell her more, and she said something to the effect that when they go to Heaven again, they will be together, and they will be the same age. "So," my friend said, "What age will we be?" Without any hesitation, she replied, "Twenty-eight." *At three, she probably didn't even know there was a number twenty-eight.* I'd love to know how she got that information. God, Angels, Jesus, a passed loved one, or maybe, if we do come as a soul to an earthly body at birth, maybe what she knew in Heaven she's not quite yet forgotten. Jesus said, "Suffer the little children to come onto me, for of such is the kingdom of heaven." Matthew 19:14

One day in December, after Jax's birth in November, I was standing in front of the kitchen sink, looking out the window beyond the enclosed patio just off from the kitchen, where, outside the patio door, some birds were feeding at the large basin-shaped feeder I kept filled for them. I wasn't really seeing the patio, the feeder, the birds, for I was thinking of Ron, missing him, mourning him. Then, for a moment something caught my eye and I saw that all the birds were gone and in their place was a bright red cardinal. He was perched on the rim of the feeder, not feeding, but seeming to look right at me. Then he flew away, and the other birds came back. It made me smile. "Thanks, Ron!" I said.

As I mentioned, I'd not seen or heard any cardinals in our yard for a long time, possibly even a year or longer, until I saw the pair in the hackberry tree, Ron's sign that he was open to a dream visit and had kissed me on the heart chakra. Now I'd just had one perched on the feeder and I was positive Ron had sent him to cheer me.

Seven weeks after Jax's birth, in early January of 2019, the dream Ron had sent me when Jax entered our world was continued in a vision at a friend's home. My friend lived about fifty miles from me and on that day had invited me over for dinner at her home. I arrived there at four o'clock and we spent the evening enjoying the good food and conversation. This friend has had some of the same kind of experiences as I've had, and as we sat in her living room, she told me of an experience that happened years ago. "I was in a library in a neighboring town and had checked out *You Own the Power* by a spiritual medium and healer, Rosemary Altea. The next day, I heard about a young man who had died in a fall. I had exchanged a few words with the boy's mother at a store a few months ago, so I knew who she was, but that was all. Still, I felt compelled to go to the funeral home where the boy was lying in state, the services to be held the next day. When I left the funeral home and got back in my car, the boy spoke to me. I could not see him, but I heard his voice clearly. He wanted me to take a copy of that book I'd checked out of the library the day before to his mother. I didn't want to. I didn't know the mother that well and she would think I was crazy, so I did nothing."

It's a long story, but suffice to say, the boy was persistent and eventually she bought a copy of the book and took it to the mother. One interesting thing the boy told her that might give others peace as well, was that although he had fallen from a very high structure and hit the ground, he told her he'd felt no pain, as he had left his body seconds before the impact.

Then I told her my story about the night Jax was born last November, and how Ron had come to me in a dream vision, walking in behind this other man, who I'd come to believe was the soul of our great-grandson just before he entered our world.

As I spoke of it, I suddenly saw Ron in a full-blown vision, right there in my friend's living room, and it was like my dream the night Jax was born, but in this vision, Ron was already in the dream, standing there looking at me, not shadowy, but clearly and in full form, like he was in my dream, but this time he was alone. And, as in the birth dream, his eyes were on me, warm, loving, and he was smiling that same happy, wonderful smile. And showering down around him were streams of golden light, like rays of sunshine, and my heart was flooded with joy. Not once had I experienced that degree of happiness since he had left me, now on this day in early January 2019 just a few weeks shy of a year ago. The tears would come again, and they have often, but in that moment, I was filled to the brim with pure joy.

Those moments come and go so swiftly, and yet while I am seeing my love, my Ron, it seems like regular time. I know it can't be, though, for when the vision fades, whoever I'm with never gives any indication that they've noticed anything unusual. My friend didn't either, and we were just a few feet across from each other, the vision of Ron in full form between us. I told her about it a few days later, but not that night. I just held it in my mind and heart, savoring the joy of having been in the presence of my love, who was showing me, in those cascading streams of sunlight, his own happiness, his joy. It would be while I was editing this chapter almost four years later, that it would dawn on me that with this rerun of the dream Ron was confirming what Kelly, who is quite intuitive, had told me: That the man who had come into that dream ahead of Ron was Jax.

I drove back to my home those fifty miles in the dark, but my heart was lit with the glow of happiness. I knew there would be deer out and my headlights did catch three beside the road, two in one place and one in another, as well as a coyote. I watched for them, but I wasn't afraid or even nervous. I had my deer whistles and, more importantly, I somehow knew I also had Ron's protection.

I was about halfway home, still warmed by the glow of happiness from the memory of seeing Ron drenched in that shower of golden light, when I thought about the Big Dream and suddenly I felt that tonight I had made it down that steep downhill grade, had escaped the deep, dark pool, and had made it back to that riverbank where I'd left my sandals. I had always understood that symbolically getting my sandals meant I had more living to do, that it simply wasn't my time to pass, but on the way home that night, I wondered if I should try writing again. My last book had been published in 2017 and with Ron's health declining, I was sure I'd never write anything ever again. But the seed planted that night would give rise to this memoir you now hold in your hands.

When I told another friend about this vision, I said, "It was just like that dream, except for the streams of sunlight, but Jax wasn't there." She chuckled. "Of course not," she said. "He's here." I laughed. Of course, he's here with us. *I knew that!*

This friend's grandmother (now deceased) used to have premonitions that came true. Now, when she sees cardinals on special days, she believes her grandmother sends them. My friend now works the business alone, but for several years she had worked with Linda, the former owner, and they had become good friends. Then Linda became ill and soon passed. The next day when my friend came home from work, as she pulled into the driveway and turned off her car, a female cardinal flew over and perched on her car's side view mirror and looked in at her. She said, "I knew Linda had sent it to let me know that all was well with her. After a while it flew up into a tree in front of her house and she got out of the car and went inside." She paused a second or two and then added. "From that window, I could see the bird in that tree, motionless, and seeming to stare right at me. Then she was gone, but I never saw her leave."

I loved that her friend and coworker had sent the female. That was the first I'd heard of the female being a sign from a loved one instead of a bright red male. Since then, I've heard of a grandmother who had passed and on her grandson's wedding day, a female cardinal flew over and perched on his car's side view mirror and looked in at him. Because they all knew that this grandmother had those special experiences and gifts, he knew immediately it was from her, and she was letting him know she was with him on this special day.

It fascinates me how often the cardinal is used by our loved ones in the spirit world. I never saw a cardinal until I moved to Kansas. They are not native where I grew up in Northwest Montana and Idaho. The birds they see there as signs from their loved ones are usually hawks, eagles, owls, ospreys, and some birds in season that "stand out," such as the hummingbird. I know of one time, though, when instead of a bird or birds, the sign was a swarm of bees.

My sister-in-law's father had raised bees nearly all his life in California. In his later years he moved with his family to Montana and continued to be a beekeeper until he was no longer able. His last days of life were spent in a nursing home in Libby. According to his family, the day before he died, he had talked a lot about his bees. At the interment in the Libby cemetery, they were all gathered around the minister for the committal service, when suddenly a swarm of bees came up out of the grass, flew over the crowd that were gathered under and around the tent, and up into the sky. My sister Mabel was at the service, and a few days later, she called to tell me. "It was truly amazing," she said. "I heard someone say, as we all stared after that swarm disappearing into the sky, that it was like planes in a flyover. And we all agreed, for it was as if they were paying tribute to that old beekeeper." She also mentioned that with the crowd there that day, how that large swarm of bees could have been there in the grass at their feet. "To me," she said, "there was no possible way a whole swarm could have been there, and yet they were."

Years later, and in light of my contacts with Ron since he's passed, I wonder if my sister-in-law's father, now free of his earthly restraints, had gathered those bees into that swarm as a sign to his family that he was once again with his beloved bees.

The woman who cut my hair those summers we spent in Montana told me that during her father's funeral, they were told later, an osprey circled above the building all during the service.

A writer friend who lives in the Northwest said that when she went out for a walk in the late afternoon after her sister's funeral, an eagle flew down from a huge pine tree and hovered in the air overhead. "It hovered and hovered," she said, "and I knew it was from my sister, letting me know she still lived."

Sometimes, a sign can be a flock of geese. Another friend told me that at her mother's internment at the cemetery, as the service ended, a flock of speckle-bellied geese flew over their heads, honking and honking. She smiled and added, "My mother's last name was Birdsong."

## CHAPTER 26

# THE CARDINALS AND THE WINFIELD CONTEST

**I KEPT THINKING** about that drive home from my friend's that night in January 2019, my heart overflowing with happiness from the vision of Ron in those streams of sunlight and how I believed that I finally had those sandals I'd left on the riverbank in the Big Dream. Maybe I should start writing again, and maybe this time, I should write about how Ron has let me and our family know, with no uncertainty, that he is alive and well and still loves us.

I thought, too, that I should also share at least some of the many stories I've collected over the years from others who have had contacts in a variety of ways that speak clearly of, not just life after death, but that our loved ones are able to pierce at will that thin veil between us, as are angels, God, and Jesus, and that they are always cognizant of us here on Planet Earth.

Although, even as I felt this need to share these many blessings from Ron, I knew there would be some who would think I was getting a bit dotty in my old age. However, I knew there would be just as many and probably many more who would read this story of my experiences and the many and varied experiences of others with pleasure and perhaps a bit of excitement, for it would, for some, validate their own experiences—experiences they've shared with only a select few, if any at all. The more I thought about the many ways Ron has contacted me, the more I believed I should not keep them to myself or just within our family. I knew the sandals were a metaphor for finishing my life's work, so maybe writing such a book was what I was supposed to do before I, too, reached the finish line. I thought about those who have not had that connection with a passed loved one and who might never know it was even possible, if we who have had those experiences don't share them. These stories could change the mindset of the nonbeliever, as well as bring joy to those who do not know how close their passed loved ones really are to them. It would also validate those who have had contact with a passed loved one, but thought it had to have been their imagination, not knowing communication between our two worlds was even possible. The more I dwelled on the idea of sharing with others, of spreading the good news that those who have passed are able to communicate in a wide variety of ways with us here on earth, the more excited I became.

The many accounts now of those who have had a near-death experience like Mary (chapter 18) have given us a vivid physical picture of Heaven and the surety that our loved ones reside there, for they have seen them and sometimes even exchanged words with them, often being told, they had to go back, that it was not yet their time. Those words they hear while having the NDE seem to imply that we all have a set time.

We wonder why some who "die" and return to life speak of having NDE and others don't, but maybe they feel uncomfortable sharing for fear they would not be believed. When those stories first came to the attention of the general public, our medical personnel had encountered many such cases, going back years and years and years, but some, maybe even most, were not convinced that it was a real event, until Dr. Moody's and others' books came out. Of course, some still aren't convinced. The psychiatrist, Bruce Greyson, in an interview by Alex Moshakis in the *Guardian*, (reprinted in *The Week*), admits to having collected those NDE experiences for decades, but they have brought him no closer to an explanation. He does say though, that in his business of helping people change their lives, it can take a long time, whereas a NDE can change them in seconds. And I have to add, as can an out-of-body experience.

Mary, who shared her near-death experience with me (Chapter 18), said that even her husband was a skeptic at first. She laughed when she told me, "Here's a man who believes an angel sat by his bedside one whole day when he was sixteen and seriously ill, and when the angel left, he began to get well. And *he* doubts my story?"

The euphoria I sailed home on that January night with that wonderful vision of Ron bathed in sunlight and my thoughts about going back to writing, began to fade as the days passed and I began to think about how my story might be received, or how I might be perceived if I did write a book about these experiences.

In the end, it was only with Ron prodding me with cardinals, that I got the job done, and in the process, felt the fear slip away replaced by the certainty that this was my job. At least, most of the time I'd think that. Not that I thought I was going to change the world, but I was sure the book would give validation to others who have had such experiences and help ease the pain of those who have lost loved ones. Maybe it would even cause some who have no belief in life after death to rethink their position. At any rate, I'm sure many will take away something from the book. Maybe some will realize they are dealing with a subconscious belief that is feeding them false information. Some may come to know that they are victims of unresolved grief and seek therapy. Maybe some who have had such experiences will begin to share, and in doing so bring an awareness to those who might benefit greatly from their experience or experiences.

Often when we share our stories of contact with passed loved ones, we free up those who have had similar experiences, but were hesitant to speak of them. As one young man said to me, "I'll tell you, but I'm not telling anyone else."

You take a risk when you tell your story of a contact with a passed loved one, but it is minimal. Sometimes you will get a slight withdraw, or as I did once, a flat out "I'm not interested." Once, a woman became angry with me. I don't know, but it's possible she believed I was dabbling in witchcraft. But in sharing with others, I've also received dozens of like stories in return. Those who have never received a message from a passed loved one and have never heard of those kinds of experiences would be skeptical, of course. I imagine I would be too.

There are some, maybe even many, who cannot pick up on signs or messages from passed loved ones and that includes the skeptics, who do not believe because they haven't had the personal experience. Some have received such signs, but believe it's just their imagination, and some do not see or recognize the sign or message. For those of us who do, this can be a gift we could share with others, rather than keeping it to ourselves, like the bushel basket that scripture speaks of in Matthew 5:17. "Neither do men light a candle and put it under a bushel, but on a candlestick; and it gives light to all that are in the house."

Initially, I was excited about writing his book and I began to share my "Ron stories" more and more, and as I stated before, I'd usually get one and sometimes two or three in return. A few years ago, I shared a story with one of my doctors and as usually happens, I got one in return. He told me that the day of his father's funeral, he had let his family out of the car at the funeral home and was driving over to the parking area, when suddenly he *knew* his dad was in the back seat directly behind him, and if he could twist around to look, he would see him, but there were cars in front and behind him, going to the parking area and he couldn't risk it. Then he heard his dad say, "I know this is hard for you son, but I'm okay, and I love you." The doctor's next words led me to choosing the title for my book. He said, "I believe that those in Heaven are so much closer than most of us realize." And to that, I say, "Amen!"

When I wrote this doctor, asking permission to use his story, and when some time had passed with no answer, I wrote him again. He answered right away, apologizing. My first letter had simply been misplaced and forgotten in the busyness of life. This one he could not forget, for it arrived on the fifteenth anniversary of his father's passing. "Amazing," he wrote. "What are the odds of that? Certainly, a higher power and another sign of the influence of those who have passed who are still involved in our lives." He also wrote that he had not heard or felt the presence of his dad for some time now. On his last visit, his dad told him how much he loved him and was so proud of him, but he would have to limit his visits now, as he was going to be extra busy working on something he needed to accomplish. Then the doctor added, "And, yet today, he visited me in the form of your letter."

Although I was excited about writing this book at the beginning, as time went by my enthusiasm began to dwindle. I would write some, maybe a page or two or more, and then delete it. I just couldn't find a place to start. My other books were historical fiction and with research of the times and my characters' input, for it is amazing how they'd step up to help me, how real they'd become and how the stories developed because of them. Fiction, I could do, but this was real, this was personal. I couldn't quite wrap my head around this.

Then on February 28, 2019, I thought about the Winfield Arts Council's "Kansas Voices contest." I was familiar with it and had even won first place with a short story a few years ago. I looked on the computer for the contest information and found that there was only a week before the deadline of March 8, and so I decided to write a short version of what I wanted to put in this book.

The limit was 4,500 words. That I could do—maybe. So, I set to work. I had no need to win the contest, only to tell a shorter version of the story and maybe that would set me on the path to getting a book written. The value of doing this contest, if it did win, was that it was not for publication, just a contest, and would not appear anywhere in print, except in the contest booklet, and only then, if it won. And even if it won, the exposure would still be minimal.

As I mentioned, I started on this contest story with just a week to get it written, so I wrote every day, and every day I questioned myself.

*Should I do this? Will I be seen as a bit eccentric, if not plain nutty? Maybe this wasn't such a good idea after all. Maybe I only thought this was something I should do. Maybe my sandals weren't for this job at all and writing it was just a waste of time.*

Now, it was just a day before the deadline and I was almost at my word limit, almost done—then doubt moved in like a steamroller and I was ready to scratch the whole thing.

You've heard the expression, "A little birdie told me." Well, it wasn't exactly like that, but sort of—close anyway. I rent a duplex now, but I was in my old house then, my office upstairs. My computer desk was between two windows on the north wall that looked out into the backyard where there are three big trees. Two are hackberry trees, and one is huge. Some of its branches close to the window on my left are plainly visible as I sit at my computer. The other hackberry, only a bit smaller, is at the back of the lot. It was where I saw the pair of cardinals when I wanted Ron's okay for the dream visit. The third tree is a large fruitless mulberry on the east side of the yard, and its branches are plainly visible through the window on my right.

So now with doubt crowding in, I glanced up from my computer, looked at the window on my right, and saw, high in the branches of the mulberry tree, a red cardinal. He stayed in that tree, high up in those branches for quite a long time, and I got a second wind and started working on the story again. As I worked, I'd look up from my keyboard every few minutes and he was always there. Sometimes he'd change to a different branch, but he'd still be where I could see him. I wondered if Ron had sent him. I thought he might have, but I wasn't totally sure. Still, I kept working on my story and soon I became so engrossed in the story that I forgot about the cardinal for a time, and when I did remember and looked up, expecting to see him, he was gone. But by then, I only had a few more paragraphs to go.

I know there is no way to prove that Ron sent that bird, but no way to prove he didn't, either. There is no way to prove or disprove that he had sent that other male cardinal to the feeder that day last

December, or the pair in the hackberry tree, but I know he did.

I proofed the story and packaged it for mailing the next day. I'd had trouble forwarding emails, and so was hesitant to risk sending it electronically.

The next morning, March 8, the day it had to be postmarked, I had the story sealed in a manila envelope, addressed, and on the table—I just needed to pick it up and go out the door. But again, doubt stayed my hand. *Maybe I should just forget the whole thing.* I stewed and fussed awhile and then went over to the kitchen sink for a glass of water. I took a glass from the cupboard and started to fill it. Then I looked out the window, past the patio windows to the bird feeder, and there perched on the edge of the feeder, was a single bird, a male cardinal. He sat there not eating, just sitting, looking, as that other one had, as if he could see me through the windows. I looked away, looked back, and he was gone, the usual flock of small birds flying in to feed.

"Okay, Babe," I said to Ron, "I got it!" I grabbed up my story and headed for the door. It didn't win, but that didn't matter, for I'd waded in and gotten my sandal-clad feet wet.

Some days later, I was at the kitchen sink when I thought about giving a copy of this Winfield story to a certain someone, and with that thought, I looked up from the sink and saw through the window the red cardinal at the feeder. No other birds, just that cardinal. He was there for a second and then gone. I guess you know I gave that person the story. She loved it and was not even aware that ADC (after-death communication) was even possible.

I still miss my Ron so very much. The tears still gather and fall, but sometimes they are mixed with smiles. Grief is not unavoidable, even when we know our loved one still lives, and even when they show us over and over. What we miss is their physical presence. There is no substitute for that. But, I'm sure that will be a different story when we too have slipped through that thin veil between us.

This Easter, the second since Ron passed, June and I were again in Logan's Methodist Church to celebrate the Risen Christ. I was, of course, remembering Ron and wondering if I would see him this morning as I had last Easter and that Sunday last September, standing at the pulpit. The pastor as always, stood down in front of the congregation, but my eyes often strayed to the pulpit, waiting, hoping... Then one of the members gifted with a beautiful voice left her pew, and, stepping into the pulpit, began her solo, and Ron appeared on her right beside the pulpit. He was in full form, but shadowy, and yet I could see him clearly and he was smiling and looking at me with love. He stayed for a part of the song and then was gone.

I hadn't worked on my story much, but about noon on May 14, I decided to try again to write this book, so I opened the document to where I had stopped, on chapter two, and began typing. I wrote steadily for two hours. Then I looked up from the computer at the window, that day open to the fresh, warm air of May, and there in the big, old hackberry tree, was a red cardinal. He sang a part of his song and then flew away. I'm sure Ron sent him to give me encouragement. I worked most of that day, and the next and the next.

I'd like to be able to write that I worked on my story every day and made huge progress, but I didn't. Sometime later, but I've no clue as to why or when, I stopped writing completely.

CHAPTER 27

# THE PSYCHIC AND DOUBLING

**STILL SKITTISH ABOUT** writing this book, I'd been thinking about contacting a psychic and asking him or her if this was really what I should be doing or if I was just interpreting everything wrong. I thought Ron would come through and I'd get a definite answer. Maybe those cardinals were just cardinals, and not signs from Ron at all. Many say these psychic people are hoaxes, but if I have a little of what they seem to possess, then it seems logical to me that some people have a lot. But right from the start we had problems. In fact, we had so many interruptions that I never got to ask her much of anything, and what I did get from her was wrong, totally wrong!

I was using my cell phone for this call and had it on speaker phone. We had talked a few minutes when I started losing the signal and would have to redial. The connection was lost three times.

After that third time, we talked a while, but I was still getting wrong answers from her. Then my cell phone rang. I looked to see who was calling and the name listed was Gary B and the number was Ron's youngest brother's, the number he'd had when he still lived in Kansas—before he moved to Oklahoma—before he passed into Heaven in 2014 to be with his two brothers there.

So, a number no longer in use couldn't be calling me, unless the call was from Heaven and the same rules probably don't apply there. I had never deleted Gary's number from my cell phone, so that probably helped. Also, according to all I've heard and read, phones are often a means of communication used by those who have passed. So, it seemed obvious that Ron, with Gary's help, was discouraging me from talking to her about the book. But why?

I told the woman that I was having trouble with my phone, which was true, so I'd have to hang up for now. I knew Ron was interfering and teaming up with Gary, but I didn't know why.

As soon as I hung up, I called that old number of Gary's and got the message that the number was no longer in service. *How little we know.* Right? This was also when I realized I'd never deleted that number from my contacts. I believed then that this experience told me, besides knowing that those in Heaven can use a cell phone, even a cell phone no longer in use, to just keep walking in my sandals and my love, my Ron would see me through. I didn't need any outside help.

About a week later, I met a woman from California who was visiting a friend of mine. Her mother had passed a few months before and she shared this with us. "When Mother was dying, she told me she'd call me when she got to Heaven. I humored her and said, 'Okay, Mama, I'll be waiting for your call.'" After the funeral and everyone had gone home, her phone rang. She answered it but all she could hear was a low static sound. She hung up, unplugged the phone, plugged it back in, and it rang again. But again, all she heard was that low static sound. This time when she hung up she remembered what her mother had said. A short time later the phone rang again and again she heard that same low static sound. This time she acknowledged her mother and thanked her for calling. She never received another call from her mother, but, one night, just as she was about to drop off to sleep, she saw her mother's face—just her face, for a second.

Sometime after my experience with the psychic, I found myself thinking about this chapter and my encounter with her. That part about her giving me those wrong answers had bothered me ever since I'd written it. So, I went back to this chapter to take another look and I worked and reworked it, but I was never satisfied. I finally decided to go watch TV for a while and maybe then with a fresh approach, I'd figure out what was wrong. I skimmed through the channels, but couldn't find anything to watch, so decided to go back and tackle that part of the story again. I clicked the power button, and the TV went off, and then right back on again and another channel was on, a channel showing the old black and white series, *The Twilight Zone* that first aired in 1959. For those not familiar with the series, it's a science fiction show where weird things happen to regular people. I soon realized I was in the middle of the show and had no idea what was going on, so I clicked it off and went back to this chapter about the psychic, and I knew immediately why that part had bothered me. I'd written all those things she'd told me, all of which were wrong, making her appear to be totally incompetent and that wasn't fair to her, for it was quite evident that Ron and Gary had been messing with her psychic abilities. Probably along with the phone interruptions, Ron was feeding her false information. So, I deleted all of that conversation I'd had with her. Thinking about it later, I had to smile, wondering if dealing with those on the other side of this thin veil could be one of the hazards of a psychic or medium's job. I'd love to hear from those in that profession if it is so.

This experience reinforced what I'd already known, although not so much on a conscious level or I wouldn't have thought I needed to contact a psychic in the first place. *Hadn't I learned by now that I had Ron to rely on and he would help me when it was needed?* Later, it would dawn on me the significance of Ron using that old *Twilight Zone* series. He always has had a great sense of humor.

Sometime, maybe a month or so after the psychic/medium experience, I was thinking about how wonderfully blessed I've been by my love's spiritual presence and I thought about the scripture in First Corinthians 13:12, about seeing through a glass darkly and that is how we see God now, but it goes on to say, "But one day we will see Him face-to-face and that will make all the difference."

In thinking about that scripture, I thought of the many and varied, often perfectly choreographed, and amazing ways that Ron has shown me and our family that he is still with us, still loves us, and suddenly the enormity of what I had been receiving from my love really hit me. It was like I'd stepped into a true understanding of those gifts he'd showered upon me, and I laughed and cried, and called out to him, knowing he had blessed me with a love beyond measure, and that sudden realization was a gift in itself. As I thought about those wonderful, totally amazing ways he has gifted me with his presence, I suddenly knew, this time without a doubt, that those messages weren't just mine to keep and treasure, but to share with others so they will find hope that their loved ones still live, still love them, and do at times pierce this thin veil between us. I realized then just how important this book could be. I would guess that thousands, probably millions or more in this whole wide world have received at least one message from a passed loved one and many have received more than one. However, there are probably many more who have not. Some simply don't believe a message from a passed loved one is even possible and if they have such an experience, they attributed it to their imagination. Like I did when I saw Ron's face on that man at the mailbox shortly after the funeral, for I'd not yet heard of doubling.

In mulling over those thoughts, I wondered if God uses those like us who can send and receive messages between each other to spread the word that He loves us and wants us to know we are not separated at death from our loved ones, just as we are never separate from Him in life, or afterward either.

As I stated, I don't know when that realization came to me, but sometime while struggling to write this book, that moment sealed for me the absolute belief that this sharing of my stories and the stories of others is why I had to go back for my sandals. That they were symbolic, not only of having more living to do, but a job too. My job? To write this book.

It was then that I thought of a memoir. A book that would include my growing-up years, for it would show that early in life, I had some extra sensory perception that often appears in young children but is not usually retained as they grow older. That I have retained mine, is, I'm sure, a factor in being able to receive those totally wonderful and amazing messages from Ron. It occurred to me that my early life was relevant to the story.

So, I went back in time—to 1942 and tried to begin my story from there, when I was a child of five and had my first (at least remembered) premonition. I wrote diligently for a few days, maybe a week, and then I began to falter and a few days later, confused and totally bogged down, I put it all away.

June 19, 2019. I had a checkup with my cancer doctor, a young man who is always eager to hear my "Ron" stories and this day was no exception. I didn't have a new one, but not wanting to disappoint him, I told him about seeing my brother, Danny, in church in 2006 and my mother in my kitchen on Angel Island in 2008 for those few seconds, both in full form. He asked if I noticed what they were wearing. I told him no, not really. I'm sure Mom was wearing a dress, as she always wore dresses, and Danny? I had no clue, but he must have worn a shirt and pants that was suitable for church. Of course, probably no one saw him but me.

The day after my visit to the cancer doctor, I had been at a store on the east edge of town and was driving west toward my home, when I saw Ron walking across the pavement of the Alta Convenience Store toward a parked vehicle near the gas pumps. He appeared to be looking down at something in his hand and walking along as real as if he were in his physical body. I immediately recognized the shirt and pants as ones he used to wear. The short sleeve shirt is white, zips up the front, and has two chest pockets. I also knew those blue summer slacks. Then Ron disappeared and another man I knew was in his place, and getting into the vehicle, maybe a pickup, I'm not sure. I don't usually notice what people drive, either. Then I suddenly remembered seeing Ron's face on that man in the pickup at the mailbox those few days after the funeral. I knew then it had not been my imagination, that he had really been there trying to make me aware of him, just as he had shown himself to me this afternoon using another man's physical body. Although I was driving while I was seeing Ron walk across that pavement, I had no awareness of driving. It was like I was in a state of suspension, as if while I was seeing him, time had stopped. Did other cars slow down behind me, or pass and go on? Or were there no cars in my lane at all for that moment in time? I really have no idea how that all works.

As soon as I got home, I started looking through the books I'd been collecting about the afterlife, and I learned about doubling. How the one in the spirit can superimpose their image over those in the physical body, and I knew what I had just witnessed was doubling, as was seeing Ron's face on that other man at the mailbox as I drove by.

The next day, it dawned on me why Ron had shown himself, superimposed over that other man, and why I knew what he was wearing. He was telling me he had been with me in the doctor's office and had heard our conversation about what Mom and Danny were wearing. Another way of saying, "I am with you always, even in the doctor's office, even though you don't know I'm there." *He's such a sweetheart!*

That day, I also looked through my photograph albums and found several photos of Ron wearing that same shirt and blue slacks back in 1989.

I was telling a friend about Ron's doubling that day and how I then remembered seeing his face on that man's at the mailbox. She told me that one day after her son, then a young man, was accidentally killed, she saw him looking out at her from the passenger side window of a car as it went by.

Later, I'd recall two such examples of doubling told to me by the two women who'd received those gifts. One of the women was in a department store when she saw her late husband walking a few feet away, pushing a shopping cart. Then he disappeared and a man she did not know was pushing the cart. The other woman saw her adult son, also in a store, standing at the end of an aisle, looking at her. Then he vanished and another man stood there in his place.

I read an account of a woman who thought she saw her deceased adult daughter in a mall, and she looked as real as she had in life. Then she vanished and another young woman stood where her daughter had been. She was so sure she had seen her daughter and yet, how could that be? She thought of it constantly in the days ahead, wondering if it had just been her imagination, or maybe she was losing her mind. Finally, she consulted a medium and she learned about doubling and how our loved ones who have passed can superimpose themselves on a living person, but they can only do so for a few seconds.

I smile when I think it's a good thing they can't stay any longer, for it could be a huge problem for those of us who are earthbound. Imagine looking like someone else for ten minutes, a half hour, a day? A whole bunch of scenarios come to mind, don't they?

One time at a football game, I was sitting in the stands when a slender man of about seventy, a stranger to me, came up the steps and stopped for a moment to scan the crowd. Then I saw that he now wore a Navy uniform, and was probably young too, but I don't recall either one of his faces. This was before I learned about doubling, so I just thought that I had picked up on knowing that the man, whoever he was, had been in the Navy. Maybe that's all it was, but now I wonder. Was there someone in the stands who had lost their loved one while he was in the Navy, and he was superimposing himself over the other man, hoping they would see him? If so, I hope they did and knew about doubling.

Ronnie's Michele had surprised him the Christmas of 2018, two weeks before his January birthday, with a gift of seven days in July at a resort on Northwest Montana's Bull Lake. The resort is just off from Angel Island where Ron and I had once had our vacation home. She arranged it all and invited every one of us. We all came, the kids and grandkids, Ronnie's sisters, their families, and me. Also, because a large share of my family still lives in the area, she set aside an afternoon for a Goyen family reunion.

A couple of incidents led me to believe that Ron was there too, at least part of the time. One morning Ally woke from a dream of her papa and his brother, Larry. She said it didn't seem like a dream at all, but real life. I understood completely, for I imagine it was like the dream I'd had of my brother Danny that Sunday morning when I'd asked him to tell me about Jesus, and later he'd stood up beside me in church. It was probably also like the dream my sister Mabel had of Ron the day before he passed, and my dream of Ron and that "other man," the night our little great-grandson, Jax, was born. I call them dream visitations. They seem so much more than a dream and I do believe they are really with us, and we are really communicating. I asked Ally what her papa and uncle wore, now more conscious of other's clothing since my visit with the doctor and Ron appearing the next day in those clothes I remembered.

Ally did not remember what her Uncle Larry wore, but she remembered her papa's shirt. She'd brought with her a small throw she had asked me for last Christmas with pictures of her and her papa. She showed me one of Ron wearing a shirt with black, white, and blue stripes, and that, she said, was the shirt he wore in her dream. Michele told me that first day when they arrived she saw Ron sitting on the deck of the resort's main house as if waiting for us. Of course, he vanished in seconds.

On one of those days, I went over to Angel Island and drove all around, a kind of sentimental journey, and as I passed where our summer place used to be, I saw the picnic table we'd left with the house in the side yard. Ron had built it at home and brought it there in sections to reassemble that first summer. I told Ronnie and he went over to try and buy it, but the owners were gone for the week. Writing this now, it seems odd that the table was in that narrow side yard, when there is a deck and whole big yard behind the house, but just driving by, I'd never had seen it there. Now, knowing Ron's amazing capabilities, I wonder if he moved it there for me to see. It would be easy enough with the owners gone that week.

At the end of the week, we all dispersed. Ally and I had driven up together, but I had plans to stay longer, so she rode home with her dad and Michele in their motor home. In Wyoming, they missed the exit to Scottsbluff, Nebraska, and went on south through Wyoming's Wheatland and Chugwater area, before turning east.

Ronnie said he felt like his dad was with them at times and I told him that by missing that exit to Scottsbluff, they had driven through the area where my mother's parents had taken a homestead in 1914 when she was eleven years old, and where thirteen years later, she'd met my dad. He wondered then if his dad had caused him to miss that exit. After all, that Scottsbluff exit is hard to miss. Sounds like his dad to me.

Ronnie went back to work at the funeral home and the evening of July 20, he was there in the chapel to put out floral arrangements for a pending funeral and was all alone in the building. Then suddenly he heard his dad sneeze. He knew immediately and he called out, "Hi, Dad!" Ron had a very distinctive, very loud sneeze that we had sometimes teased him about. Ronnie was pleased that his dad had let him know he was there, and I'm sure his dad grinned big time when his son recognized the sound and acknowledged his presence.

Writing this, I thought about one time when Jordyn, Ronnie's daughter, was six or seven and she and her cat, Sophie, were staying with us. This one day, she was in the living room, sitting on the floor by the bookcase looking at the kids' books I had there, her cat curled up beside her. Her papa was in the dining room, just around the corner from her. I was upstairs in the bedroom and was just starting down the stairs when I heard Ron sneeze, that very loud, distinctive sneeze, and then I heard Jordyn say, "Scared hell out of the cat."

# CHAPTER 28

# MORE SIGNS AND MY HOUSE SELLS

**SEPTEMBER 7, 2019** would have been Ron's eighty-seventh earth birthday. The kids all called to let me know they were thinking of me and remembering their dad. It was late evening when Kathy called. She told me she asks her dad for quarters now and then and always finds one and knows it's from him.

I had hoped for a sign from her dad all day, although I hadn't asked for anything specific, feeling certain he would do something that would resonate with me, but I had pretty much given up on the idea of receiving a sign from him and was feeling kind of blue and missing him so much.

After talking to Kathy, I went into the main bathroom and there was a quarter on the counter by the sink. Ally was staying with me at the time, and we each had our own side of the counter. The quarter was on my side, but Ally had a handful of change on her side, and I figured it had come from there, and so I set it over on her side with those other coins.

I had been in and out of that bathroom several times that evening, always barefoot, as I usually am at home in warm weather. Then just before I went to bed, I went in, stepped up to the sink, felt something under my bare foot, looked, and there was a quarter. I laughed, knowing it was from Ron. I told him I loved it!

Some days later, I thought about that quarter I had found on my side of the counter. Had Ron put it there for me and when I didn't get it, he'd waited until bedtime, then took that quarter back from Ally's pile and dropped it on the rug for me to step on?

A few days before her dad's birthday, Kelly thought about posting on Facebook the head and shoulders studio portrait of him in his Air Force uniform, but she was afraid it would make me sad to see it there. After Ron passed, the kids and grandkids had all wanted a copy, so they all had that 8x10 photo. That day, Kelly was discussing it with her daughters in Emily's apartment. Kelly was lying on the bed, which had a high headboard that is flat on the top. Emily has several objects and photos on display on this ledge, including that photo of her papa in his uniform. Both Emily and Lizzie assured her I'd not be upset, but Kelly still hesitated, saying, "I'm just not sure." And with those words, that photo on Emily's headboard fell over. Nothing else moved—just that photo.

"Thanks, Dad," Kelly said.

It was also on his birthday that I asked Ron for a yes sign if he agreed with me on a situation, and I needed to know by a certain date. The sign I asked for was a cardinal. A few days, maybe a week or so before, I'd received a sample copy of a *Birds and Blooms* magazine in the mail. I had skimmed through it and then laid it aside and basically forgot about it. So, on this day that we celebrated Ron's birth, my request already made, I began to watch each day for a cardinal. On the September 11, I thought about that magazine, and although I did not remember seeing a single cardinal in that issue, I thought it wouldn't hurt to look. So, I picked it up, turned the cover page, which featured an owl, and there as the background photo for the table of contents, was a full-page image of a red cardinal, and I knew that was my sign. Then I noticed at the top of the page in the righthand corner, a number thirty-eight, but I gave it no thought. I just closed the magazine and thanked Ron for the clever way he had given me my sign.

Two days later, I thought of that number 38 and turned to that page in the magazine, and there was a duplicate full-page picture of that cardinal. Wow! I asked for a cardinal and got two identical ones. How could I have missed seeing those cardinals when I'd leafed through that magazine the day it had arrived in the mail? Both were so "in my face" in size and color, and even a page number for the second one. I just shook my head and smiled and pictured him smiling back at me.

Later that day, Ally came home from work at the retirement center so excited, for she had seen the birds, like the ones her papa sent her the morning he passed, flying overhead. "Some darker birds and that white one flying in middle of them," she said. And she knew her papa had sent them too.

On September 17, while reading in bed, I dozed off, waking suddenly to the smell of Old Spice, the shaving lotion Ron always used. I'd loved that scent on him. In seconds it dissipated. I talked to him for a few minutes and then laid the book on the end table, turned out the light and went back to sleep.

Diane, an acquaintance of mine, told me about going back to the farm where she grew up, the land now farmed by others, the house abandoned. As she walked through the old, empty house, she stepped into a hallway and suddenly smelled her dad's aftershave. Her father had passed years before, but she knew with that scent he was there. I saw her daughter one day and mentioned it. She smiled. Yes. She knew the story.

Another woman told me she often catches the scent of her husband's aftershave and takes comfort in knowing he is there with her.

The months passed and one day in mid-December I found myself struggling, depressed, and singing the blues, when my friend called to invite me to a pre-Christmas gathering she was hosting that night. I drove the fifty miles, my spirits lifting and was there by five o'clock that evening. My friend entertains at "The Farm" a place in the country she inherited. There were ten or more of us there, two talented musicians, one on guitar, the other, the violin. We were a mix of Black and White, some that I knew and some that were strangers.

We visited, ate a lovely meal, sang Christmas carols, and laughed a lot. It was great! I was finishing my meal when I suddenly knew Ron was there! Some of the guests had finished eating and were beginning to move around, the rest, including me were still at the table. Then one of the guests, a Black man visiting from California, a very nice, soft-spoken man, probably in his sixties, came out of the kitchen where, having finished his meal, he'd taken his plate. He stopped in the doorway to talk to a couple seated at the opposite end of the table from me. I looked down at my now empty plate, laid the silverware on it, looked up and saw Ron in that man who was now leaning against the side of the doorway. Not really, not visibly. He wasn't doubling. It was the man's pose, a sort of "at ease" pose that was exactly like Ron's, and for the rest of the night, to see that man was to see Ron. Even when the man looked at me, his eyes seemed to be Ron's. Although I did not really see Ron and can only describe it as the essence of him. It did not make me sad, just added to the joy of the evening, for I felt he really was there and enjoying the party with me.

It was dark when I left for home, and I was reminded to watch for deer, but having felt Ron's presence all evening, I felt totally protected, and I had my deer whistles. I did, however, see something I have no definite explanation for. It flew past my driver's side window, going in the opposite direction. My first thought was of an owl. It was a light tan with some filmy off-white material like gauze, floating out from it like wings, but it was as large as a person and stretched out way too long to be an owl. It didn't surprise or scare me at all. I can't say for absolute certain, but it did look like an angel stretched out in flight. I didn't really think about it, until later, after I was home. That's when I realized it had to have been an angel. An angel sent by Ron to let me know I'd be protected on my way home.

I am certain he sent me another angel seven months later, on July 6, 2020, when I was lost in an unfamiliar town and needed help. In the following chapter, you will read about her and other angels who have come to our aid in times of distress and need.

Ron has amazed me in so many ways, and I feel that nothing is beyond his capabilities. Not only do I believe he sent that angel to protect me on the way home from the Christmas party, as well as the one in the next chapter when I was lost, but he even came to my aid three times when I needed help with my granddaughter's dog.

Sometime in 2018 I had gone to Ally's house to leave something for her. I don't remember what, but that doesn't matter to the story. I knew Ally wasn't home, and I expected her dog, Willow, to be in the fenced-in back yard. She wasn't. When I opened the door to set the item inside, the dog zipped past me and out into the front yard. I tried to get her to come to me, but she wouldn't, and every time I'd get close, she'd dance around me, but she'd never let me get close enough to catch her. Then she took off running straight north, parallel to the highway, and I ran after her, one block, then two. Now and then she would stop to sniff at something, but as soon as I got close, she'd take off again. I was so afraid she'd alter her course and run out onto the highway and get hit, and finally, in desperation, I called in my loudest voice on both God and Ron to stop her. She ran a couple of feet, stopped, and let me walk up to her. Which one stopped her? I imagine God let Ron do it, but I thanked them both profusely.

About a year later, Ally was living in another house, this one without a fenced area, so one day I was walking Willow for her. We were back at her house and up on the front steps, but instead of opening the front door and taking her in before I unleashed her, I absentmindedly reached down and unhooked her. She took off like a shot and I ran after her. Same story, however, she'd run only a block before I called on Ron, just Ron this time, and she ran a few more feet, then stopped and let me walk up to her.

It happened one more time. This time I got her inside, unhooked her from her leash, went into the other room, came out, and she was gone. This time the door was open just enough for her to slip out. How that happened, I had no clue. I could not believe I had not completely shut that door. I ran out to look for her, just as Ally, in between the two jobs she had that day, drove up. When I told her what had happened, she jumped back in her car and took off to go look for her dog. When I had walked Willow earlier, we had come across two long, bare bones. I thought they were probably leg bones from a deer. Immediately, Willow had hopped on them and started chewing. I'd pulled on her leash, dragging her away, and we went on. Now carelessly, I'd let her get away again, for the third time. Knowing it was next to hopeless to find her, I called on Ron and immediately I both heard and saw the words just in front of my face, "She's over by the deer bones." And she was just chewing away. I thanked Ron and promised to be more careful from then on. And so far, I have been.

February of 2020 came, now two years since Ron had passed, but never really left me. The first of the month, I had moved into a rental duplex and put my house on the market, as I no longer needed such a big house and yard, nor did I want the hassle of the upkeep home ownership required. Ron and I had purchased our home in April of 1961, and we raised our children there, but it was too big for one person and without Ron's physical presence, just too lonely. Someone mentioned the years of memories created in that house, but memories go with us, carried in our hearts and minds, and in my case, also a diary, a stack of DVDs, forty-two photograph albums, some slides, and home movies. I'm sure Ron approved of my move, in fact, I'm pretty sure he took care of some of that house-selling business, and probably had a hand in getting me to pick this place, for it is perfect for me in every way.

I started the process on Saturday, February 1 by thinking about the realtors in town and on February 7, I made my choice. I didn't really know Jessica, although she and her family attend the same church I do. We sit on opposite sides of the sanctuary, but for some reason, on February 2 she and her family sat on chairs against the back wall across from me, instead of in their regular pews, but the next Sunday, they were back where they always sat. I saw her several times around town that week and noted the real estate office where she worked. Although I'd seen the name, I didn't recall being actively aware of it before now. I had known her husband's grandmother for years, but we had been little more than acquaintances. So, suffice to say, we were pretty much strangers. So, on day one, I decided to find a realtor. Day two she sat where I could see her with her family, and in the week that followed, I saw her several times, once with her kids, the other times either walking into a store or driving. Then on February 7, I was in the grocery store over near the deli, when I realized she was standing right behind me. It seemed like an omen, and I turned to her right there in the store and asked if she'd take the job. I did enjoy working with her. She is very down to earth, very personable, and she sold my house in record time, although at first there was a hitch.

My granddaughter, Ronnie's daughter, Jordyn, and her husband Brandyn, asked to look at the house on February 17, for they were pretty sure they wanted to buy it. However, they'd have to sell their house first. I told the realtor about the kids wanting to buy my house. She said there was no problem, she'd hold off showing it until they decided.

I should have been delighted to have Jordyn and her family live in my old house, but I wasn't. I had developed an uneasy feeling about them buying my house that had developed into a totally unreasonable fear—the fear that their little son would fall down the steep, concrete steps that led from the garage to the basement and I made Ronnie promise to build a gate at the top, if they bought my house.

Two and a half months went by, and the kids had not had an offer, so they decided they'd stay in their house and look for another one later.

"I think," Jordyn said, "I wanted your house for sentimental reasons, as I have so many happy memories of my growing-up years in that big old house of yours and Papa's."

I relisted my house with Jessica and this time signed a paper, and she was soon showing it again.

In early May I found myself dealing with some situations that had me feeling worried, depressed, and sad. So, I went to the park late one afternoon to pray to God and talk to Ron. For years, I've taken my special prayers to the park, crossing the old walking bridge that arches over the small creek, and there on the west side among the trees I petition the Lord in prayer. Since Ron passed, I stand in the middle of the bridge and facing upstream, I talk to God. Then I turn and facing downstream I talk to Ron. Today, as I talked to Ron, sharing my anxieties with him, my eyes on the trees that grow along the creek bank, I suddenly noticed a male cardinal sitting on a branch in one of the trees directly in front of me. It was as if he had just materialized on that tree branch, for he was suddenly just there, and I knew Ron had sent him. Usually, the cardinal does not stay long, but this one stayed and stayed, his eyes focused on me, or so it seemed. He never moved, never sang a note, but stayed motionless, looking at me. The minutes passed and my voice faded until I was no longer talking to Ron. As I stood there, mute, my eyes fixated on the bird, I began to get a little nervous and I kept waiting for him to move, to look away—do anything but just sit there, still as a stone, and stare at me. Finally, I just wanted him gone, and I began to slowly walk to the end of the bridge. Then I stepped off the west side of the bridge and took a slow step or two and he was gone. I never saw him fly away. He was just gone. I suppose I took my eyes off him for a second, I don't really know, and I guess it doesn't matter, for however he got there and left, I believe Ron sent him to remind me that he is always with me, will never leave me, and knows my worries, my cares.

On May 31 a couple looked at the house, then came back several days later and made an offer. We signed the papers on July 20, 2020. I found it interesting that those two and their little girl would be living in my house, as his mother had illustrated most of my books and stories. Also, he was the nurse on duty at the hospital when Ron passed in that early morning hour on January 25, 2018. I don't remember his actual words when he woke me that morning, just the sound of his voice and his demeaner, so soft, so gentle, so kind. Fast forward now to August 14, 2020. That day, Jordyn and Brandyn began moving into their newly purchased home. This house had come up for sale a little less than three months after they decided not to buy mine. They had listed their house again and it had sold right away. I really like their new home and it feels to me like it belongs to them. I think, too, of how they had no bites on their house when they were planning to buy mine and got a buyer right away when this house came on the market.

I'm sure that Jordyn's papa knew it was the memories, not so much the house itself that had tugged at her, and just as I am as sure that daylight comes after dark, he worked it all out for us, perhaps even for the young family who now lives in our old home. I did so hope those two and their little girl would enjoy living in our old house, and one day, some months later, I saw her uptown and I asked. She smiled and said, "It's awesome."

# CHAPTER 29

# ANGELS

**A MUTUAL FRIEND** introduced me to Anna and after learning she and I had some similar experiences, we talked about getting together. Her home is sixty miles from mine, so it was nearly a year before we could arrange it. She called early on a Sunday to see if I would mind driving over that afternoon. She gave me her address and the directions I could follow when I got to her town. But when I arrived at the house that was supposed to be hers, there was a different name on a plaque by the door. No one was home, so I went on, wondering how I could find her house. She had called my land line and I had not thought to put her number in my cell, or I'd have called her. I drove around awhile and was ready to just start for home when I thought about Ron and right then and there I asked him to help me find Anna's house.

A couple of minutes after calling on him, I turned onto another street, just as a car coming from the opposite direction pulled up to the stop sign. The woman driver waved at me as I drove past, but I didn't think anything of it. If I thought at all, I probably just figured she'd mistaken me for someone else, as I knew no one in this town, except Anna—and I didn't really know her, having met her only briefly that one time, now nearly a year ago.

At the end of the street, I looked in my rearview mirror and the woman's car was still there at the stop sign. This street was a dead end, so I turned around to start back up the street and I saw her make a U-turn, which was illegal there at that stop sign, and start down the street toward me. She slowed to a crawl, and I saw she had her window down and was looking at me, so I assumed she was going to ask me about something, or maybe she thought she knew me, as she had waved to me. So, I stopped, and she did too. I lowered my window, expecting her to ask me something, but she didn't. She just looked at me and smiled. She was a slender, smallish woman, maybe in her seventies with white hair. As I'd seen Anna only briefly, I didn't recall much of her appearance or size, but I did think she was a bigger woman, younger, and with dark hair. However, because I could think of no other reason why this woman was looking at me as if expecting something from me, I thought maybe she was Anna. Maybe she was older than I remembered, and she could have been coloring her hair. I also thought that maybe she'd somehow picked up on the fact that I was lost and had come to look for me. Of course, she probably didn't remember what I looked like either. Anyway, I said to this woman, "Are you Anna?" She smiled and said, "No," and gave me her name, but even as she told me a first and last name, I didn't retain it past the telling. She then added that she lived over there and waved her arm in, I assume, the general direction of where she lived, and that it was next door to Virginia somebody, I didn't get that last name either, but it wouldn't have meant anything to me anyway for I didn't know anyone in this town.

Then after establishing herself as a resident, she just sat there and smiled at me, like before. So I told her I was looking for that Anna and gave her full name and the address she had given me, but I told her that it was the wrong address and it had led me to another house. Now, the woman had just told me she didn't know Anna, and I'd told her that the address I was given wasn't the right address, but she started to tell me how to get to Anna's home anyway. That was odd, but it only seemed odd later— much later. Then she changed her mind and said, "I'll just go down and turn around and come back up and lead you to Anna's house." So when she turned around and came back up the street and pulled in front of me, I followed her, and she led me directly to the right house, slowing down as she approached it and then she stopped and stuck her arm out and waved toward the house. I wish I had watched her go to see if she disappeared or drove on down the street. But I was then still unsuspecting.

I parked in front of Anna's two-car garage and then it hit me as to how odd that whole encounter had been, and suddenly I *knew*, and I said out loud, "Ron! *You* sent her, didn't you! And she was an *angel*!" I sat there in Anna's driveway and went over that whole event, and I knew it only made sense if she was an angel sent by Ron in a direct response to my plea. In that context, the encounter made perfect sense. Otherwise, it made no sense at all. To me, it even fell outside of the realm of coincidence. For she had driven straight to Anna's home even though she told me she didn't know Anna, and the address I was given was wrong, so how did she know who Anna was and where she lived?

I apologized to Anna for being late. I told her that I got lost, but I didn't mention my mysterious helper. She apologized for giving me the wrong address. I never really got an explanation, just a lot of how sorry she was. I wonder if she had given me a former address without realizing it. As we visited, we didn't seem to connect at all, and she told me she would soon be moving away. I wondered if she was having memory problems, hence the wrong home address. I am sorry for her if she was having memory problems, but I was blessed to have had that angel encounter, thanks to Ron.

When I told my daughter Kelly that I believed her dad had sent me that woman and that she was an angel, I added, "But how does an angel get a car?" She laughed. "Well, Mom, I imagine, only you saw her and the car. If anyone else had been there, they might have just seen you and your car." I had to laugh at the picture that made in my head. Me just sitting in my car midway on that street, the window down and talking to no one. It was then that I realized no other cars had turned down that street. Of course, it was a dead end and a Sunday too, so it wouldn't have had much if any traffic. When I told Ronnie about it, he said it was too bad I didn't get those names because then I could check and see if those women really lived there. That's probably why I didn't retain the names, for it's likely the angel set it up to let me think she was a resident, so her presence would appear normal—at least for the time she was with me. Only later would I realize that *normal* didn't quite fit the situation.

There are lots of stories about angels coming to our rescue. Years ago, one such angel helped Kandy when she had car trouble. She was headed for work one morning when her car stalled at the top of a two-lane overpass. Cars whizzing past her, the overpass closely monitored by guard rails, there was no place for anyone to turn out and come to her aid and no place to walk. There was a parking area at the bottom of the overpass, and she wondered if she could push her car down into that parking area. But as she opened the door to step out, a voice from behind her said, "Stay in the car and steer, and I'll push." She jerked around to look back and saw a man standing there. *Where had he come from? There was no car behind hers.* "But, she said, "I wasted no time in speculation, and with me steering and him pushing, the car rolled down that incline and into the parking area."

She said she looked in her rearview mirror then and waved, and he waved back and then he stepped out from behind her car and said, "It will be okay now." She saw him turn and start to walk away and got out of the car and hurried around to call her thanks to him, but he was nowhere in sight. She said there were only a few cars in the parking lot, and she had a clear view in all directions. She knew there was no way he could have disappeared in that small span of time unless he was an angel. Her car started right up, but she did have to get a different one a short time later. She remembers him as being Hispanic, but didn't have an accent, and he wore a plaid shirt. She said she saw his facial features clearly while he was helping her, but later, she only had a kind of hazy image of his face and could no longer remember any of the colors of his shirt. She calls him her angel in the plaid shirt. Indeed, there seems no other plausible explanation.

Sometimes angels visit and we know they are angels, especially if we are kids. Kids seem more connected to the spirit world than adults. One of the nearly two hundred stories I've collected over the years, mostly from people I know, or from people who know people I know, was about this little girl of six or seven who one day burst into the kitchen where her mother was fixing dinner and said, "Mom!" Come quick, there's an angel in my room!" Mom, being busy as moms often are, suggested she go back and look again. She did and soon came running back. Yes! He was still there. So, her mom wiped her hands on a towel and followed her daughter into her room. "Isn't he beautiful?" said the little girl, looking to where she obviously could see him. Her mother looked but she saw nothing out of the ordinary, let alone an angel.

One Halloween this same little girl wanted to be a princess, so her mother made her a princess dress and then they went shopping for a gold crown, but no crown could be found. With only one store left to search, her mother was doubtful, but this store did have a crown, a single gold crown on a top shelf in the back of the store. Her mother was delighted, but the little girl was frowning. Just yesterday, her best friend had also decided to be a princess, so she'd told her they'd get her a crown too. "I'm sorry," her mother said, "But there are no more crowns." Then, her mother looked up at that high shelf again, and there was another gold crown. The work of an angel? I suspect so.

Some years ago, Sally was having trouble deciding whether she should keep her job as an RN at the local hospital or move out of state where she thought she would like to live and get a job at a hospital there. One day, still undecided, she took a basket of soiled clothes to the local laundromat and proceeded to stuff them in one of the washing machines. There was no one else in the building, or so she thought, but as she turned away from the washing machine, she saw an old man sitting on a chair nearby. She should have heard him come in, as there was no one else in the place and no other machines in use. The man did not have any laundry with him, so she assumed he was there just to rest a bit. Somehow, they started talking and she told him about her indecision. He listened and asked questions, but he did not give advice. When the washing machine stopped, she went over and took the clothes out and put them in the dryer and then turned to continue her visit with the old man. But he was no longer there, and at that moment, she knew what she would do, her decision was made. Later, she thought about how he was just suddenly there on that chair and how he had just as suddenly disappeared, and she knew he was an angel.

Esther told me about her nephew who was riding his motorcycle across the country and was in the Mojave Desert when he realized he was dangerously low on water. He rode on, knowing he was in serious trouble. Then a man on a motorcycle appeared. "Just out of nowhere," the nephew told her. The man handed him a container of water, saying something like, "Looks like you could use this." After he drank the water, the man gave him some more to take with him, and then got on his motorcycle and rode off. The nephew saw him go and then both man and motorcycle just simply disappeared.

I sent a friend a photo of an angel cloud that another friend had taken one evening near Christmas as the winter sun was setting. A kind of dark filmy formation against a blue sky, it looked for all the world like an angel flying over the town. The Christmas lights were on, and the angel's arm was outstretched, and it looked as if she was lighting one of them. I sent a copy of the photo via email to a friend whose husband had passed and wrote, *Remembering you tomorrow on Adam's birthday.*

I was confused, as I thought her husband had passed in April and his birthday was in December. But it was the other way around. This was her reply:"Wow! Adam's first birthday in Heaven! Is there such a thing as coincidence? Well, sometimes, I suppose, but not in this case. I love it! It gave me goose bumps. So now a light that went on by itself, a flower blooming in the snow, and an angel picture!" She'd told me about the lights that kept going off and on in those early days of his passing, just as I had experienced after Ron passed. She had also told me about the flower that had bloomed in the snow, like the daffodil Ron had bloom a week after he passed for my artist friend and also for me. The angel picture was taken with a camera that dates the photos. I looked again at the photo and saw what I had not noticed before. It was dated the day her husband passed. Amazing!

Libby and her daughter recently returned from New York City with this story to tell. "We wanted to go to Battery Park and see the Statue of Liberty, but we took the wrong bus and ended up in a rough part of the city and we were totally lost and a little scared as well. A few minutes before, a bus had come by, but the driver said he was at the end of his shift. He assured us another bus would soon be there."

So they waited, their nerves getting a little more on edge as the minutes ticked by. Then they saw a policeman cross the street and come toward them. When they explained their situation, he told them he'd wait with them until the bus arrived. Libby said as they were getting on the bus, she saw through one of the windows, their policeman standing there. She looked away for a second, looked back, and he was gone. Later, although she thought he was about thirty years old, she no longer remembered his face and he had disappeared from that bus stop so fast. A little too fast. Then it dawned on her that she and her daughter had surely been in the company of an angel.

These experiences, mine included, seem to point to a need, at times, for an angel to help us through some difficulty. I wonder though, if the angel who comes to us is our guardian angel, the one Jesus in Matthew 18:10 said was assigned to us at birth. The Bible isn't totally clear on that, unless I'm missing something. In that scripture, Jesus says, "See that you do not despise one of these little ones, for I say to you that their angels in heaven continually see the face of my father who is in heaven."

So, in defining the worth, the value of children, He said that each of them has an angel assigned to them. Does that mean the angel stays with us to the end of our life, or do they leave us at say, eighteen or twenty-one? And if when we are adults and if we no longer have a guardian angel, then when God, Jesus, or a passed loved one sees a need, do they just call on the next available one to help us?

While the pages of the Bible are filled with angelic activity, there doesn't seem to be a direct answer. But, the Bible does say in Psalms 91:11, "For He shall give His angels charge over thee in all ways."

CHAPTER 30

# QUARANTINE, JAX, PAPA, AND COOPER

**SEPTEMBER 7, 2020. THIS** would have been Ron's eighty-eighth birthday and Kelly came to spend the afternoon with me and brought me a special gift. She is quite artistic and has done some neat drawings and paintings, and her gift for me was a painting of the cardinal I saw that day at the park. The cardinal that stayed and stayed, never moving, his eyes seeming to be totally fixed on me. I knew Ron had sent him. I'd told her the story and sent her a picture of the creek and the trees and asked if someday she would paint it for me with the cardinal in one of the trees, but I'd forgotten I'd asked her. She said it had just come to her last night and so she'd stayed up late and painted it, wondering if her dad might have prompted her to do so. If he had, she probably wished he would have done it a day or two sooner. She also brought me the molded form of a big, fat red cardinal that had sat in her bookcase for years, and lately I'd begun to covet it. I didn't know she knew and maybe she didn't, but I bet her dad did. It sits on my kitchen counter and keeps an eye on me. Kind of like that cardinal at the park. My other three kids and the grandkids also acknowledged Ron's birthday, each in their own way.

The Sunday afternoon before, I had invited a friend over to watch a movie. She called five days later to tell me she had Covid, so I'd have to be in quarantine. At that time, the recommended time was fourteen days. Since it had already been five days, I hoped I could just do the nine. I'd had a mammogram at the hospital earlier that day and my temp was normal, so it should be okay just to finish out the next nine days. I'd check with County Health.

I had one day left in quarantine when I walked into the living room and on TV, running at the bottom of the screen, was a notice that the Center for Disease Control advocated getting tested when the quarantine ends, to be sure you weren't a carrier.

I had talked to my friend that day. She'd been quite ill but was now feeling better. She said she'd had some dizzy spells at the beginning of her illness, which reminded me that I'd had some dizzy spells the day before. Only a few and only lasting a few seconds, although one might have lasted a minute or two. I'd even laid down on the bed for that one. Then she told me about her next-door neighbor who said she had a relative who was a carrier and had unknowingly infected several people with Covid. *Coincidence, or what?* I called County Health, and they sent me to the hospital to get tested. However, for some reason not exactly clear to me, I could not get tested. I called County Health again and they said to be sure, I'd need to stay in quarantine ten more days. So, I did. Which turned out to be just what I needed, for on day one of that second quarantine, I started again on this book and this time I would finish the task. I wrote every day until I arrived at the beginning of the last chapter and then I had a mini breakdown, but Ron soon got me back on track again.

On September 18, Ronnie was keeping his little grandson, Jax, who was then just shy of two years old, and they were outside in the yard when a monarch butterfly flew over and landed in the grass in front of Jax. "Look," Ronnie said, "A butterfly." Jax pointed at it and said, in a happy voice, "Papa!" Jax calls Ronnie "Papa" just as our grandkids had called Ron, but Jax wasn't pointing at him, and the only explanation that fit, Ronnie said, "was that he was seeing my dad, the other 'Papa,' there with the butterfly."

When Ronnie told me, I thought of that dream when Jax was born, the dream when Ron showed me that he and our new great-grandson had known each other in Heaven, and I thought, *they still do.*

A few days later, Ronnie told Jordyn about her little son and the butterfly. She told him that just a week or so before Jax had seen a picture taken at their wedding of Ron and I, her Papa and Meme, standing with her and Brandyn, and he had pointed to Ron and said, "Papa." And no one had ever told him about this Papa.

Shortly after the butterfly event, I had Ronnie, Michele, Ally, John, Jordyn, Brandyn, and Jax over for dinner. Ally took Jax into my office and showed him photos of Ron. She'd hold them out to him and say, "Who's this?" and he'd say, "Papa," every time and without hesitation. Since then, I've shown him photos of Ron from age twenty-three through eighty-five and he knows they are all of Papa.

I was keeping Jax a few months later, in January of 2021, and we were in my office looking at funny videos on the computer. I've saved the ones he likes, and I was sitting in my swivel office chair with him on my lap while we watched one about a fox diving headfirst into deep snow in search of field mice. Jax was totally intent on that fox when suddenly he jerked his head up and over to look at the wall beside a bookcase, just a few feet from where we sat, and called out in a loud, happy voice, "Papa!" Then he slid off my lap and ran over to look up at the space between the copier and the bookcase as if someone were standing there, but all I could see was the wall. Again he said, "Papa!" Then, as if Ron had squatted down closer to his level, Jax lowered his gaze and stood there a second or two looking as if seeing him there and Ron was engaging him in some way. He then turned to the bookcase and picked up a 4x6 unframed photo of Ron and me that was stuck at the bottom of a larger framed photo of us. Holding it in his little hands, he looked up at me and said, "Papa." Then he looked back at the photo and up at me again and said, "And Meme." We stood there a little while, then seeing the moment was over, I took the picture and stuck it back in the larger framed photo and we went back to the computer. Because they can't stay very long, I think Ron used the picture of us to divert Jax's attention from him. I don't believe Jax would have picked it up on his own, for he pays no attention to those photos he's shown, except when asked to identify Papa. I absolutely knew Ron had been there, but I still wish I had asked Jax.

Later that summer of 2021 was an exception to what I wrote about Jax paying no mind to the photos of Ron in my home unless we call his attention to them. He was with me today and we were on the computer again, watching another video he likes, when he paused, looked over at the photo in the bookcase of Ron and me, the one he'd picked up and held that day the previous March, and said softly and sweetly, drawing out the word, "Papa."

Now, it is two years later and as I am editing this chapter, I think of the other day when little Jax, now two months shy of four years old, was here and he looked up at a family picture of some ten years ago and said, "That's Meme's Papa." And he was talking about Ron being mine. And I wondered how he knew that.

As I've stated before, young children seem to be more aware of the presence of those in the spirit world than adults. I have no doubt that Jax knows Ron, this *Papa* who passed months before he was born and who sent me the dream the night Jax came into our world, and that they knew each other in Heaven. I recall that other little boy who looked up from his play to tell his grandmother that he knew her before he was born.

In visiting with a man just the other day, I shared a "Ron Story" with him, and he had a story to tell of when he was a little boy and had an imaginary friend. One day he and his parents went to visit his widowed grandma who lived in another town. While he was there, he saw a picture of his imaginary friend and asked his grandma where she got that picture. "Why, that's a picture of your grandpa," she said.

It amazes me the many stories of children who see God, Jesus, angels, and passed loved ones. Even some who have had no exposure to Christianity at all. The artist Akaine Kramerik was just four years old when she said to her then nonbelieving parents, "Today, I met God." Soon she began her painting, saying to her parents, "God teaches me to paint." By age eight she had created the beautiful, now famous painting of Jesus, titled "Prince of Peace: The Resurrection."

A woman named Gail was worried about a situation her granddaughter was caught up in. When she saw the painting "Prince of Peace: The Resurrection," she ordered a book about it. Knowing there was little she could do for her granddaughter but pray, she decided to pray for the child at a certain time every day for forty days. Then she printed a small copy of that painting of Jesus and took a same size copy of a picture of her granddaughter and glued them together back-to-back. Each day, the combined photos in hand, she prayed. At the end of that forty days, she took the connected photos to a small stream near her home, asked Jesus to watch over her granddaughter, and then laid them in the water. The combined photos floated over to the opposite bank and stopped, then Jesus's photo curled around her granddaughter's and there it stayed. Gail said she felt that Jesus had heard her prayers and that curling of his picture around her granddaughter's was a sign that she was in his care and keeping. After a while she went over to the opposite bank and gently moved them out to the middle of the stream, and they floated away. She told me the situation slowly began to improve after that.

When I read that book, written in 2006 by Akiane and Foreli Kramarik and simply titled *Akiane*, I was caught by the words that small girl had said after she told her mother that she had met God that day. "What is God?" her mother asked. "God is light—warm and good. It knows everything and talks with me. It is my parent."

One Sunday, some years before she became Ron's and my daughter-in-law, Michele and her children were in church when Elyse, the eldest daughter, then about five, leaned over and whispered to her mother that there was an angel standing behind the choir. Michele looked, but all she saw were the choir members. "Where?" she whispered to her daughter. "Just behind Bridgit," she said. Michele looked, but still she saw no sign of an angel. Bridgit is our niece. Her father is Larry, Ron's brother.

Bridgit was delighted when I told her that story and then shared with me a time after her dad had passed when she was going through a really difficult time. That day, alone in the house, and feeling so hopeless, so miserable, she was lying on the floor, sobbing and praying for some relief in the situation when she heard the creak of the back door opening. She looked up and saw her dad standing there. "He didn't say anything," she said, "And in seconds he vanished, but I knew he had come to comfort me. Maybe even to let me know that in time everything would be okay."

In July of 2021 I asked for a sign of confirmation from Ron, and I asked that the sign be a cardinal. Then, I said, "No. Not a cardinal." I wanted a sign I could be certain was from him, and so I decided on a dime. First, I said a brand-new shiny dime, then I said, "No, just any ol' dime will do."

Every night, after I write in my diary and pray to God and Jesus, I talk to Ron. I stand before the old antique wardrobe I have in my bedroom where I've set a small oval-framed photo of Ron's face, the bottle of Old Spice he didn't finish using on one side and the plastic figure of a cardinal on the other. First, I pick up the bottle of Old Spice and remove the cap for a whiff of that old familiar scent, then recap it, set it back and pick up the picture of Ron in the oval frame and holding it, I talk to him, remind him of my love, and then I kiss him goodnight. But, this night, as I reached for the bottle of Old Spice, I barely touched it when it fell over, bumped the picture frame, and it too fell over, and there where the picture had sat was a dime—a 1976 dime, the date holding no special meaning for me, so it was just any ol' dime.

There was no way that dime could be there, unless someone put it there, and I was the only one in the house. It had to have been from Ron, in direct response to my request, and he must have agreed with me. Later, although I knew it was from Ron, I tried to reenact that situation, but the Old Spice bottle wouldn't fall over with just a touch. It had to be pushed quite hard and then it only hit the photo once out of several tries and even then, it only pushed it aside a little, but not enough to show the dime. This had been too precise, too perfect. It had to have been Ron—besides it was exactly what I had asked him for.

In 1993, I served as chairman of our church's centennial committee and received a music box as a thank you gift from the church at the Saturday evening banquet. In the shape of a church, it has a key on the back that needs to be wound manually to play its song, "Amazing Grace." I've had this music box all these years, and when I moved to this duplex, I may have turned the key on the back to play the song one time before putting it in the bookcase I have in my bedroom, but I was sure I hadn't since. On the last day of July, a few weeks after Ron had left me the dime, I was selecting a few items to take to the thrift shop and while in the bedroom, I noticed the music box and wondered if I really wanted to keep it anymore. I picked it up and held it in my hands, then I looked up at one of the pictures of Ron on the wall in my bedroom and said, "What do you think?" Should I, or shouldn't I? Immediately, it began to play its song. It played a few seconds and stopped. Startled, I turned it over and up and around, but it never played another note. That is until I turned the key on the back. I laughed and told Ron I would keep it forever.

When I told Kelly, she said that when her husband's mother, Betty, passed, the evening after the funeral, family and friends had gone home and Alex, her father-in-law, now alone in the house, was suddenly startled to hear Betty's music box begin to play. Some years later, when Alex was going to marry again, Betty came to Kelly in a dream and told her it was all right with her.

Jordyn and Brandyn gave us our second little great-grandson, a sweet little six pound bundle of joy on August 17, 2021, named Cooper Dean. There was no dream this time, of course, for Cooper arrived in the afternoon. Even so, we know from the dream Ron sent when Jax was born, that Cooper came from that world where Ron now resides. I talked to Ron about this new little guy, about how I knew he was around Cooper, just as I know he's around Jax, and I smiled to think of that day when this little guy would start talking. I then wondered if one day he'll look at those same photos of Ron, and when we ask, he'll say, "Papa." It struck me then that maybe he was with his other great granddaddy, Brandyn's grandpa, and it will be the photos of *that* paternal great grandpa he will recognize.

November 21 was Jax's birthday party. He had been sick on his birthday, so the party had been postponed until today. I had purchased his gift and a bright blue gift bag to put it in and had put it away when the party was postponed. Now as I got his gift and the gift bag out, I realized I had not thought to buy some tissue paper to stuff in the top of the gift bag.

I looked in the box where I keep my gift wrap and ribbon, but the only tissue in there was green. So, I thought I'd need to stop at the store on the way to the party. It would probably make me late, but not by much. Then, no thought in my head at all, I walked over to a closet where I keep picture frames, candles, boxes of old slides, DVDs, VCR tapes, and other similar items, opened the door, and there, on the middle shelf on the top of a box of DVDs, in plain sight, was one sheet of light blue tissue paper—exactly what I needed. "Thanks, Ron!" I said, "I know you don't want me to be late." Then I tucked the tissue in the gift bag and went to the party. When I told Ronnie, he said, "Dad would do that for you and Jax." Kelly said, "Dad's still looking out for you." Kandy added, "He's still hurrying you along, isn't he?"

I had been in that closet just a day or so before and I know there was no tissue paper of any color in there. Then, one sheet of light blue, just exactly what I needed appears? Of course it was Ron.

# CHAPTER 31

# OUR SONG AND THE ANGEL BOY

**I WOKE THE** morning of January 26, 2022 with just this last chapter to write, but I had not slept well, waking often, worrying about the story, and I wanted only to stay in bed and try to sleep the day away. Finally, I dragged myself out of bed and into the kitchen, took my pills, stuffed a piece of toast down my throat, went into the living room, and dropped down in my recliner. There I spent the rest of the morning, staring at the TV and dozing off and on. Every hour or so, I'd look up at the photo of Ron on the wall and whine to him about being tired, and each time I would promise that soon I would get up and get to work—maybe when this program was over.

Then it was midafternoon, and I was still in pajamas and robe, my hair resembling the proverbial rat's nest, and I continued to stare at the TV and try to calm my worries about the book. Here I was about to tell the world, or a part of it anyway, that I hear voices, have out-of- body experiences, and so on. I had not had one of those bouts of anxiety for some time, but today, nearly to the finish line, and with push about to come to shove, I was plagued with doubt. Did I do a good job? Could I have done better? Would my family like it? Would I get a good publisher if I did get it published? Would a vital sentence be inadvertently dropped out, as it had been about my siblings in that article about my dad years ago? I kept looking at that picture of Ron on the wall and telling him that soon I'd get up and get to work. Now, though, I was thinking that I would wait until tomorrow. Maybe I'd feel better then.

I knew I shouldn't be worried, for I was certain Ron wouldn't let me fail, at least I'd been certain until then. With this chapter I would cross the finish line and what would be, would be. There would be no other day, no other week, no other month; except for this last chapter, my time had run out. I knew I needed to get up and get with it and what happens after that, I could worry about later. But I had one more way to drag my feet a little while longer.

I looked up at Ron again and said, "Okay! I'm getting up, but first I want Alexa to play our song. As I mentioned in the Big Dream, back in our dating days we had chosen "our song." Probably neither one of us had thought about it more than a few times over those sixty-two years we were married. But since Ron passed I have resurrected it and every now and then, I ask my Amazon Alexa to play our song. So that afternoon, I said to Alexa, "Play 'Hold My Hand' by Don Cornell." She answered, saying, "Here's 'Hold My Hand' by Don Cornell on Amazon music." But nothing happened. Or so, I thought.

"Oh, what the heck," I muttered and got up to go take a shower and get dressed. I got out of my robe and pajamas and was ready to turn on the water when the phone rang. So, I went in my all-together to answer it. It was Kelly, who lives sixty miles away. She said, "Mom, did you ask Alexa to play yours and Dad's song?" I told her I had, but nothing happened. She said, "Yes, it did. It played here." I laughed and mentally said, *okay, Ron, I got the message.* So, I got my robe, and told Kelly the story. I told her I knew it was her dad, saying in jest, "Oh, sure, Eun. Then it'll be another excuse."

I knew it had to be Ron's doing and I loved it! There was no other explanation. Like all his messages and signs, this one too, was perfect. He had it go to Kelly, who is retired and who he knew was at home, because he knows everything, and who, knowing it was our song, would call me about it. I loved it! He always was so darn creative.

One afternoon about a month later, little Jax came over to play with me. While he was here, he gave me further proof that he knows his Papa in Heaven. That day, too cold to play outside, we were in the office coloring and cutting and pasting, when I remembered a book I'd been meaning to look at again. It was in a bookcase in the office, stuck behind a framed photo of Ron taken two years before he passed. We had used that picture for the folder handed out at the funeral. It wasn't one we'd ever shown Jax and it's on a shelf at my eye level, so a little high for a three-year-old, but he might have noticed it. I didn't even think about asking him that day as I went over, picked up the photo and held it while I pulled out the book I wanted. When I set the photo back on the shelf, Jax, who had been watching me, said, as I turned back to him, his eyes on the photo, "That's Papa."

One March afternoon a few weeks later, I was sitting in my recliner, my feet up sort of watching TV, but kind of drifting, too. Usually, I kick off my shoes, but I hadn't yet. Then for a second, I felt the toes on my right foot being squeezed through my shoes. It startled me and for a moment I was stunned. *Had it really happened! Had someone really squeezed my toes?* But I had felt it. It was as real as if someone in the room had squeezed them, and I was the only one in the house. I knew then it had to be Ron. He had stopped by to give me a little love squeeze and I laughed and called out to him, telling him I loved that little squeeze. It was such a sweet endearing gesture.

The following is a Ron intervention story from some time ago that I couldn't fit into the story before, but it's too good not to share. One afternoon, worried about a particular situation, I was tipped back in my recliner watching TV, when I fell asleep and dreamed about a hog, an enormous gray hog with dark gray and white spots. I'll skip the details, but suffice to say it was an emotional dream, and I woke to find Ron, in shadowy form, standing there beside my chair looking down at me a second or two before he vanished. I always write down everything that I know is from him, and so I muted the TV and went into my office to type up the dream. From my computer, I can still see about half of the large screen TV in the living room, needing only to lean forward a little to see the entire screen. As I was typing, a flicker of something on the TV screen caught my eye. I leaned forward and saw the head and shoulders of an enormous hog, that same hog that had been in my dream, now filled the screen. Then he vanished and a program about people showing their prize-winning dogs was playing.

I know Ron superimposed that hog's image on the screen. There was a definite point to that dream, and I knew exactly what he was telling me, and I knew he had given me the dream to spur me into action, and it did. Right away some changes were made, and the situation began to improve.

On May 17, 2022, I got a haircut at this beauty shop I've been going to for years. My friend and owner of the shop, with whom I've shared many of my Ron stories, asked if I had any new ones. I didn't and said, "No, not lately." After she finished with her clients that day, she and her daughter were going to give the shop a thorough cleaning. Two hours after I left, I got a call from her.

They had pulled out one of the bulky hair dryers to clean behind it and there on the floor, where the chair had been, was one of the programs handed out at Ron's funeral with the order of the service inside and his picture on the cover, the picture Jax saw me take out of the bookcase last February. Nearly four and a half years had passed since his funeral, and I wondered if it had been under that hair dryer all that time. I could see how every time they'd pulled out the chair to clean, the folder could have slid out with it. Except, this time it didn't. So, was this Ron's doing? Did he, when he heard me say "No, not lately" decide to change that no to a yes?

I was told the program had some lint and dust on it as though it had been under the chair a long time. It's certain Ron knew it was there, so maybe this was another sign from him. I think of all those times I had my hair cut and I never knew it was under that chair. Or was it? Did Ron, hearing our talk, decide to plant it there for them to find when they cleaned that afternoon? If so, he could have picked up one of the copies from my office where I have some in a drawer, along with his memorial book, or he could have just pulled one out of his file at the funeral home. He could then have swished it in a little dust and lint as he stuck it under the chair for them to find. Only Ron knows which it was. I can only speculate.

After church on July 21, 2022, two of my friends and I stayed, standing at the back of the now empty sanctuary to visit for a while. Then a little boy, about five years old, came in and over to where we were talking. He stopped a few feet away and stood there looking up at me with a big smile on his face. I didn't know him and had no idea which family he belonged to, and I was sure he didn't know me either. When he continued to look up at me with this happy, and (I'd swear on the Bible) "Let's play" look, I acknowledged him and asked if he needed something. He didn't answer, just looked at me, still with that playful look, and then he darted away and out the door at the back of the sanctuary. I turned back to my friends, and then he was back, just like before, grinning up at me with that same playful look on his face—like a puppy dog joyfully wagging its tail. So, I stepped toward him, and he backed up, still grinning, and as I moved closer, he stopped and in a stance that suggested he was about to take off running, and still looking at me, he began to weave from side to side as if teasing me about which way he was going to run. I got it then. He wanted me to play with him, to chase him around the sanctuary and so I laughed and chased after him and when we got near the door at the back of the sanctuary, he ran out and down the hall to where some people appeared to be waiting for him and as he joined them, I went back to my friends.

I don't remember having any thoughts about it the rest of the day and I had dinner with one of the women that evening and I slept well all night. I don't even remember dreaming. When I woke up the next morning, Monday, August 1, I still didn't think about it. It was as if it had completely slipped my memory. Then suddenly, about midafternoon, I remembered it all and I was caught between amazed and horrified. For to think I'd been chasing a little boy around in the sanctuary yesterday was crazy and not to realize it until now, was even crazier.

In thinking about how weird that whole encounter had been, I did not at first attribute it to Ron. That little boy coming up to me, a woman he didn't know, and wanting me to chase him, to play with him. And me, a grown-up, chasing after him in the sanctuary—not just the church, but the holiest part of the church, the sanctuary, for gosh sakes. I remember that when I went back to my friends, they didn't say anything about me going off to play with the boy and no way could they have missed seeing that. But, as I wrote in earlier chapters about those out-of-body experiences, those with me see nothing unusual and I appear to still be there with them all that time. So, it must have been an out-of-body experience and it had happened in the church on Sunday, but why did I not remember it until now?

Then I thought of Ron. Had he sent that little boy to play with me, and was he an angel? But, why? It had seemed totally real, like those other out-of-body experiences. Except I didn't go anywhere as I've always done before, the little boy came to me. And when I came back from those other ones, I knew what had happened and why. This one, if it happened on Sunday I should have remembered it then, not Monday afternoon. Why did I not remember until then? I had to know, so I called one of the friends who had stood with me and the other friend in the sanctuary, the one who had invited me over for dinner at her home that Sunday evening. No, she had noticed nothing unusual and had not seen any little boy, let alone me chasing him.

On Saturday, before that experience with the little boy in the church, I had decided to end this book with Ron's funeral program being found in the beauty shop last May, for in a way it was a kind of ending. It was when Ron passed that he began to send me all those messages that eventually led to me writing this book, so now finding his funeral program could signify the end of the story, making it, in a way, come full circle. So, I was prepared on Monday to take the manuscript to the local print shop to have them make a few proof books for the editing process.

Then that episode with the little boy happened. My memory says it was Sunday but was it? I finally decided it was from Ron and it was an out-of-body that probably happened that afternoon on Monday, and it took me back to that Sunday morning where I'd stood with my friends. It had to have been an out-of-body experience, so time and place can be anywhere—any time. Later, talking to my friend again, she told me then that I'd said when I called her before, "Well, whatever it was, it's a perfect ending to my story."

I didn't remember saying it and I still don't. But it was then that I understood. When I thought that finding Ron's funeral program had brought the story full circle, and as far as the book was concerned, it had. But this memoir had begun with my first premonition. I was a child of five and was suddenly thrust into a world of terrible loss and fear, beginning with that premonition that my daddy would leave us. That continued through his death and my mother's breakdown, leading to the panic attacks and fainting spells. It was the out-of-body experience years later that finally set me free.

Now, these many years later, in a kind of rerun, a little, laughing boy—an angel boy, I guess—is coaxing me to run and play with him, and I run after him, as if I am indeed a child again, happy and carefree as all little children should be. And that's what really brings me and my story full circle. I like to think that the setting, planned by Ron, the sanctuary where I played with that little boy, was also symbolic of the story having God's blessing.

Now only the publishing is left and only Ron knows when that will be, and with what publisher. I'm also certain he will be with me throughout that process, and for however long I am to be here. Then one day my love will come and part that thin veil, holding it open for me to step through and into that amazing world beyond.

# EPILOGUE
# IT HAPPENS EVERY DAY

**AS I WAS** writing this book, I thought about all the people all over the world with many different belief systems, races, and cultures, who leave this earth and take up residence in the afterlife. So where do they go? Is it possible we all go to the same place? If so, I'd think it would have to be to different sections. Just like we'd want to go to where our loved ones are, not to strangers who came up from China or maybe the South of France. Nor would they like landing in the midst of us and our passed loved ones. Just thinking of the enormous job it would be to get everyone all over the world in the right section of Heaven boggles my mind. Thankfully, it's all in God's hands. He created the world and all that is in it, so it's probably no big deal for Him. Besides He's been doing this for a very, very long time.

In 1975, Ron spent six weeks in India as the leader of a Rotary group study exchange team. Among those he encountered was a Catholic sister who believed her life's work was converting the Hindu people to Christianity, even though it could mean her death. One must honor her devotion to God. I imagine few of us could be so brave for the Lord. I wonder, though, if we believe God created the world and all who dwell therein, is He not the God of all people and might we all end up in the same place? Figuratively speaking, of course. My friend, who had the near-death experience said that Heaven seemed unending, so maybe there is room for us all, no matter where we live in the world. Another friend, who was from an Asian part of the world, was met by

Buddha when she had her near-death experience. He told her it wasn't her time, and he summoned an angel to take her back to her home. We have different cultures and speak different languages, so it makes sense that we all have a different name for God.

A Hindu couple from India visited us sometime after Ron returned home. We talked about their religion and ours. We shared the differences as well as the ways we were alike. They were lovely people. I can't imagine a door in Heaven closed in their faces. They told us the Hindu's have a trinity. The first is Brahma, who they believe is the creator of the universe. The second is Vishnu, the preserver. The third is Shiva, the destroyer, who, when the world gets too bad, will destroy it. Then Brahma, the creator, will rebuild it and Vishnu will then step in and work at preserving this new world. They also have a big flood story.

I suspect that those of different faiths and religions compared to our Christian faith, is like my dad would say, "A horse of a different color, but it's still a horse." I believe we all go to the spirit world by whatever name we call it, but how it all works is beyond my comprehension, and I am sure, the rest of us humans as well. For to know that one would have to be as smart as God. I think of my friend who met Buddha when she had her NDE. Years later she moved to America and was a Christian when she passed, which brings some questions to mind.

I know there are many whose belief system differs widely from mine, but none of us really know how it all works. I like this quote from *The Cowboy and the Cossack* by Clair Huffaker, first published in 1973. "I believe that people who are devoutly religious, within any specific religion, have no true respect for the ultimate vastness that is God."

How can we, mere mortals, limited in so many ways, know the mind and heart of this maker and master of the universe? Even the brightest of those coming out of the seminaries can't hold a candle to God's infinite wisdom and power.

I do so appreciate those who gave me permission to share the following stories, as well as those scattered throughout the memoir.

They validate those of us who have had such experiences and bring comfort to those who have not had contact with a passed loved one, or even thought it was possible. I am sure there is a great number of the world's population, Christian or otherwise, who have received in some manner a message from a passed loved one. I'm also certain that a great many of them have had contact in some manner with God or Jesus, by whatever name they call them, and in those ways have come to believe that there is but a thin veil between us who are earthbound and that world beyond.

It happens every day.

All of the following shared memories are anonymous, the names are fictional, unless the contributor requested I use their true first names.

### THE WHEAT PENNY

Janice's parents passed within a few months of each other and soon she was faced with the sad task of clearing out their house and putting it up for sale. When she and her husband had given away or sold off everything but her parents' personal belongings, they were loading those boxes in the back of their pickup, pushing the boxes across the tail gate and back toward the cab. She picked up the last box and carried it out to the pickup while her husband locked the doors. As she started to set it down, she saw a penny on the tail gate. She pushed the box up next to the rest of the boxes and picked up the penny. It was a wheat penny, and her heart was flooded with joy and tears fell from her eyes. A wheat penny! Somewhere in those boxes they'd carried out and put in the pickup was her father's collection of wheat pennies. She knew without question he had put it there for her to find as a sign that he and her mother were still with her and still loved her.

## A JOYOUS REUNION

Karen had received word that her adult daughter was to be removed from life support and not expected to live more than a few days. She arranged to fly to her daughter's side and was packing her things when suddenly, exhausted and overwhelmed with grief, she dropped down on a chair and immediately saw a vision of her daughter running in joyous abandon toward her grandfather, Karen's deceased father, who was holding out his arms to receive her. Her daughter passed soon after Karen arrived and she held on to that vision, so comforted to know that her father had let her know he'd be there to receive her daughter.

## FROM A WRITER FRIEND'S BLOG

One night, Laurel dreamed that she was with her grandfather at his cabin at the lake and he was getting ready to go fishing. She wanted to go with him, but he said he couldn't take her this time, that he had to go alone. He told her he loved her and when it was time, he'd come back and they'd go fishing together. She woke that morning to find he had passed.

## JESUS KEEPS HIS PROMISE

Over the years, Ed's drinking had led him to become addicted to alcohol and he had grown dreadfully sick of its hold over him. But he could not stop his drinking. He had seen those delirium tremors in others trying to kick their addiction and had known some who had died from alcohol withdrawal, and he feared he was too far into his addiction to survive trying to get sober. Eventually Ed joined Alcohol Anonymous and stayed in it twelve years, but he was never able to stay sober for any length of time. Then one day, sick with despair, he went into his bedroom and, flopping down on his bed, an arm flung over his eyes, he began to sob and beseech the Lord to help him. As he lay there awash in tears of despair, he saw a sudden burst of white light. The walls of the room disappeared, and he saw the form of a man in that still glowing bright light. Amazed, he sat up, his eyes on the form as it came over and sat down on the bed beside him. He saw the bed give way as the figure of light sat down. Then the figure began speaking to him, quoting some scripture and then told Ed that he would not die if he quit drinking if he would just give it over to Him. He would be with him through it all. He would never forsake him. He told Ed that He loved him and would always be with him, so there was no need to fear. Then the bright white light and the figure disappeared, and the walls of the room reappeared. Ed never drank alcohol again and he did not have the delirium tremors or any other adverse reaction. He knew he had been in the presence of Jesus and that He had kept His promise.

### A DAUGHTER BANISHES HER MOTHER'S FEAR

Marsha is a devout Catholic and when her daughter committed suicide, she was devastated. Not only was she mourning the loss of her beloved daughter, but she believed that because her daughter had taken her own life, she was now in purgatory. Several weeks after her daughter passed, she was praying and crying and praying and suddenly her daughter appeared before her in full form, and she was smiling.

"Don't cry, Mama," she said. "I'm fine." Then she vanished.

### A HEADSTONE FOR TRIPLET BABIES

Charlotte was born some years after her mother had given birth to triplet boys in 1926. The three little ones all passed before they were a year old. The boys had never had a headstone and Charlotte decided that even though ninety years had passed, she should get them one. After the stone was set, she went out so see it, and as she walked toward the gravesite, she saw her mother standing by the new stone holding a baby. Then as she drew closer, her mother and the child vanished. Charlotte said, "I know she was thanking me and letting me know that she knew what I had done."

### HER DAD CROSSES OVER

Several weeks after Jennifer's father passed, she dreamed that she and her siblings were sitting around the kitchen table with their dad and mother, as they had done so many times, listening to their dad tell stories of his cowboy days. But this time he was telling them that he had to leave them, that it was time for him to cross over to the other side. This was unusual, as he wasn't a churchgoer, nor did he speak of religious things. Jennifer said that when he spoke of this crossing over, she reached for his hand, and it felt warm and solid, the skin leathery. She even felt the bone structure. Then he got up from the table and walked away, and it seemed that a wall of their kitchen was now gone, and she could see a three-strand barbed-wire fence and beyond the fence, a beautiful scene of fields and mountains, much like the country around their ranch. And as she had seen him do so many times before, he pushed the top wire down a little ways with his hand and swung a leg over the wire and then the other. He had crossed over. She woke then feeling as if he had been there in spirit telling them goodbye. She had at times sensed his presence after he had passed. But after that dream, she never did again.

### A FEATHER AND A FLOCK OF BIRDS

Carol and Marilyn had been close friends since childhood, having grown up in the same neighborhood. Both married local young men, and the two couples remained friends all through their lives. So, when Marilyn passed, Carol was devastated. A few weeks after Marilyn's passing, Carol stepped outside to take the dogs for a walk and noticed a black feather in the yard. She picked it up, wondering if it was from Marilyn. She had heard that feathers were often a sign from passed loved ones. A few minutes later, she and the dogs walked past an old building, and she saw a black bird perched on the roof top. They walked on and the bird flew off the building and over to land in a tree nearby. They walked on and the bird flew to another nearby tree. And so it went, the bird flying along as if keeping up with her and the dogs. When they turned to head back home, a whole flock of black birds flew over and the bird flew away with them. Carol is certain the feather and the bird were both signs from Marilyn, a way of saying "I'm still with you and still your friend." She is also certain that the flock of birds that the bird who had followed her flew off with, symbolized the many friends and family she's with now in Heaven.

### A LETTER FROM GRANDMA

After the feather and the flock of birds, Carol received another message from Marilyn. The feather Carol found in the yard and believed was from Marilyn, she kept in a small vase on a cabinet in the living room. One day, she noticed the feather was no longer in the vase. She pulled out the cabinet to look for it and saw it there on the floor next to an old letter. She picked up both items and was surprised to see that the letter was one her deceased grandmother had written her back in the fifties. Carol keeps all those old family letters in a box on the opposite side of the living room from the cabinet where she'd been keeping the feather, and she'd not opened the box in months, possibly even a year or two. As children, she and Marilyn had often played together at this grandma's house. She believes her friend put that letter there and dropped the feather beside it, so Carol would find it and know that her friend was telling her that she and Carol's grandmother were together in Heaven.

## SOME BEDSIDE VISITS

It appears to be quite common for a loved one who has passed to appear at one's bedside. Sometimes they speak and sometimes their facial expressions speak for them. One woman was anxious about a biopsy she was to have the next day and that night, she tossed and turned, too worried to sleep. Then her deceased mother appeared at her bedside and, although she doesn't remember the exact words, her mother said, in essence, that the lump was benign. Jane was sleeping beside her husband when she suddenly woke and saw her husband's father standing by the bed looking down at his son. Frantically, she reached for her husband, trying to wake him, but before she could get him awake, his father had disappeared. A friend of ours told me that he woke one morning to see his wife standing by his bed smiling down at him, and then she vanished. One woman woke to find her deceased brother standing at the foot of her bed. He told her to stop smoking. She'd been using the nicotine patch, but wasn't quite motivated enough to totally stop, until her brother dropped in from Heaven and that did it.

## AN OLD AUNT'S REASSURANCE

Alan's old aunts, Claire and Esther, had lived together in the family home for years. They had always been totally self-sufficient, and both had declared that they were never going to a nursing home. Eventually though, time caught up with them and when Claire passed, Alan knew Esther could not manage alone. Although both he and his wife were heartsick about it, they put her in the nursing home. Soon after, Alan's wife dreamed that she was at work, when Claire opened the door, stepped inside, looked at her and said, "You did the right thing for Esther." Then she went back out the door and Alan's wife woke up.

### HER EX-HUSBAND'S FATHER

Debra and her husband had divorced several years before his father passed. One night, she dreamed that her ex-father-in-law appeared to her in full form, standing before her, but as a young man in a military uniform and she did not recognize him. "Who are you?" she asked. He told her he was Pete, her ex-husband's father, and he had tried to get his family to see him, but they could not, and so he had come to her. He wanted them to know he was all right. Later, the family showed her a photo of Pete as a young man in a military uniform, and he looked just like the man in Debra's dream.

### HIS HANDS ON HER SHOULDERS

Denise lost both a son and a husband within a few months of each other. She was so devastated that she could barely function and on one of those terrible, awful days, she decided to go to her church, hoping in some way to find even the smallest bit of relief. The church was empty and if the priest was anywhere near, he did not make an appearance. She sat in a back pew and leaned her head on crossed arms on the back of the pew ahead of her and cried until she could cry no more. Then she lifted her head and saw a prayer card on the seat of the pew she'd been leaning on. On it was a photo of a woman sitting in a pew and leaning on crossed arms on the pew ahead of her—the exact same position Denise had been in while she sobbed her heart out. But the woman in the photograph was not alone, for standing behind her, his hands on her shoulders, was Jesus.

### A PASSENGER ON HIS MOTORCYCLE

Shane and a few of his friends enjoyed riding their motorcycles, so much so that when their pal, Lee, passed, he evidently wanted to take one last ride. One day, as Shane was riding his motorcycle, he suddenly realized Lee was sitting behind him. The ride, of course, was short, as

Lee disappeared in a few seconds. Later, one of their other friends told him that Lee had also appeared behind him on his cycle.

## A THUMBS UP, GRANDMA

A friend of mine told me this story about a friend of hers. She said this friend, I'll call her Fran, lost her mother to cancer a few months before Fran's little son turned two and was beginning the potty-training process. The little guy wasn't too cooperative, but his attitude changed one day when she put him on his potty chair and, as usual, closed the lid on her toilet and sat down to read to him from one of his little books. Suddenly, he looked past her and up at the wall behind her and the sudden happy expression on his little face made her twist around and look, but there was nothing there. She turned back to her son, and he was still looking at the wall and still smiling that big happy smile. But now, the little boy was also holding one tiny hand up high and making the "thumbs up" sign. "What are you doing?" she asked, thoroughly puzzled. He dropped his hand and said, "The grandma—who is dead—is behind you and she's doing this to me." Again, he grinned up at the wall and made the thumbs up gesture. I imagine he was soon successfully potty trained.

## SUDDENLY HEALED

Kay told me she used to have fibromyalgia, but one evening, she suddenly felt as if her skin, her whole body was on fire and she hurried to the bathroom to splash water on her face, her arms, and her clothes in an effort to cool down. At last the heat began to fade and finally went away. The next day, she no longer had the aches and pain of her illness and in the years that have passed, it has not come back. She knows God healed her that day.

### TWO DREAM VISITORS

Alice was suffering from cancer, and it was uncertain as to whether she'd survive it, but she took all the treatments and her friends and family prayed and slowly she recovered. Still, even though the doctor told her she had licked the disease, she felt as if she were dangling over a precipice and could go either way. Then one night a friend who'd been killed in an accident appeared to her in a dream and told her that she was fine. Still, she worried. Then some nights later, another friend who had passed appeared in a dream and said, "It's time." She believed the friend meant it was time to stop fretting and get on with your life. It's been some years now and she is still cancer free.

### TWO WOMEN IN THE FLOWER SHOP

Martha worked in a flower and gift shop and one day she was kneeling down, putting some gift items on a low shelf when the door opened, the bell overhead jingling, and a woman walked in. Martha told the woman she'd be with her in a minute, but the woman made no response or even appeared to notice her presence as she walked past her and up to the counter. Martha stood up to go over and wait on the her, but as she took a step, the woman disappeared. She described the woman as having had short white hair and wearing a white shirt or blouse with thin blue stripes and dark blue pants. Another time while Martha worked at that shop, the other woman who also worked there said she saw a woman with dark hair in the shop one day and went over to wait on her and as she approached the woman vanished.

### LITTLE GIRL SEES KYLE'S FRIEND

When Kyle decided she wanted to work in Social Services, she went back to college to get her degree while working part-time and raising a family. She was pregnant with her first child when she was assigned to drive a ten-year-old girl to her foster home. They had not gone far when the little girl said, "You had a friend that died. What was his name?" Surprised, Kyle said, "What are you talking about?" The little girl then said that he was in the car with them, in the front seat beside Kyle and described him by hair and eye color and even the month he had passed. Then she added that he stays around and is always watching to be sure her baby stays safe. Kyle's friend had indeed passed, and the little girl had described him accurately. Later, Kyle would name her child after that friend. I love that Kyle also shared this story on Facebook.

## A BUBBLE OF PROTECTION

Joanne told me this story about the time her husband was seriously ill and was taken by ambulance to Denver. She took care of things at home and then headed for Denver. As she neared the city, the traffic picked up and, not used to city driving and so worried about her husband, she felt like she just couldn't do it. So, she called out to God, asking Him to put her in a bubble of protection all the way to the hospital. The traffic soon thinned and what there was stayed out of her lane, or far enough ahead or behind so as to pose no problem and she made it to the hospital. Now she wondered if she'd be able to find a parking spot in the huge parking garage, several floors high. As she drove in she saw that the very first slot was empty. She wondered if it was reserved for the doctors or other medical personnel but seeing no sign, she pulled in, parked, and thanked God over and over for His protection. Although the bubble was invisible to her, she knew it had been there protecting her all the way. Her husband recovered and was eventually able to come home.

## SHE SEES HER FRIEND PASS IN A DREAM

When Sara worked for a company in Seattle, she became acquainted with Evie, a coworker, and despite some thirty years difference in their ages, they became good friends. A few years after going to work for the company, Sara took her vacation time to visit relatives. While she was away, she dreamed one night that Evie came out of her house wearing a blue dress, got into her car, and suddenly slumped forward over the wheel. Dismissing it as just a dream, she enjoyed the rest of her vacation. Back at the office in Seattle, she learned that Evie had passed, and in the manner she had seen in her dream, even to the blue dress.

### A STAR IN THE SKY

Helen and her longtime companion had split up over some serious differences and soon after his health failed, and he went into a nursing home. Helen worried about him and visited him often, for she knew he was basically a good man who'd made some bad choices. He died a year later. When she heard of his death, she was saddened, but also glad that he was free of his earthly bonds. That afternoon Helen stepped out her back door and saw in the clear blue cloudless sky, a huge, hazy white star. She sat down on a patio chair and watched it, believing it would soon fade away, but it didn't. Finally, she went back inside and checked often to see if it was still there, and it always was. She went back to sit on the patio after dinner and watched it still hanging there in the sky. Then as the sun set and evening's shadows gathered, the star began to fade and when darkness covered the sky, it was gone. Helen believes he sent her that star to let her know he was all right and, perhaps more than that, that he was sorry for his actions that had split them apart.

### A NEW HOME AND A BLESSING

Carolyn and her husband had moved to Kansas because of his job and they had recently purchased a home there from a Mrs. Davis who had moved into a rest home. When the family held a yard sale to dispose of her belongings, Mrs. Davis had requested Carolyn's presence at the sale. Perhaps she had wondered what the young woman might purchase for the home, for when Carolyn bought a mirror and two sconces that had been on the wall in the living room, Mrs. Davis maneuvered her wheelchair over and looking up at her, said, "You like those things, don't you?" About two weeks later, Carolyn hung the mirror and the two sconces in their original places on the wall and when she finished, she looked in the mirror and suddenly felt a hand on her back between her shoulders and for a second or two felt a gentle backrub. Without even a thought, she said, aloud, "It's okay, Mrs. Davis. I promise to take good care of things." Later, that day, her husband came home and told her that Mrs. Davis had passed that afternoon and Carolyn cried.

### A DOG ATTENDS TO GRIEVING PET OWNERS

Scruffy and Buddy were two little dogs who lived side by side and had spent many years playing together outside in each other's yards. Then Scruffy died and a day or so later, Buddy began a nightly ritual that lasted well over a month. Every night at seven o'clock, Buddy went to the door to be let out. He'd then go next door to Scruffy's old home and bark to be let in. He'd stay several hours with them and then he'd go to their door to be let out to go back home.

### THE DOG AND THE DAY OF THE DEAD

The Day of the Dead is a Mexican tradition during which deceased loved ones are honored in a memorial service. Derek, who is White, and Carmen, who is Hispanic, fell in love and married. Early on that Day of the Dead, their first in their own home, Carmen showed her husband how they honored their dead by setting up a display on the mantel of their fireplace. They arranged candles and photos of those who have passed and mementos representing what their loved ones enjoyed in life. Because the grandmother liked a glass of vodka now and then, they poured a little in a glass and set it by her photo. Later that day, they noticed the dog had been sitting there looking up at the display for some time. In fact, he stayed there all day. Throughout the day, they'd literally have to pull him away from the display to take him outside. Afterward, he always wanted to come right back in, and he'd go back over and stare up the mantel again. At bedtime, they blew out the candles in the display and it was then that they noticed only a tiny, tiny bit of vodka remained in the grandmother's glass.

### HER PARENTS DANCE IN HER DREAM

Louise told me that after her mother passed, she often saw her in her dreams. Her mother passed before she and her husband were married, but sometime afterward she dreamed of her wedding and her mother was there. After her father passed, they would appear together in her dreams. In one dream, she and her husband were at a party where there was dancing, and for a few seconds, she saw her parents dancing among the other dancers.

### A LITTLE BOY'S "COOL!"

Frank's sister's son was born with Down Syndrome and passed from the measles when he was five. Frank often visited his sister and her family and always told the little boy about where he lived in the mountains and someday, maybe he could visit him there. That never came to be, but Frank said when he left to go home after the funeral, he felt the little boy's presence in the car and the feeling stayed with him all the way back to his home. When he drove into their driveway, where there was a clear view of the mountains through the windshield, Frank said, "See, those are the mountains I told you about." And he heard the little boy say, "Cool!" After that he no longer felt the child's presence.

## A BEAUTIFUL BLUE HERON

Peggy was born several years after her brother had drowned in the creek one hot summer day when he was seven. She had never known the exact location and now fifty years later, she got the location from the brother who had been with him that fateful day and drove to the creek. The day her brother drowned, a heavy rain had flooded the creek, but this day the water was running slow and shallow, and there, standing in the water was a beautiful Blue Heron. He stood there awhile and then his powerful wings lifted him up and he flew away. And in that moment, Peggy felt that her brother had used that bird to show her the exact place where he had passed.

## HER DECEASED BROTHER DRIVES BY—TWICE

Jenny had just been told she had breast cancer and would be meeting with a cancer doctor in a few days to find out about her treatment. She was worried and anxious, but she tried to stay optimistic. She thought about her brother who had passed a few years before and wondered if she'd soon be seeing him again. The next day, she took her grandkids to school and had just dropped them off when her brother drove by in the car he used to have before he passed, and she heard the words, "You will be okay." Later, she came out of the drug store and got in her car. She was ready to back out when her brother drove by again. And again, she heard the word's that she would be okay, and she was. She finished her cancer treatment and is now cancer free.

## KATE'S DAD HELPS HER OPEN THE GATE

Kate and her husband owned, among other properties, a fenced-in storage facility. One day, she needed to get inside, but she couldn't get the heavy chain that was wrapped around the gates and fastened with a big padlock to give up under her efforts. She struggled and struggled, getting more and more frustrated. Finally, she said, "I called out to my dad. Why, I don't know. He had passed twenty years ago." Nevertheless, she begged him to help her. Then she tried it again and this time she had no trouble opening the gate. "All I had to do was ask," she said.

### GOD'S HANDS

Elaine's son was addicted to drugs but was able eventually to get off the drugs and in the process named his dealers. He was found some days later, face down in a small creek. An autopsy revealed he had not drowned but had been murdered. When she went to identify her son's body, Elaine was so full of tears of despair, she could hardly see to drive, then a hand, a hand she knew was the hand of God appeared outside the windshield of her car and she knew that God was with her, and her son was safe in His kingdom. Even as the image faded, it stayed clear in her mind and she made it through those sad, trying days ahead. The crime was never solved and through the years that image gave her peace and comforted her, for she knew her son was in His hands.

### A TAP ON HER SHOULDER AND A VOICE

"My grandmother worried and worried about my brother when he was in Vietnam," a friend told me. "Then one day while praying for his safety, she felt a tap on her shoulder and then heard a voice say, 'He will be all right.'"

### A BROTHER TEASES HIS SISTER

My friend's brother was killed in a vehicle accident, a week before her dad became ill and was sent to a hospital in Kansas City. She stayed with her dad through those sad and worrisome days, going to her hotel each evening. One evening, she got on the elevator intending to go down to the lobby and back to her hotel room. But instead of going down, the elevator went all the way to the top floor. The doors opened and she saw she was on the floor of the psychiatric unit. She knew immediately that her brother was there. She told her dad and the days that followed, while he was recovering, were a bit easier, knowing their son and brother was obviously alive and well and had tried to ease their sorrow with that little joke.

## HER CHILDREN HEALED IN HEAVEN

Lois and her first husband had two children who died of cerebral palsy. The little girl was blind with one unseeing eye turned outward. She was three when she died in her mother's arms. "Seconds before she died," Lois said, "she looked straight up at me, the outward eye in a normal position, and she smiled." Her son was eight when he passed. Sometime later she had this beautiful dream of him running and playing with other children in a grassy meadow and he was happy and healthy, but he still had his crutches. In the dream, she asked him why. He laughed and, tossing them aside, said, "Oh. I don't need these anymore."

Lois also told us that she sometimes sensed her late husband and could smell his pipe tobacco smoke, as could her present husband. She said they were lying in bed one night and smelled his pipe tobacco again and she said she called his name and told him that she loved him dearly, and she liked knowing he was around, but would he please stay out of their bedroom. He came around for quite a while longer, but he never again entered their bedroom.

## A VOICE TO BE HEEDED

Cora was having lunch at the senior citizen's center when she heard a voice say, "Move your car." She was puzzled and hesitant to follow the directions of a disembodied voice. How does one explain that to a table full of others? So, she sat still and maybe had her meal finished before her car got hit.

### "GO FIND THE KIDS"

My sister's husband heard a voice that told him to "Go find the kids," and he obeyed immediately, for he recognized the voice. It was his dad's—his dad who had passed some years before. They lived in the country and the two kids were five and seven. He found them wandering off in the fields and not very far from a nearby pond.

### CARDINALS AND RAINBOWS

Betty and Gerald loved each other, their children, grandchildren, and great grandchildren and showed it. Betty loved birds and always kept a full feeder. Her favorites were cardinals. One winter day after she passed, her grandson, who took care of keeping the feeder full, forgot and early the next morning there came a tap, tap, tapping at the living room window. The grandson looked toward the window and saw a female cardinal tapping at the window and the empty feeder. He laughed and called out, "Okay, Grandma Betty, I'm coming."

The day Betty and Gerald were married, and years later when their son, Dan and his wife, Shani exchanged vows, there appeared in the sky, a beautiful double rainbow. Throughout their lives, in moments of joy and in times of difficulty, they or their children would receive in answer to prayer the assurance that all was well by the appearance of a rainbow. At times, even a double rainbow would arch across the sky.

### GRANDMOTHER APPEARS OUTSIDE HER FORMER HOME

He was three years old when his grandmother passed and two years later, his grandfather moved to a house across the street. Now five years old, Tommy was visiting his grandfather one day when he looked out the window at his grandparents' former house across the street and saw his grandmother walking there in the front yard. He was only three when she passed, and now it was two years later, but he recognized her. Was it from pictures, or in those two years had she kept in touch with him?

### A STRAW HAT AND OVERALLS

Lacy lost her beloved Grandpa when she was just out of her teens. Over the years, her grandmother would mention that she knew her husband, the man she'd loved for many years, was still around, for she often got a whiff of cigarette smoke and Grandpa had been a smoker. Lacy always wished she could smell the smoke too, so she'd know Grandpa was nearby. Then one night, she woke from a dream and the smell of her grandpa's cigarettes, and she knew he was there with her. The dream had been so real. Her grandpa had stood there smiling at her, wearing the clothes she remembered so well, the clothes he had worn in life when out working in the fields—a straw hat and overalls.

### THE LAYING ON OF HANDS

Beverly and her husband had moved to another town and had recently joined a church. Soon after, Beverly woke with the sudden onset of rheumatoid arthritis and the doctor put her on medication. One day, three women from the church came to her home and told her they had felt compelled to come lay hands on her and pray for her healing. A few days later the arthritis was gone. The doctor was amazed. It's been thirty years or more and the arthritis has never returned.

### DID THE CAT WAIT FOR HIM

When John and Charlotte's cat died, they would sometimes see her in the house. The dog seemed to see her too. The two had never liked each other and now the dog would at times stop and stare and growl as if seeing her. After John passed, Charlotte no longer saw the cat and apparently neither did the dog, for he stopped his growling. Charlotte believes the cat waited for John and left with him.

There are thousands, probably even millions of these stories in the whole, wide world, all evidence of this thin veil between us. I hope those of you with a story or stories to tell will consider sharing them with family, friends, and even strangers. Some will turn away, even the most devout, as well as the nonbeliever, but many, probably most, will have a story they will now feel free to share with you. And I hope for you, as it is for me, like finding hidden treasure.

www.ingramcontent.com/pod-product-compliance
Lightning Source LLC
LaVergne TN
LVHW041907070526
838199LV00051BA/2538